Living Exponentially

UNLOCKING THE POWER OF EVERY MOMENT IN YOUR BUSINESS AND LIFE

To Karen + Jean and the best, Exponential version of yourselves. #BExponential

Jennifer Davis

Jennifer Davis

Published by Spotlight Publishing

ISBN: 13:978-1-7320409-2-2

The Publisher has strived to be as accurate and complete as possible in the creation of this book.

This book is not intended for use as a source of legal, business, accounting, or financial advice. All readers are advised to seek the services of competent professionals in the legal, business, accounting, and financial fields.

In practical advice books, like anything else in life, there are no guarantees of income made. Readers are cautioned to rely on their own judgment about their individual circumstances and to act accordingly.

While all attempts have been made to verify information provided in this publication, the Publisher assumes no responsibility for errors, omissions, or contrary interpretation of the subject matter herein. Any perceived slights of specific persons, peoples, or organizations are unintentional.

Dedication

This book is dedicated to each and every Exponential thinker, who is chasing the dream to measure success by the joyful pursuit of life. You've come to the right place.

And of course...

I dedicate this book to my parents, who were the example of Living Exponentially. They gave us the opportunity to live like free-range chickens, while knowing we were exuberantly loved, by parents who were the models of hard work, empathy, creativity, ingenuity, and adventure. I am grateful for your example and the love that gave me the confidence to become uniquely me. Your greatest success is in the reflection of your children and making us #FriederickStrong.

Alongside of my parents, this book is dedicated to the eight siblings, I proudly own. In addition, I add Tony to this dedication. He is my brother from another mother. Our mutual love is the example of Exponential loving. Each one of you holds a special place in my heart and in my journey. When God picked my siblings, I am grateful he picked you.

Furthermore, this book is dedicated to my insanely huge extended family of aunts and uncles, in-laws, cousins, nieces, and nephews. The ingenuity and accomplishments are remarkable. The commitment to adventure, hard work and living large is your version of Exponential Living.

To my St. Catherine of Siena Catholic School community, our chapter together has ended, but I will be permanently shaped by the joy our family has experienced within your walls. I dedicate my work to each and every athlete that I have coached throughout my career. I hope my influence parallels the joy that each of you gave me.

Next, I dedicate this book to the Davisware family of customers, partners and employees who supported me in my journey to Exponentiality and the fruition of writing this book. Thanks for trusting Dan and I to pilot our journey together, and for holding on tight and riding sidecar on this adventure. Your commitment to us created it all.

Next, this book is dedicated to all of the kids we call our own- those who have grown both in and under my heart. You are the why in our journey. Thanks for your patience and support, even when it was undeserving. I hope today, your mom's new title as an author makes you proud.

Finally, I dedicate my work to Dan, the guy at the bottom of the totem pole, often carrying an unhuman load. You've always been the one who believed in me far sooner than I believed in myself. My work is dedicated in gratitude for your exuberance to helping me learn to take risks, create adventure, and find my passion in all that I do. Thanks also, for helping make all of those kids. I like them a lot- most days anyway.

Lastly and most importantly, I dedicate my work to God the Father in heaven, who created the circumstances for me to write and share what I have learned. His blessings have allowed me to live freely in America, writing our version of the American Dream.

This small-town girl never knew to dream this big. The best is yet to come.

Special Dedication

In humble dedication to every solider, both past and present, who served to preserve our freedom. This book is being released today, September 11, 2021, commemorating the 20th anniversary of the day the world was shaken by the evil terrorist attacks on America.

In loving memory of everyone who died in the wake of those horrific events and to each person who has been impacted or died from that day on, continuing to carry the torch of freedom. Freedom isn't free. We are indebted for your service.

Table of Contents

Foreword

It is early on a Tuesday morning in late January 2021. I text Jennifer Davis a quick question. She responds immediately, letting me know that she is about to drop her daughter off at school and will call me right back. Later that same morning, I am on a 3-hour video conference with Jennifer, where she leads a group through the 2021 strategy for Davisware, the software company that Jennifer co-founded with her husband, Dan, over 30 years ago. The meeting is well planned and executed, with a clear and strong sense of what to expect in the coming year. Jennifer has a "hard stop" at the end of the meeting so that she can get to the airport to head from Chicago to Texas for a customer visit. Later that evening, I decided to call Jennifer to see how her day was and reflect on the morning strategy session. She answers the phone and lets me know that she has just finished dinner with members of her family in Breckenridge, Colorado. "Breckenridge?" I ask. Once again, I am in awe and just can't figure out how she does it all. It doesn't seem possible.

To say that Jennifer Davis is unique would give too much credit to the word "unique." Jennifer is one of the most interesting and fascinating individuals I have ever met. She is a business founder, a business leader, a wife, a mother of ten, a coach, a servant of the community, a friend, a mentor, and so much more. She lives a big, full life filled with adventure, achievement, and uncommon concern for others. She is one of those rare individuals that just seems to find a way to get more done than what seems possible. A long-time ago, another mentor of mine emphasized that ***TIME*** is the most precious commodity we have – don't waste it. Jennifer is one of those extremely rare individuals that truly honor this principle.

If you work in or around the foodservice equipment service industry, you have probably met Jennifer (or at least heard of her). I have known Jennifer for about 17 years. I am Chief Executive Officer of Parts Town, the global market leader in foodservice equipment parts distribution. We are headquartered in the Chicago area, have over 2,000 team members world-wide, and over $1 Billion in annual revenue. We are a high-tech distribution business that has delivered 35% compound annual growth over the past 18 years and are recognized as one of the fastest-growing privately held companies in the U.S. We have been a customer and partner with Davisware for many years and consider Jennifer and her team close strategic partners and great friends.

When I heard that Jennifer was writing a book, I couldn't wait to read it. ***"Living Exponentially"*** gives the reader a powerful glimpse into Jennifer's world. The book provides lessons, examples, and a roadmap to help unlock your full potential in business and in life. For me, it helped to answer that question, "how the heck does she do it?" More importantly, it gave me some practical insights to bring into my life and help me become a better leader, husband, father, and friend. If you are looking to better optimize your time in a way that improves your business performance and your quality of life, you have come to the right place.

Preface

For many people, 2020 will long be remembered as a year to forget. It involved considerable, unexpected changes in almost every area of our lives. We have new words that have filled our vocabularies, such as uncertainty, social distancing, quarantining, and lockdowns. These are phrases we may have never heard of before 2020. For all of us, the year 2020 has brought a complete global reset.

Not since the start of Christianity has this happened without a world war. This yet-to-be-named chapter in global history is one that we witnessed firsthand as we pivoted our businesses, families, and lives around the new version of normal.

2020 the Year to Forget (or Reset)

When we look back at 2020, almost every aspect of our lives had a reset. Here are just a few:

- Social reset. For the first time in modern history, we were told whom we could meet and how we could meet them in addition to where.
- Health reset. The world's health became everyone's top priority as we learned about social distancing, masks, elbow bumps, self-quarantining, temperature checks, and contact tracing. We learned a new definition of being in it together and saw virtual appointments and self-assessment improve medicine.
- Economic reset. The global pandemic altered how goods were bought and sold at every business level, from international trade to the local mom and pop stores. Businesses closed or learned to survive by changing their established methods of operating. Recession-proof businesses such as restaurants and gas stations learned of a new risk to their business. The supply chain was altered in ways that will become the new normal.
- Educational reset. We learned that education is far less rigid than it once was, and we can achieve quality education in various ways other than a simple classroom. Teachers, parents, and

students used innovative technology to meet learning objectives. New risks and benefits entered the educational scene as students in every imaginable classroom experienced disruption to their learning and adapted to new systems and learning platforms.

- Calendar Reset. The global pandemic created restrictions around planning around traditional holidays, vacations, activities, and events. Professional sports had to reinvent how they competed. State and local restrictions changed how we celebrated traditional family events, including holidays, weddings, and funerals. We learned to be far more flexible in everything we were doing and far more efficient in how we were doing it.
- Entertainment Reset. Streaming, social media, and virtual events replaced in-person, large-scale events. The entertainment industry pivoted with new ways to stream and new types of virtual events and interactions.
- Priority Reset. For the first time in decades, families had family meals seven days a week, riding bikes, going on picnics, and doing puzzles. They discovered the new normal that brought more balance and joy to families.
- Travel Reset. Airplanes went from every seat full to only a handful of flights and only a handful of passengers. Businesses started to re-think how to do business better without travel. Families used technology to connect to avoid travel altogether. Some adventuresome people abandoned their home lives completely for an adventure on the road.
- Spiritual Reset. For the first time in modern history, churches were closed. So, worshipers looked to technology to connect with their faith and find a way to worship. Online services and bible studies allowed international faith communities to form in ways never seen before.
- Clothing Reset. Seemingly irrelevant, people's clothing changed from office attire and professional gear to "waist up" professional, then semi-professional, and then just dressed as the pandemic continued into 2021.

- Housing Reset. With more people at home, houses started to feel smaller and needed a different blueprint, where office space became mandatory and internet speeds critical to education and livelihood. With the ability to live anywhere, families took advantage of the opportunity to leave their homes and move out of the city. Or they moved to a new town that was a part of their lifestyle, not driven by their careers.

This list is not exhaustive, but one that puts in perspective the change management every human on earth was experiencing in some way. For us, 2019 was where so much had changed in our lives; we were looking forward to 2020 for stability and "normal." Davisware had just executed historic changes. Dan, my husband and Co-founder of Davisware, took on equity partners in our business as we sold the majority position in our company. Dan left day-to-day operations, leaving us to find new technical leadership. For me, it was coming to work each day without my 30+ year business partner. We now had investors and a board of directors to answer to and many new faces in the previously family-owned business. The changes we had leading up to 2020 were enough to give us the confidence to survive the changes that 2020 brought us.

Like many companies, Davisware made both short and long-term pivots to create security and prosperity in the short term and years to come. We executed the company's first-ever large-scale layoffs, salary reductions, and benefit changes. Our long-term pivots included closing office space and focusing on what we could control. In addition, we strategically invested time and money into new tools and reporting tools to make us stronger for the next chapter. The chorus of changes in these subsequent years tested the organization in many untested ways. It tested me as a leader and my ***Exponential Mindset***.

It was a perfect storm for Davisware leading up to 2020. In the face of all these challenges, our results could have been very different than they were. In the wake of what we faced, I documented what I had known to be *Exponentiality*.

Our organization perfected what it meant to have an *Exponential Mindset,* and now, I get to share it with you.

Davisware became a better and stronger organization with our culture, customers, tools, technology, and teams due to the global pandemic, as did many organizations who saw it as an opportunity.

2021 and Beyond

The world looked longingly to the flip of the calendar, hoping for an instant reset back to the way it was. We soon learned that wasn't going to happen for many reasons, but the most important one was because we have all changed. We have come to expect different things, have different goals, and so has everyone around us. Our society and each of us have evolved. While we long for many of the things we loved, like social gatherings, concerts, and seeing each other's smiling faces unmasked, we also are grateful for the many innovations that have resulted from the global pandemic. Positive shifts in how we live and do business surround us, including:

- Businesses aren't limited to hiring staff based on geography. Hiring pools in many industries have become almost limitless.
- Retail businesses can sell and service their customers 24/7 beyond their brick-and-mortar locations.
- Doctors can see patients while they are in the comfort and safety of their homes.
- Sales calls can happen remotely without spending the time and costs of traveling for the customer or the rep.
- When, where, and how children get educated have been altered. Families have more freedom in planning vacations and time off. Missing school is no longer a dilemma. An internet connection and a computer are enough to keep almost any student up to speed with their class.
- Families have broken the boundaries between work and home. Kids are a part of their parents' workday and parents a part of their kids' school days. Dogs or cats crashing a Zoom meeting are the rule now instead of the exception.
- Families re-defined what a workday looks like and how productivity is measured. Eliminating the 9-5 paradigm and the

tyranny of the clock has created better balance and joy in our lives.

Just as we have forgotten about some of the pains of our old reality, we have also forgotten how grateful we are for the new one. Over halfway through 2021, our new normal is still being written. Whether 2020 was your best year ever or one you would like to forget, there is no question that it was a year that changed you.

In any period where there is so much disruption to normal, there is equal opportunity.

Leveraging and embracing these changes has leveled the playing field in many ways, allowing those individuals and businesses who want to live boldly to create their social contracts to create their success.

Small Changes and Big Impact

Each changing social contract represents opportunities to improve our well-being and make us more productive. While the world around us has changed dramatically, the small changes you choose for your own story can create a significant impact. How many minor changes could you make that could dramatically transform your day? The global reset you've just lived through created many opportunities for your life transformation if you take advantage of them.

Post pandemic will present us with a vast array of choices around when we work, where we work, how we work, and how we spend our time away from work. Our lives are now blank slates, and we can write our own scripts. For some, this is exhilarating. For others, it is intimidating. For others, like myself, we didn't wait for the pandemic to end to start to write our own scripts. Instead, we used the new freedoms to write our own stories. For small business owners and anyone with an entrepreneurial spirit, I hope this book gives you confidence in your dream and that you take this time to write your own story. The secret to *Exponentiality* lies within these pages. No dream in 2021 is too outlandish. In 2019, if I wanted to be the CEO of a software company and live in my tiny, rural hometown of Potosi, Wisconsin, it would have been an impossible dream.

Today, people are making decisions like this one every day. The social contract has changed, and people chose where they want to live, not their career. As a result, we see the reversal of the Great Migration that started in 1916. Instead, people are fleeing large urban areas and moving to smaller urban communities like Salt Lake City, Nashville, and Austin, where they find a lower cost of living and a higher quality of life. They are leaving behind high-rent districts for closer geography to family and friends.

Whether you have come to this book as an entrepreneur, an organizational leader, or a part of the support community for one of these people, my goal is that you walk away from this book with a glimpse into how *Exponentiality* changed my life and my business and the mindset that it can change yours too. I hope you find tools in these pages that make your business better and your teams happier. Most importantly, I hope that this book helps you find joy and balance in your life.

You've only got one life. Stop waiting. Start living it.

Enjoy your journey.

Acknowledgments

Where does one begin on acknowledging all of the people who took me on this journey to Exponentiality?

The list is long and disorganized.

I was once given the advice to thank everyone who needs to be thanked because you may never write another book—so here it goes.

The pages of this book are filled with stories that were penned by the authors I am acknowledging.

Through careless omission or my fifty-year-old memory, there are still many others who have been left out. What this journey has taught me is how profoundly impactful small conversations have been. The person on the other end of that conversation often has no recollection of the conversation, much less its profound impact. We never really know who we impact or how we impact them.

Here is my best effort…

Starting with my inner circle, our tribe puts the *why* in all that I do. I always wanted a big family; God decided it was "go bigger" than I dreamed and with a far higher degree of complexity. For Dan, the man, you are the one who started it all. You were willing to take the risk, starting with those first days on those starry Texas nights. You've driven ten million miles to get us safely to our destinations.

You've always pulled the hair from the shower drain and been the first one to wake up when there is a bump in the night or a baby crying. No challenge has ever been too big, and no idea too crazy. You are a force to be reckoned with no matter what you do.

To Greg, our firstborn, your existence created fortitude that was beyond my years. It was through the experience of adoption I became who I am.

Thank you to your parents for loving you nearby while I prayed for all of you from afar. The joy of being reunited with you has made every hard day worthwhile. Thanks, too, for adding Morgan to the tribe. She is a perfect first-mate.

Next, to Austin, our ~~first~~ second born (sorry about springing that one on you), through your curly red locks, you fulfilled the gift of being a mom. From little league baseball to motorsports and your passion for gaming, there is no question that you won't be outdone in finding fun. When you brought home Melissa and told me that *"it's scary how much she is like you"* (me), I knew she was perfect for you. Thanks for giving our family someone else who knows how to execute a plan.

Mary, our "test drive teenager," when we finally and permanently added you to those I call my own, we learned as much about being parents from you as you did from us. The rest of our kids had better parents because of you! It's God's miracle that we have always looked (and acted) alike despite no bloodline.

And Troy, thank you for being the puzzle piece that goes with Mary. You are perfect for her and our family. We immensely love each and every one of your brood and love teaching them all of the things we can. (BTW… there is nothing wrong with Jake learning to drive the Red Bus at age 7. Just ask him.) It's payback for some of your pretty challenging teenage years.

Next up- Hannah Pearl. Your beautiful and innocent spirit is one I hope the world never steals from you. It is a gift. Your pure joy can be found in the kindness and empathy that come naturally to you. God made you special. Don't let the world change that. You have no idea how much you have helped me grow. Hopefully, you will see a lot of your wisdom in the pages of this book!

Chas, you came into our world unannounced and without reason. I prayed to God, asking him why, as I thought I could do no more. Those were really challenging days. God answered my prayers by explaining why— because you were exactly what our family needed. God, with the help of Coach Ro, put you right where you belong. Not only have you been perfect for our family, but you have also done a great job of keeping Adam alive. Thanks for that too because I like him a lot.

Adam, the tumbleweed, we are never sure where you may land. You've been the family CEO since birth. Your magnetic charm causes you to be surrounded by a dozen friends in 2.5 seconds. My evening prayer is that God keeps you safe from all of your horrible ideas for another day. He's done well by both of us so far. Thanks for your encouraging spirit, for our late-night talks, and for being the one I am positive I can count on, no matter what. Your talent is only impeded by what your heart allows you to do. Your work ethic is unstoppable, and if there is a crisis, you are the one we all turn to. Work hard, be humble and kind, and God will reward you.

Gabrielle, you are my mini-me in so many ways. Who knew that those childhood tantrums would turn into the beautiful, confident, and athletic human you are? Thanks for all of our early morning chats. They are a nice way to start the day. I find the joy of motherhood by watching you grow every single day. Be proud of who you are. Learn it faster and do it better than I did. You are capable of amazing things. Be patient with where you are today. Don't trade today for a perfect tomorrow. God has you right where you belong.

Eva, you always fill my heart with wonder, astonished by your next experiment (and mess, of course). Your gentle, nurturing spirit surrounds all that you do. You are a perfect horse mom to Nikko. I hope you never sell yourself short to the potential that God has given you. Your natural curiosity gives you an unparalleled wealth of knowledge. Don't waste it on tomorrow. Use it today. The world is waiting for you to change it.

And finally, the caboose, Amelia Don Anne. God sent you to us in the dark days of losing Green Grandma and Tickle Grandpa. We lost both unexpectedly with so much more life to live. God sent you to us to soothe my most broken heart. Your loving and playful spirit always adds to the joy in whatever we are doing. I love your creative energy and spirit. I can't wait to see what happens when you find your passion in life.

The village it took to write this book is the village that it took to live this life. As a mom, when your kids are happy, you are too.

Through the Au Pair in America program, our family was forever blessed. We had outstanding childcare from our 24 years of au pairs, PLUS we gained an international family. These women were my companions on the long days while Dan was traveling. They were my pinch hitter for whoever was left behind when I was coaching or serving the community, and they were my substitute whenever work took me on the road. Jasmin, Katrin, Kate, Esther, Caroline, Kathleen, Natalie, Natalia, Megan, Yasmin, Mellissa, Jelva, Rebekka, Leah, and Tamryn, there are no words to describe the gratitude. Without you, this literally would not have been possible. If I had to worry for a moment about my kids, none of the other success would have found us. Thank you, thank you, thank you. We are forever indebted to you. Some of my most joyful adult moments have been watching each of you become mothers and seeing the reflection of you in your own kids.

The foundation for everything you will read and learn came from the humble beginnings of Potosi, Wisconsin, and the #FriederickStrong family. Your ingenuitive, industrious, resourceful, insanely hard-working, thrill-seeking, gear-headed, faith-filled lives served as a demonstration of the way to work and how to live. My aunts and uncles are an extinct breed of community servants. My fond memories of them served as examples that you don't look for the path; you pave the way. These memories include Uncle Joe & Uncle Ralph's farms, Uncle Earl's electric shop, Uncle Carl's hardware store, Aunt Esther's corn husk art business, and Uncle Kenny's God only knows what farm, machine shop, log splitting business and whatever other junk he could find and make new. Thanks for so many amazing childhood memories in all of these exquisite places. And the memories don't end at childhood with my recent tour of Uncle Carl's chicken coop and ambushing Uncle Kenny. (Uncle Kenny, that's the last time you will leave me behind, I can assure you.) Aunt Janet, you are a highlight of our weekends in Cassville. I am so glad Uncle Leo forced us to buy that house. It was one of the best decisions we've ever made. Finally, Aunt Esther, our spirits are aligned in a quest for beauty and hard work. I am grateful to have you as my aunt. My Dad loved you so much.

This crew is not to be outdone by the other side of my family and the pioneering work that started with my grandfather in the baking industry and my grandmother, a highly educated, career woman born in the early 1900s. They stood as the example that dozens of my cousins followed into highly successful journeys of joy, faith, family, and career success (important in that order).

Out of this group spawned a few cousins who inspire me. Lee Friederick, you have no clue how much your daily Bible writings inspire me and so many others with whom I share them. Cousin Ronda, how is it you find so much joy in all you do? I aspire to be like you.

Cousin Sue, while I was terrified of you as a child, what I learned as an adult is that we are kindred spirits, and I look forward to our mutual *Next*. I treasure the moments we find together and am so happy you are part of my village for my SLC kids.

Finally, Cousin Rick, you are a bad-ass example of how to rise above all, never lose your focus on family, and when the world tells you it's not possible, you just quietly make it happen. Thank you for inspiring me to find our birth son and for always being my biggest fan. This book was motivated by you. Thank you. I can't wait to figure out what God has in store for our *Next* together.

When I think back to my childhood, there are not enough words of gratitude and acknowledgment for every minute of it. Our parents worked hard and played hard. We struggled a lot and found a lot of joy. The good days and the bad days and the horrible days all shaped where I landed in life. For the first 18 years of my life, the best gift I received was each and every sibling I had (yes, Jason, even you).

Mark, you've always worn a cape as the leader of the family. You put in the same level of effort at Davisware too. You have always been my hero. Thanks for bringing us your sidekick, Kris. I was instantly hooked with her back handspring. Who knew someone that old (what, maybe 25?) could still do gymnastics?

Mike, your visits to Chicago, buying cars were some of my favorite memories together. I am insanely proud of the success you created, succeeding against all odds. Sometimes in life, you just need to drown out the noise.

Missy, thank you for the introduction to Dan. Without you, the story would have been entirely different. I know I wasn't quite the little sister you ordered, but I am glad you decided to keep me anyway. I'm sorry for all of those years I kicked you all night long. It was the horrible mattresses' fault—really.

Jeff, my hillbilly philosopher brother, your wisdom is far beyond any degree you could hold. The testament to who you are is in the reflection of those beautiful boys you have raised.

God had someone special in mind for you— better late than never. It was all on God's time. Cindy showed up on cue, perfect in every way for you and our family. She is the daughter you've been dreaming about since we were kids. Clare—you are beyond lucky.

Jerry, thanks for teaching me a passion for Cubs baseball and old cars and even for the insane summer bike trips. They (mostly) came out all right. Carol, you have more grit than anyone I know.

Jason, the best decision you ever made was marrying Janet. You are the quintessential American Dream, high school sweethearts, both passionately successful in your careers and raising diverse kids. The fruit of your work will result in the same. In case you are wondering, Jason, the childhood fight record is Jenn 116,428 and Jason 1. I am proud to say I was smart enough to stop after I lost once. I'm still scratching my head trying to figure out why you started all of those fights to begin with? I am proud to say I am likely the only person on the planet who ever beat you up.

Finally, Molly and Melissa- I prayed for a decade to have a baby sister, and God blessed me doubly with the two of you. You slept in my arms from birth and went everywhere with me. I didn't know that I could love other humans so much until I met the two of you. Seeing each of you today as a mother is my joy.

The final finally in this tribe is my dear brother, Tony. He is a brother from another mother, but one we cherish as ours. You showed up on the scene long before I remember. When you finally came to live with us permanently, I thought I had caught a shooting star. I'm still waiting for you to visit but maybe if I write that in this book, you will feel guilted into actually coming. 😊.

From this brood produced the nieces and nephews that filled my cup before we had our kids. Bobby & Mitchel, thank you for your hard work helping us with our house and Tegan and Jessalyn for doing the same round 2. Brittany, Blaine, Brandon, Ryne, Brett, Rebecca, Bryce, Catrice, Caleb, Brooklyn, Roman, Bailey, Lucy, Kaia, and Aspen are each a source of joy, pride, and love. Each of you is #FriederickStrong.

Finally, Brett, thank you SO much for being the first editor of this book. I cherish our relationship and the fact that we connected so that you became the first safe person with whom I could share this book. Putting your writing in the hands of the public is very scary.

An introduction thirty-three years ago by my sister Missy, yielded me the addition of more family to endear. Dan's 12 brothers and sisters added to my circle and granted me the title of aunt dozens of times over. Joe, thank you for being part of the connection that made me whole. Without you and Missy, none of this would have happened.

Green Grandma, I hope that you are looking down from heaven with pride. I can see your shining smile, telling the whole world I wrote it. I bet book sales in heaven will skyrocket.

Aunt Irene and Aunt Louise, each of you have been the source of inspiration in your own right. Aunt Louise, thanks for allowing Dan and me to share that single mattress in your living room so many years ago and for introducing me to teaching. Your classroom was where I first saw the vision of how I wanted to inspire kids. Aunt Irene, your adventuresome spirit shows me that, without a doubt, you are who I want to be when I grow up. The memories of the Grand Canyon stay close to my heart.

It would be reckless if I didn't mention Aunt Christine. Thank you for always being such a vital part of our kids' lives. Exuberant love is how I would describe your love for them. I am so thankful that God allowed my kids to be yours exclusively. He always has a grander plan.

And finally, "my boys," PJ, Jonathan, Brandon, and Ryan- each of you continue to be mine. Thank you, Mary, for graciously sharing them. It is blissful to see how you have each grown up and are now thriving in your own right.

Jonathan, thank you for being a raving fan and for helping kick this project off. Your talent overflows. Nothing in life limits you but the decision to limit yourself. Use Christiana as the wind beneath your wings and soar.

The same goes for you, Ryan, and PJ. You've all married so well. Make sure they all know it and soar together. Brandon, take that gentle spirit and continue to create joy wherever you land.

With all of this human horsepower behind me, it is easy to see how Dan and I were able to find success.

When I talk about our big, beautiful family, every adjective is accurate. We are a lot of people!

This immense group of people is only one element of our human family. Team Davisware makes up the rest. Every person who wore Davisware blue created the story that follows. Because Dan and I were just children when we started, our teams were trusted comrades, and our customers were often our business advisors.

First, hats off to Cheryl.

Thank you seems to be insignificant in describing how you changed the trajectory of my career. The world sees us as yin and yang. I know that you've heard this before, but I hope you *know* it. You gave me the ability to use my talents and be successful by using yours. Very few people in their careers find someone like you to be a sidecar in the journey. You changed my life.

Following immediately behind is Lisa. While your career at Davisware is short, the magnitude of your impact withstands. Without your scheduling skills, ability to fact-check my time management, and creative problem solving of how to stuff 100 hours of work into a typical work week, this book would not have happened.

Both you and Cheryl should have your names on the front cover too. You helped me survive the global pandemic and drown out the noise. It was often lonely at the top, but having you two beautiful women, changed that.

Alongside you, the Davisware 2020 Global Pandemic Leadership Team was world-class. We made the business a better place during global chaos. Very few companies got to say that. What I've said throughout this journey is if I had to choose a team to row with, I would pick you. Ram, Mark, Derek, Madhuri, Terry, Curt, Amy, and Adam- each of you served a role in allowing Davisware to turn the page to another chapter of our story.

There are other significant cheerleaders in our organization that I would be neglectful if I didn't mention helped us row passionately against some powerful storms. Thanks, Nancy, Trent, Justin M., Gopi, Justin S., Beth, Heather, Dorian, Jim A., Shridhar, Jeff, Melody, Mark S., Sharon, Sudha, Shridhar, Janelle, Serina, Jennifer P., Molly, Team Cramer, Phi, Cam, Kay, Denise, and Kevin P. for being the doers that got it done. I am positive I missed someone here, but know whether your name is listed or not, your contributions to creating the opportunity to create this book are real.

Some of this crew laid the foundation, and others will continue to carry the torch. Nancy, you've been with us since the very beginning, first as a customer and then on our team. Your commitment to us has been unparalleled. I learned from you that it is always important to get margaritas, appetizers, and dessert. You were a part of the crew who was with us during the most challenging times. Your sister Janet, Bruce, Therese, and my brother Mark made sure we paddled together.

Thanks to Ross Arroyo, Sean Hyott, and Dan Restivo for creating the foundation of the Davisware acquisition story. I hope you have been proud of what we have done with your work. Thanks to the team at FieldEdge for carefully taking on our cherished Wintac customers. We are grateful they are in good hands.

To our leaders in India, I treasure the time we spent together during my visit. Murali, thanks for being the ultimate host, introducing us to your culture and way of life. Sandeep, thanks for being our tour guide. Our kids still talk about our time together. I am happy to see you now have a family of your own. Prasad, your contributions are often an untold story.

During our celebration event, I was able to meet so many of your families, hug your babies and absorb the love and admiration that was evident. I will cherish these moments forever. Many others remain nameless, not for lack of wanting to call you out, but for lack of ability to spell! Thanks to each of you for sharing your culture and teaching me that there is much to love in India.

Finally, I want to thank the brand-new Davisware leadership who will control the pen to write the next chapter.

Curtis, your opportunity is expansive, your teams are quality, and this business is well-positioned for Exponential growth. I have confidence you are the guy to help make that happen.

Thank you to the names behind the brand at our investment firm. You've all had a pen in this story.

For the Davisware Board of Directors, both past and present. Jean Choquette and Ken Beasley, you blazed a trail before all others. Thank you for your friendship, kindness, and guidance in helping get our business to a significantly better place. Bill, Steve, Adam, Dan, and the PE firm folks are proudly some of the best board members I have ever witnessed. It takes a village to do what we are doing, and I am thankful that you are in our village.

Thanks to Glen and Kevin at GCA, who connected us with a great partner for our business.

The list of customers who have impacted our world is long. The impact is deep. Thanks to Bruce Hodge, Roger Kaufmann, John Culkin, Gary Potvin, Greg & Karen Leisgang, Rusty & Phyllis Kolodziej, Gene Hara, and Jean Choquette. The organizations you lead were the foundation for Davisware, and your leadership taught Dan and me so many early and valuable lessons. To Rick White, Ken Beasley, Gary Scherman, Ed Stack, TJ Coker, Tina Reese, Marc & Brian Pittas, Tony Rapanotti, Pete Farnum, Mike Buelow, Kevin Schoenheider, Adam Smith, Mark Turvene, Bobby Ring, Dave Wenger, Dennis Dettman, Jim Kramer, Adam McCollough, Kristen Novak, and Wells Whaley, thank you for being early adopters to the mission of Davisware and for believing in the story that continued to unfold.

Our village includes many people to whom our story belongs. Our circle of friends we have ridden sidecar in our insane adventures helped us, parent, when kids were in too many places (or possibly forgotten somewhere) and who have stepped up and stepped in just about every way possible.

Thank you to the teachers and coaches who helped build my foundation— Mary Fiorenza, Steve Chandler, Al Carius, Mr. Downs, Mr. Heck, Mr. Shuckert, and Mrs. Jonas.

Your impact is far-reaching. Thanks to the childhood friends that carried me, including Christina “Tina” Brown-McAdams, Theresa Bennett, Jeanne Schwab, Joe Hoffman, the Timmermans, and the Essers. Childhood can be hard. My friend list was short, and I was grateful you were on it.

Your tribe sets your vibe.

The crew I go through life with have the passion, loyalty, kindness, and ability to navigate any waters that come our way. Victoria Hucek, you are cut from royal cloth. Thank you for loving me, our family, and our home. Thank you for your lectures for me and everyone who resides at the Davis Sunny Acres. There are not enough words of gratitude to express the joy you bring to everyone around you (except, of course, during the lectures).

John Dennison, thanks for being Dan's friend who actually became mine. Thanks to Sterling Hicks, the example that random kindness pays off, just like in the movies.

To my fellow coaches, Scott & Mary Robbins, Julie Hart, Dan Smith, Dean Ott, Stacy Brown, Coach Pleticha, Lea Gueavara, and Mike Ellsworth, you helped me teach these kids so much more than just sports. Thanks to each of the kids who created that joy and the parents who allowed me to impact their kids.

Thanks to those who coached me, including the entire Cross Kicks Fitness crew, my beast mode partner, Steve O'Neill, Don Stumpf, the Elgin Sharks, and Lana Kalinowski.

Each of you helped pave my journey to fitness.

Thanks to Dr. Tom Mitchell, Dr. Chung Rim, Dr. Mark Wright, Dr. Guo, Dr. Gary Kazmer, Dr. Hobie Summers, and Dr. Mark Turner, as well as Stacy Brown, my resident (almost) doctor, each for contributing to putting me back together when my natural clumsiness won out over my aspiring athleticism. Without health, you have nothing. I am forever grateful for each time you put me back together.

Thank you to Joe Giagnorio for every contribution you have made to our lives, personally and professionally. You have literally been with us through it all, from acquiring kids to businesses and houses, helping us rebound from near bankruptcy to business success, and everything in between. We always knew you had our backs—even if we weren't making it easy.

To Hugo & Selina, Coach Pleticha, Karen Langsam, Lalita Janke, Anna Kaufmann, Tom Kearns, the Bautsch's, Shodji Boldt, Kelli Bucci, Jodie Charlop, and the Moy family, thank you for being a part of our adventure.

Very importantly next, thank you to the influencers in my life who very likely don't know I exist but have had a profound influence on me and this book. Craig Groschell, your podcasts are my morning routine.

Chris Voss, you are a master among masters. I hope someday I get the opportunity to study alongside you.

Mike Roe, the first time I heard you speak was the first time the world of education today made any sense. My passion mirrors yours. I hope we get to make a difference together someday.

Rory Vaden, my personal growth story was to force myself to read books I thought I would hate. I choose yours because I hate procrastinating, only to find out it was profound. That is why growth exercises rarely create wasted effort.

Reed Hastings, your ability to begin again, innovate again, and remember not to get sucked into praise or discouraged by criticism is something I aspire to mirror.

To Doc Hendley, your spirit, your mission, and your passion have impacted my life.

Dr. Suess, your profound wisdom is captured in joyful print and pictures. I can recite nearly every book.

Mother Theresa, you are my favorite role model. I aspire to find ways through humility and kindness to change the world.

And last, and most importantly, to God, my Creator. Thank you for the gifts, the opportunity, and the talent to create this work. I pray that you look with favor on my use of the talents you bestowed upon me and continue to look upon me and my entire giant circle with kindness.

Phew… that was a lot of people to thank. I am absolutely positive I've missed some. My apologies if that was you. Now get to work on your journey to *Exponential Living.*

If I Just...Join the Movement

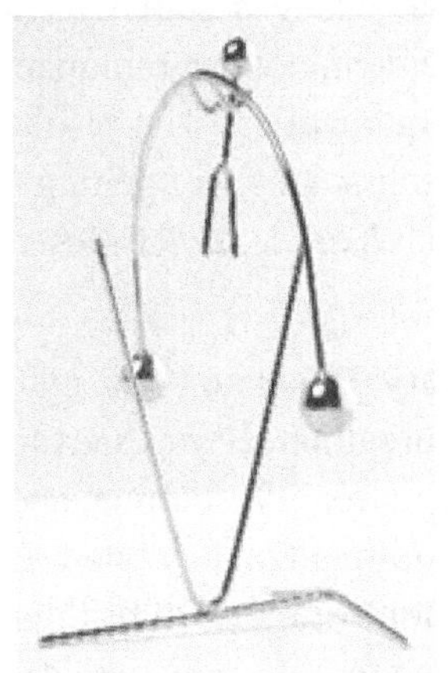

The *Exponentiality* movement is the result of watching service and contracting business leaders grow their businesses and seeing the tribulations and triumphs that came with the process. I have witnessed technicians become entrepreneurs. Those entrepreneurs become small businesses. Those small businesses grow to mid-market contenders. Those mid-market businesses either start acquiring companies or decide that they have created value in their business and choose to exit.

While Davisware holds some impressive statistics on customer growth —over 50% top-line revenue growth in partnership with Davisware; what is most amazing is that we have helped business leaders break through business milestones that limit their ability to *Live Exponentially*.

The average Davisware customer adds nearly a million dollars in annual revenue and is seen as an industry innovator. In many cases, at each business threshold, that tech in a truck (this is you) trades a bit more of their personal success (joy) to gain the next level of professional success. Sound familiar? At each threshold, there is this elusive idea that if I *just* hire a few more technicians, if I *just* implement a new ERP system, if I *just* sign on a few more national accounts, you will finally gain relief and success. It never happens because there is a foundation missing— 7 of them, in fact. *The 7 Elements to an Exponential Mindset* will create the relief and realign the success journey

I want you to join this Movement because I want you to find these successes in tandem. The business leaders I have witnessed are community and industry servants— having scaled their personal lives in many of the same ways they have scaled their businesses. I targeted this Movement to those leaders who want success in every aspect of their lives. These pages are the instruction manual for how to grow a successful business while having a joyful personal life.

What does it mean to join the Movement? The success I have witnessed happened because the leaders of our customer's businesses are committed to incremental changes. These changes progressively make their business and lives better. These incremental changes start with a commitment from the top, but for this to be a movement, not just minutiae, *Exponentiality* needs to proliferate through the organization. The results may be implementing new software, hiring new technicians, or opening a new business branch. Still, these are the results of an *Exponential Mindset*, not the solutions to the problems of the business.

Exponentiality is not a big bang. It's evolutionary. If you go to the gym once, you aren't going to be able to complete a marathon. If you start to run every day, you will slowly see changes in your strength, stamina, and physique. In my case, it took ten months. My commitment on day one was that each day I would run one step further. In 10 months, I was 90lbs thinner and completed the Chicago marathon. I had also found a new passion. What I did that first day was **COMMIT.** I committed to changing my exercise. I committed to changing my diet. I committed to changing my work methods. I committed to changing my sleep schedule. I changed my travel habits. I changed what I did for fun. Success was impossible without every aspect of my life changing.

Joining this Movement means you are making a decision for your organization. You are committing with your family to *Exponentiality* in your personal life. *Exponentiality* in a business cannot happen alone.

Exponentiality cannot happen professionally without a commitment personally. The membership to join this Movement needs to be "*all in*".

Every member needs to see and understand it. Bring your significant other on this journey. Bring your kids (mine can tell you all about it). Bring your friends. Bring your organization. The examples in this book are my journey. I have thousands of examples. This process does work.

Your commitment to opening this book is the start of the process.

COMMIT. Your success will be when you bring your teams and family along for the journey. Join the Movement. Start today. You've got this...

Introduction

It's 8:15 pm, and you're still working. You've missed dinner with the family and won't leave your office in time to read with the kids. You want to get out of there, but you still have contracts to review, bills to pay, and emails to answer. So, you do what you do best. You grind. You take a deep breath and put your head down, and plow forward, convincing yourself that the extra effort tonight will make tomorrow a better day.

When you started your career, you expected long hours, sacrifices, and hard work.

As the months of long hours and sacrifice turned into years, you're beginning to wonder if there truly is a light at the end of the tunnel. You love what you do but would like to do less of it with more joy and less guilt. You want more harmony between your work life and your home life.

If this sounds familiar, take a minute, and ask yourself some self-reflective questions. Are you using your evenings to "play catch up"? Are you working harder and longer to get the same or even lesser results? Does managing your people feel like a distraction? Does it feel like you are coming up short for both your family and your team? Are you finding your "To-Do" list longer at the end of the day than it was at the start? Do you feel like you are the lone problem-solver? If you answered "yes" to any of these, I invite you to read on. If you have answered yes to many of these, I am excited to help you create *Exponentiality* in your life.

I wrote this book for entrepreneurs, business leaders, organizational, and leaders of families. I wrote it for those who lead and those who support the leaders both at home and at work. Finally, it is written for anyone looking to find more joy and more balance in their lives.

It was written for you.

You Are Not Alone

According to a report from the Global Entrepreneurship Monitor (GEM), sponsored by Babson College and Baruch College, finds that 27 million working-age Americans--nearly 14 percent--are starting or running new businesses.[1]

Whether you started the business you lead, came into a family business as a part of an entrepreneurial legacy, or are a business leader trying to find a means to a more balanced life, this book can help. No matter which of the paths you took to get to where you are, you have likely hit a threshold of change. You have a growing sense of feeling overwhelmed by responsibility. You work to balance work and personal demands meticulously. Your trajectory for the business and your life are competing priorities to get the results you want. You want the company to grow to the next level, but that feels like it requires more of your personal time commitment that you simply don't have. At the same time, your family is growing or growing up, and you want to be there for key moments that always seem to get snatched away one crisis at a time.

"The definition of insanity is doing the same thing over and over again and expecting a different result." The journey you are on is how to find a **symbiotic** relationship between these two passions - your career and your personal life. You have seen others figure it out, so you have proof that it is possible. How do they do it? What's the recipe for the secret sauce that they have found that continues to elude you?

I don't have a magic wand of success, but by creating an *Exponential Mindset*, you will find your own magic wand to create a life of *Exponentiality*.

Invest in yourself, your organization, and your family by taking the lessons I have shared in this book. You will find your own secret sauce. Soon it won't be a secret to you.

Why You Should Listen to Me

My journey has taught me to be an expert *Living Exponentially.* As the Co-Founder and former C.E.O. of Davisware, LLC., I have figured out how to balance a robust career while being an active parent, community volunteer, and coach hundreds of kids on dozens of teams. In addition, I have been an engaged aunt to my 113 (and counting) nieces and nephews, a good sister, and sister-in-law to our combined 20 brothers and sisters, and have traveled the world on our endless quest for adventure.

Like most moms (and often dads, too), I usually hold other significant titles. Since 1992, I have been our family C.O.O., the dispatcher, coach, laundress, uber driver, security officer, logistics coordinator, accountant, and janitor at home. We are parents to 10 kids (and no, that's not a typo. We have ten kids). These ten kids brought home ten friends, and they brought friends who then brought friends. Our house has always been full of energy, laughter, laundry, and dirty dishes. After a very short lull of only our youngest three daughters at home, the global pandemic has refilled our house with college kids e-learning, or so they call it that. This time, it feels more like a frat party than the daycare it once was. Those kids have taken every resource and ounce of energy on any given day. They have forced me to level up while learning to be *Exponential* myself. I have lived *Exponentially*.

Before we had kids, it didn't matter if I spent most of my time working. I loved working alongside Dan, doing what we did, so it was my hobby and career. However, when the kids started arriving, it created competition for my time and energy. Our family and our business were growing simultaneously, creating more and more demands on me. I knew I needed to get more out of the same twenty-four hours.

Time is the great equalizer. Whether you are the President of the United States, a fifth-grader, stay-at-home mom, a recent college graduate, or a business executive, you have the same 24 hours in a day.

My passion for small business and the entrepreneurial dream were born from serial entrepreneurship within my family heritage. My parents and most of my relatives have owned their businesses, often from a very young age.

Davisware's humble beginnings in a small, family HVAC business is where our passion for helping small businesses with technology began. We founded Davisware because we wanted to help small businesses become *Exponential* through the use of technology. We found that adding technology to very non-technical companies was like adding water to seeds. I have personally watched *Exponential* growth in more than 2000 small and medium sized businesses. Our technology and expertise were used as tools in their businesses to grow their businesses more than 50% on average during our partnership. That's *Exponential* growth! The growth we witnessed was *Exponential*.

Our 31 years of passionate pursuit of excellence created three assets in our business--our team, customers, and culture. Along the way, these assets allowed us to produce great technology solutions. Today, thousands of contractors have managed, organized, and grown their businesses through Davisware technology. Our team of nearly 200 empathetic and creative problem-solvers delivers services while passionately defending our intentional culture in 16 states and three countries. Even though I was only 17 when it all began, this business fueled my passion for serving and creating *Exponentiality* in any way I could. Since its inception in 1988, Davisware grew *Exponentially* together with our customers' businesses.

Alongside Davisware, Dan and I grew up too. We added kids, houses, and pets, creating epic complexity. Out of necessity, I learned an *Exponential Mindset*. That *Exponential Mindset* has allowed us to *Live Exponentially*.

In 2019, Dan and I started the next chapter of our version of the American Dream by taking on a private equity partner. *Exponentiality* for Davisware meant that the next chapter required a co-writer to continue positioning the business for growth and success. Each of our successes, failures, risks, moves, challenges, and teams got us to where we are today. Through our business, we have *Lived Exponentially*, but that is only part of our story.

As Paul Harvey would say, here is *The Rest of the Story*. Dan and I live passionately while working feverously in our business. We worked hard and played just as hard. We embraced our roles as community servants and exuberant volunteers. We have learned from our mistakes and built a business while building a life. We took on too much and slept too little. We often took a long and winding road to find our version of *Exponentiality*.

As I already pointed out, each of us has the same 24 hours each day regardless of what we accomplish. Successful and happy people find a way to make the **highest and best use of that time**. That is what I wanted to do too. Without sacrificing my quality of life, I challenged myself to figure out how to get more joy and harmony out of my 24 hours than those around me. I didn't want to settle for what many other business leaders and entrepreneurs did. I didn't want to become enslaved by the unrealistic demands of both the business and our family life. I didn't want to continue disappointing everyone around me, personally and professionally, with unrealistic expectations. I wanted to make sure we never forgot to live while retaining the passion for what we did. I wanted to live life to its fullest—a life that embraced both our family and our business. I knew it was possible. I just needed to figure out how. It has taken me some time, and I don't always get it right, but our life is a testament that I have done it right more often than I have not. There are seasons to my success and the great balancing act that I will touch upon later in the book, but overall, I have found success in *Living Exponentially*.

So, why did I write this book? I believe in small businesses and the entrepreneurial spirit, like the ones I grew up in. I love to see the growth of companies from a small entrepreneurial family business into a mid-size market contender to one that is ready to be handed off to investors to continue the story. The small companies that sponsor our little leagues and keep our local food pantry stocked are the lifeblood of our economy. When small businesses are healthy and prosperous, the communities they serve also prosper. I see this in my tiny hometown of Potosi, Wisconsin, and equally in my Chicago suburban home. There are over 30 million small businesses in the U.S. that employ just over half of U.S. workers. ***Firms with fewer than 20 employees employed 20.2 million and created two-thirds of the 1.8 million new jobs in 2019***. Twenty percent of small businesses are family-owned. Married couples like Dan and me run 1.2 million family-owned businesses.[2]

Once I figured out what *Exponentiality* looked like in my life, I wanted to share it with those who could benefit from what I learned the most - people like you.

If my knowledge can contribute to your success in capturing joy and creating harmony, then that is what I want to do. I love helping people. Whether you are one of the customers we assisted with our technology or are new to my journey, I wrote this book to help you learn to *Live Exponentially*. I want to help you, your business, and your family. I want you to grow your business and create more harmony in your life so that there is more joy in everything you do. I wrote this book because I want to help you find balance sooner, learn it faster, and do it better than I did.

Success by Choice, Not Chance

Like I said before, I've been where you are. Fortunately, I discovered a mindset and skills that gave me the freedom, confidence, and success to open the doors of opportunity in front of me for our family and business for the joyful pursuit of success. Of course, everyone who knows me knows I always work hard. But I just learned to work smart also.

By following me, I'll share my experiences and secrets so that you, too, can eliminate the barriers that stand between you and the rewarding experiences your hard work and your family deserves. As you work your way through this book, I'll share secrets to help you:

- Make the highest and best use of your time.
- Solidify your **non-negotiables** around your time and your commitments.
- Measure your success *both* in dollars and in joyful harmony in the personal and professional investment of time.
- Purge guilt from the use of your most precious resource - your time.
- Work *on* your business, and strategically choose where *in* it you will work.
- Leverage tools and technology to create sustainable results.
- Gain control of your business by giving up control without abdicating that control through process, organization, and a leadership team.

For you to be successful in this journey toward an *Exponential* life, you'll need to embrace the following:

- ***Triumph.*** *Expect success.* See opportunities with the perspective of success. (Our world has never had more of them than right now).
- ***There is a way to make the highest and best use of your time.*** Your time is your most valuable commodity. You have deviated on your journey toward an *Exponential* life anywhere you are not making the highest and best use of your time.
- ***You will fall but not fail.*** Accept that this journey will be full of missteps. Those failures are steps on the journey toward *Exponentiality*, not failures.

- ***There are always problems***. Commit to the expectation that difficulties are ever-present, even when you are successful. Please find comfort in chaos and joy in solving them, not the exasperation in their existence.
- ***All solutions are possible***. See the world through a lens of flexible solutions. You will need to stop dismissing potential solutions because they don't feel reasonable or possible.
- ***Let go***. Realize that *YOU* are the person who got your business and your life to where you are. You must grow as a leader before your organization can grow, and your life will find harmony.
- ***Share what you learn***. The business leaders in your business are counting on you to figure this out and share it with them. They will watch you and take your lead.
- ***Be purposeful***. Purposeful intent will be a part of your daily decision-making and your everyday culture.
- ***Everything needs a process.*** Systems and processes are foundational to *Exponential Living*. Anything you expect to have consistently needs a process associated with it. This fact is equally true personally and professionally.
- ***Use tools***. Technology and organized information are the critical tools that you will need to implement. Again, this is not limited to your professional pursuits.

Warning!

What I am about to share with you changed our business and my entire life. It will change yours if you pursue it. Once I learned to harness the power of *Exponentiality*, I saw harmony between my pursuits, my family, and my career.

I was able to find more joy in the time I spent with all of them. It is my sincere hope that you realize every benefit I have. Success at *Exponentiality* won't happen overnight. It will grow out of a conscious decision to *Be Exponential*.

This process won't be easy. Nothing you are proud of is.

Knowing that others have been down the same path will give you the confidence to complete your journey. So, let's solve The *Exponential Mindset* and *Living Exponentially* together.

Let's get started!

Chapter Summary: Introduction

Lessons Learned

- Measure your success both in dollars and in joyful harmony in the personal and professional investment of time.
- Gain control of your business, by giving up control, not abdicating control.
- Time is your most valuable commodity. That is why we refer to it as "spending" it.
- You will fall, but not fail. Accept that this journey will be full of missteps. Those failures are steps on the journey toward *Exponentiality*, not failures.

Statistics to Ponder

- 27 million working-age Americans--nearly 14 percent--are starting or running new businesses.
- There are over 30 million small businesses in the U.S. that employ just over half of U.S. workers.
- Firms with fewer than 20 employees employed 20.2 million and created two-thirds of the 1.8 million new jobs in 2019. Twenty percent of small businesses are family-owned. Married couples like Dan and me run 1.2 million family-owned businesses.

Action Plan

- Are you ready to commit?
- What has you motivated to take the next step?

Good Quotables

- *You are not alone.*
- *Don't allow the key moments in your business to be snatched away one crisis at a time.*
- *The journey to Exponentiality isn't easy. Nothing you are proud of is.*
- *What is the highest and best use of your time? Do that.*
- *The definition of insanity is doing the same thing over and over again and expecting a different result.— Albert Einstein*

Supplementary Learning Recommendations (Read/Listen/Watch)

- *Paul Harvey's the Rest of the Story* – Paul Harvey, Jr. — https://www.amazon.com/Paul-Harveys-Rest-Story-Aurandt/dp/0553259628

CHAPTER 1

Cultivating an Exponential Mindset

One of the biggest challenges I faced in writing this book has been taking something I have done instinctively for so many years and converting it into a step-by-step process that anyone with the right motivation could accomplish. In this chapter, we will focus on how you can begin to cultivate an *Exponential Mindset*. It will be the foundation for all other lessons shared in this book. This chapter is the most crucial chapter of the book. I highly encourage you to read it in segments. Set it down and come back to it. Highlight what you need to focus most of your efforts on. Work alongside this book with a notebook and document how you can apply this in your own life. There is no value in reading this book to be inspired unless it inspires you to action. Let's take action!

Defining Exponential Mindset

If we address an *Exponential Mindset*, I think it is necessary first to set the expectation and understanding of *Exponential Mindset*. What are we *actually and explicitly* talking about here? Is an *Exponential Mindset* something that applies to business life, home life, or both? Getting a clear understanding of what the *Exponential Mindset* is should be the first stage in your journey. Spend time on this section to make sure you are clear on what *Exponential Mindset* actually is so that in later sections, we can talk about how to apply it to your life.

In May 2019, the Commercial Food Equipment Service Association (C.F.E.S.A.) asked me to participate in an event to share my *Exponential Mindset* journey. It would be the first time that I attempted to share my revelation with the world. When preparing for a presentation, I often spend much time with Professor Google, checking facts and ensuring that my line of thinking is in line with the message I am trying to deliver. In that research, I learned that I couldn't find a satisfactory definition of the word Exponentiality related to an *Exponential Mindset*. I could not find any definition of it in Dictionary.com at all (as of this date, it still does not exist). Any description I could find centered around using the word *Exponential* as a part of the definition. If this was going to be the word that I used to describe my mindset, it needed a proper definition. So, I set out to create one on my own.

Ex·po·nen·tiality / ˌek-spoh ˈnen shuh-a-letee noun

Exponentiality is a mindset using skills, tools, and technology to make the highest and best use of an individual's time and talent. In business, it is creating replicable processes with skills, tools, and technology. An *Exponential Mindset* means making a conscious effort to get the most out of every moment, every minute, and every interaction. *Living Exponentially* is living life to the fullest.

When most people hear that definition, they think about it in terms of their business. You may be thinking right now about a process surrounding servicing a new product line or improving your customer experience in your company. While these are great applications of *Exponential Mindset*, they are just the beginning. An *Exponential Mindset* applies to all that we do. It needs to be used in your work life AND your home life if you are going to be successful. One does not work without the other. It's a mindset with a toolbox of skills. Theoretically, you could have the skills, but if you don't have the mindset, you're not going to know how to use them in the appropriate situations. If you have the mindset but don't have the skills, you will not execute effectively. This book is about bringing them both together.

Sharing an Exponential Mindset

For many years, people have asked me, "How do you do it all?" Fellow parents, friends, relatives, customers, and colleagues saw me as the unicorn-as the unique being that somehow could piece together a world that they were all struggling to build.

Desperate moms who were trying to piece it all together were hoping I had some magical answer. Unfortunately, until recently, I didn't realize that I did have the answer. In my journey, I found the answer out of necessity, not individual brilliance. The answer was there the whole time. I was just unaware that it existed. Once I realized what I had, I wanted to share it. That has proven harder than I would have imagined.

Not because I didn't want to share it, but because *Exponential Mindset* comes instinctively to me. Like many of our natural skillsets, it is hard to describe to someone else how to do it when it has not been something I have consciously done. Unconsciously, I executed a strategy of *Exponential Mindset* in everything I do.

The process of writing this book required that I figure out how to make the unconscious—conscious. In doing that, I became a better leader and improved my personal life. In addition, through this journey, I gained more insights into the art of being Exponential in my own life by cultivating a conscious *Exponential Mindset.*

I have always had a natural tendency to do things *Exponentially.* I'm organized. I like processes, and I love technology. So, naturally, I gravitated toward a subconscious *Exponential Mindset.* What I did, without conscious knowledge, was execute a unique perspective. I was also unaware that others didn't think in the same way. Over the last three years, I slowly came to realize that what I had been asked by many to share was the art of the *Exponential Mindset.* I just needed to figure out how to convert my unconscious thinking into a system and process to impact the world.

The Joy Triangle to Living Exponentially

The **Joy Triangle** is a graphic to demonstrate the relative importance of every step of this journey. Each part of this journey is foundational to the next and builds upon your previous successes. As you go through this journey, you will change your thoughts. If you have never done this type of work, you may refine your core beliefs. Throughout your life, you will undoubtedly change your goals. Expect all of this. The more time you invest in this process, the better you will become at each step. What is important to realize is that while developing an *Exponential Mindset* is evolutionary, its elements do not change. Once you learn them, you will need to discover how to execute them, not necessarily learn something new. Your core beliefs, goals, and *Exponential Mindset* will create the opportunity to *Live Exponentially* in joy and harmony.

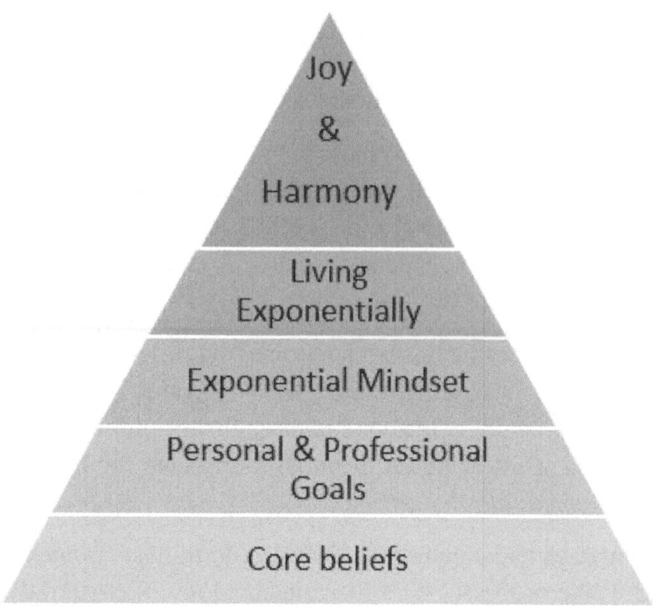

Exponential Mindset & Core Beliefs

What are your core beliefs? I think it is essential to start with a definition to avoid confusion about a core belief.

According to Betterrelatoinships.com, core beliefs are fundamental beliefs about us, other people, and the world we live in. They are things we hold to be absolute truths deep down, underneath all our "surface" thoughts.[3] Essentially, core beliefs determine how you perceive and interpret the world. My core belief is to ***live my life to the fullest***. I know that I live my life to the fullest when I feel genuine **confidence, joy, and harmony**. I also know that I cannot segregate my work life and home life. I know that there must be symbiotic between them for confidence, joy, and harmony. I am motivated to continuously find ways to feel this way as much as possible every day.

Here are some of my core beliefs that contribute to my ability to create an *Exponential Mindset*:

- Nothing is impossible.
- The human mind is our most significant inhibitor to what we can accomplish.

- Failure provides our most significant lessons learned.
- I seek continuous improvement and learning.
- Doing a repetitive task that offers no value beyond the job is a waste of time.
- I need to know that I made a difference in the world.
- I value my time and the time of those around me.
- Wasting time robs me of being able to do something more meaningful.
- Doing what is important gives me the confidence that I made a difference in the world.
- We are burning daylight and have no guarantee of tomorrow. There is an urgency to today.

Take some time to reflect on your core beliefs. Catalog them.

Put this book down for an hour or a day, or a week and create a list of your core beliefs. Having a conscious knowledge of your core beliefs is foundational to the success of an *Exponential Mindset.* There is no right or wrong answer, except to not write them down. Your core beliefs may change over time as you gain clarity or life experience, but you need to start with something. As you become more aware of your core beliefs, they will likely change. My favorite place to write them is my bathroom mirror (a fat Sharpie works perfectly for this). On your mirror, you will see them multiple times a day, literally, in your face. Your core beliefs influence your life. If you discover core beliefs that don't serve your goals or, even worse, are conflicted with your goals, you can change them with a commitment to doing so. Replace them with ones that support what you want out of life.

Goals on the Journey to Living Exponentially

As a part of the journey to *Living Exponentially*, goals are foundational. If you are like me, you have made (and likely failed) at many goals you set in your life. Often, these goals are created in a vacuum between your personal commitments and your professional pursuits. As you develop your goals, seek goals that are complementary, not contradictory to each other. Your goals will change. The critical takeaway is to have goals that align with your core beliefs and that are copacetic to each other. You cannot find success in your dreams if one goal makes another impossible.

Why Cultivate an Exponential Mindset?

The value of an *Exponential Mindset* is that you are taking your most precious resource, your time, and protecting its use- focused on what creates the most joy and harmony in your life. Time, being the great equalizer, is the thing we cannot change. For that reason, we must create all opportunities for success in constructing our mindset. In the same way that you would not knowingly overpay for the same product at one store as you did at another store, so too, do you want to use every moment in the best way? Of course, you do! We just often sabotage ourselves, forgetting to stay focused on our goals. It is no coincidence that we refer to what we do with our time as "spending" it. If we can cultivate a mindset that protects our time in the same way we are taught to protect our money from a very young age, we would already have built our *Exponential Mindset.* If your time were money, this would not be a necessary conversation. We don't naturally value our time in the same way we value our money.

Think about the need for this a little bit differently. If we were both shopping and we both had $100, and both chose the same sweater. My sweater was on the 50% off the rack. Yours was on the full price rack. You would never be OK with paying double for the same sweater.

In the same way, why wouldn't you want to do that with your time? Every human on earth has the same quantity of hours in their day. So why wouldn't you continuously want to get the best value for every moment that you spend? The best deal doesn't mean being efficient and productive every minute of every day. Often, the best value is gaining more joy in life.

7 Fundamental Elements of an Exponential Mindset

Now that you have defined the *Exponential Mindset* as a mindset to get the most out of life, you can use it to achieve your personal and professional goals. These goals are built upon your **core beliefs**. In each of these cases, a successful journey requires **conscious awareness**. You may have come into this book already there. Or, like me, it may be a journey in and of itself.

Once you have created a conscious awareness of your core beliefs, the fun of building an *Exponential Life* can begin.

From there, it's about putting into action what you've learned. Ask yourself, "What can I do to improve any aspect of my life. It could be my morning routine, my configuration at the office, or my business?" You can improve all of these with an *Exponential Mindset.*

Being *Exponential* doesn't necessarily translate into producing more work. Instead, it means making the highest and best use of your time. It's doing everything you do to the fullest.

In my world, it allowed me to be more fully engaged in more things and do a better job at them. An *Exponential Mindset* created a framework for always making the best use of my time and my talents.

Fundamental #1: Triumph. Expect the possibility/probability of Defined Success.

Whether you are defining the likelihood of successfully improving a process or applying an *Exponential Mindset* to your lifestyle in balancing conflicting priorities, both start with your belief in the possibility.

You must believe that success is possible. Beliefs influence our behavior. When Henry Ford said, "Whether you think you can't or think you can - you're right," he emphasized how much our beliefs and attitude influence our outcomes.[4] Beliefs mold our expectations of what we do and what we won't do. Not only do you need to expect the possibility of success, but that success also needs to be defined. *What does success look like?* So often, we set ourselves up for failure by committing to better balance in their lives without clearly describing it. Does balance mean that three nights/per week, you will be there to put the kids to bed? Does success mean that you will delegate through a systemic process the cash management in your business? Regardless of what you see as success, you need to define it and then believe that there is a means of getting there. Those sound easy… until you start to put them into action. This step is likely one of the most challenging parts of developing an *Exponential Mindset.* Once you genuinely adopt an *Exponential Mindset* in your life, you will find it comes as second nature. The concept of an *Exponential Mindset* will encompass your whole life, not just a solution for work or home. Why is that?

In the example of putting your kids to bed three nights per week, what keeps you from doing that today are commitments at work. You can make a proclamation that you will do this, but you will not sustain this decision unless you make a change at both home and work. You will set yourself up for more failure.

Finally, once you have established the definition of success, the belief that you will find success is the single most important contributing factor to that success. The concept of "fake it 'til you make it" isn't far off. I wish I had learned this much earlier in life. Throughout my life, there were things in which I was very confident. In hindsight, those are the things I always found success in because I believed in success, AND I had a clearly defined image (although likely an accidental image) of success. I did not define success or fully believe it would happen in many other areas, and the results showed for themselves. The truth is that defining success is key to feeling confident and believing in that success. Today, I know that I will make that happen if I think I will improve our business process to save time/money. If I want to be both at the meeting AND the soccer game, I will figure out how. These core beliefs drive my tenacity to find a solution. This core belief forces me to define success in every element of my life, personally and professionally. Once I have described what success looks like, it is easy to aim toward achieving it.

Fundamental #2: Leveling Up. Expect others to meet you at your level.

I have spent most of my adult life coaching kids from elementary school through high school. I have mentored hundreds of adults as direct reports, consultants in their businesses, and as a coach and friend to them. I have noticed that the world around us, especially when it comes to kids, does not set the expectation to meet at your level. As an employer, we often "level down" when working with subordinates. What we are doing in both cases is selling them short. Just like in a race, you don't want a head start. That would undermine the value of winning. So too, does it jeopardize your success by not choosing to force everyone to Level Up. Your organization, team, and kids will surprise you if you ask them to come to your level instead of the opposite.

Fundamental #3: Goal-Driven Focus.

Goal-Driven Focus is merely staying focused on the original goal or objective. Do not allow yourself to get distracted by obstacles or redefine what success is.

We like to sabotage ourselves. We change what we define as success to create failure. Instead, it is essential to remind ourselves of our original destination and make sure that it is concisely defined.

This fundamental is not just about the big things. Practice it with the small ones so that you are good at it when it comes to the big stuff.

I will share a real-life example of how I tried to sabotage myself recently on one of those small things.

With the global pandemic, the world is upside down, as we all know. So, this past spring, our family decided we would dig deep and go try to do something "normal." We packed up our brood and headed to Breckenridge, Colorado, to try to enjoy a ski vacation, as we have done for 20+ years.

Giving up this tradition became a non-negotiable. We committed to making it happen however we could. Our longtime season passes now came with new rules and restrictions.

The new processes were messy and not well-orchestrated. It felt like at every turn; I encountered frustration and a roadblock. Finally, after more than 40 hours on hold, waiting for assistance, unanswered messages, and staying in cue for online chat literally for days, we took the risk and headed to Colorado without a plan but with an expectation that we would ski.

I had defined success as getting our family on the slopes. While Dan and the kids spent the first day getting acclimated to the altitude and gathering equipment and gear, I spent my time on the phone, on the computer, and at the ticket window, not once, not twice, but four times seeking success. After the third try, the staff and I had come up with a solution to get us skiing. It involved paying additional fees for ski school so that we could garner a reservation for the hill. *This roadblock is where I began to sabotage myself.* Rather than staying focused on my commitment to "getting our family on the slopes," I changed the perspective that I wanted to get us on the slopes without added costs. While it wasn't fair or right that I should have to pay additional fees, I had to realign myself to the original goal and consider myself successful when I had lift tickets in my hand for everyone, *despite the added expenses.* In the end, we skied. I nearly took my joy away in that experience by redefining success as something different from what I had initially defined it. No matter how awful the experience was getting there, the responsibility to stay the course of my *Defined Success* was on me. It cost me more, and I gave up days of my life to make it happen, but it happened, and we got to do "normal" for that week.

Another example many of you can probably relate to this year is the reaction to the global pandemic. Each of us has our journey to share here, and I am no different. On February 25, 2020, our board of directors officially approved our 2020 budget, forecasting a year of escalating success. On March 13, 2020, we closed our physical offices and entered crisis management. Our business focus has long been commercial HVAC, restaurant equipment repair, and petroleum services. Obviously, with these businesses being some of the hardest hit, we aligned ourselves to 1.) Controlling what we could control, and 2.) Saving our business.

Throughout 2020, we did both. We measured our success in organizing our company for growth and controlling all costs while watching the story of 2020 unfold.

In the end, our revenue was nowhere near where we had initially projected. Still, we had an overwhelmingly successful year in preserving culture, stabilizing products, executing implementation backlog, managing risk, and overall emerging from 2020 as a better organization than we were when we went into it. Despite this, it is easy for me as the business leader to be distracted by revenue failure even though we decided to measure success differently for 2020.

Do not allow yourself to become prey to failures by redefining success. Instead, stay *Goal-Driven* in your focus on your ***Defined Success.***

Fundamental #4: Jenga. Solution-Focused Flexibility.

When people see the word "flexible" as an element of this process, they usually think about changing goals or personally being flexible. This perspective is entirely false. The concept of ***Solution-Focused Flexibility*** is that there are <u>many</u> options for problems that people rule out before considering them. My strong push in this process is to train your brain away from ruling out what you have deemed impossible until proven that to be a fact.

Throughout the years of formally or informally coaching *Exponential Mindset*, most people could find a means of embracing many of the other elements of an *Exponential Mindset*. What they struggled with, and you likely will too, is the art of *Solution-Focused Flexibility*. Do not define success, boundaries, or balance by a clock or what the world expects. Instead, look at every situation as possible, with enough flexibility. What exactly does this mean? *Solution-Focused Flexibility* does not mean that WE need to be more flexible. Focused flexibility It's like playing ***Jenga***.

For those unfamiliar, the game of Jenga is a physical and mental skill built on the simple premise of stacking interwoven wooden blocks. The object of the game is to extrude wooden blocks without causing the tower to collapse. I have played this game hundreds of times. Often the tower that seemed impossible of standing, still standing. These towers remind me of *Solution-Focused Flexibility*. If we looked at the blocks like they would come tumbling down in our *Jenga* game, we would never pull the bottom piece out, when really, that was the only one where there was no pressure. In *Solution-Focused Flexibility*, we must look at the situation as though we can move every block, and then one by one, we stress-test them, poke at them if you will, to see if we can make them move to get the result for which we are looking.

There is a great deal of timeliness to *Solution-Focused Flexibility*, having just endured 2020. **Before March of 2020**, if someone would have told you that you could:

- Do a tele-visit with your doctor.
- Get prescriptions via Zoom.
- See every church in America online and watch any student take classes from wherever they had wi-fi. You would have responded with a hardy chuckle.

We saw all of that and more in 2020! The societal crisis we were living through forced us to look at inflexible things and make them flexible. It forced us to see them differently. Before 2020, did it *really* make sense to have sick people come into a doctor's office? And why haven't churches

all gone remote before 2020? The truth is that until we are forced to do so, we don't think flexibly. Train your mind to do this every day. You will find innovation for your business and a balance in your life that others deemed impossible. This year has given us many real-life examples to provide you with confidence in this way of thinking, so you have a hand up in this process that others before you haven't had. While there has been much heartache associated with 2020, history will definitely remind us of the massive innovations in flexibility that came out of this year. We have genuinely redefined harmony and balance!

Fundamental #5: Protagonist Power. Expect Conflict. Confront Conflict. Get Comfortable in Conflict Chaos. Expect Solutions to Conflict.

When I think about this Fundamental of an *Exponential Mindset*, I think about the great protagonists of the world—James Bond, Bugs Bunny, Darth Vader, Rocky Balboa, Marty McFly, Scooby-Doo, and even Shrek. These characters can take action, causes the story to happen, and move the plot through their actions and choices. Even if they're trapped in a cell, they're able to find a way out by picking the lock or breaking the bars. They don't just stand there; instead, they make solutions happen. Fundamental #5 is setting the right expectation. Conflict will happen, and you will need to expect it. Chaos will come with challenges and problems on the road to success. Expect challenges and welcome the chaos that comes with them. These go hand-in-hand in your professional and personal life.

Once you have set the expectation that these can and will happen, the most crucial element is being willing to confront them. The sooner you address the conflict, the more time you have to solve the problem. So often, we fixate on the barriers or obstacles between us and the goal that we forget what the goal was. Your goal in this book is learning to lead an *Exponential Life*.

Solving conflict will be part of that.

Fundamental #6: The Slingshot Effect.

One of the most important mechanics of progress is that often you need to go backward to go forward. I call that *The Slingshot Effect*. Anyone growing up in the 70s has seen or played with one. In case you haven't, a slingshot requires that you pull backward on a stiff rubber band to catapult whatever you put in front of it.

In my case, it was usually a rock and aimed at a brother. The farther back you pulled, the harder the object was catapulted. When converting your thinking to an *Exponential Mindset*, it is essential to realize that what many people would see as sacrifices or setbacks, you should see as pullbacks. These are conscious decisions or sacrifices that you make to get to your ultimate goal.

The year 2020 has provided many current examples of *The Slingshot Effect*. Davisware had to "pull back" on trade shows and events due to the global pandemic. As a result, our online presence broadened our audience to a far greater group. Our shot forward was that we impacted ten times more people with our presentations. My personal "pull back" was that I could not attend Easter Sunday Mass for the first time in my life. The shot forward was that we got to watch mass in 3 states instead, being inspired by very progressive local pastors from which we would have *never* had the luxury of learning.

The expectation when using a slingshot is that you must pull back. The further you pull back, the further your shot goes forward. So too, in developing an *Exponential Mindset*, you must get comfortable with the expectation that you will sometimes need to pull back. That creates forward movement at a significantly higher rate of speed than would have occurred otherwise.

Fundamental #7: Process-Driven. Always Drive Toward Process.

Personally or professionally, I am continually trying to create a process and drive toward it and making an effort to constantly assess situations to improve them in every aspect of their lives. Anything you do that doesn't have a process associated with it will happen TO you instead of allowing you to control it. In business, it is common that there is a check and balance to every process in the company to ensure quality and **closed-loop communication**.

In your personal life, many of the same results can happen. Standard processes on who is responsible and when the cars have their oil changed prevent situations where it doesn't happen or does it long before needed. Standardizing the facility that does it, documenting what services you choose, having a single person responsible for all oil changes causes you to make fewer decisions and better-quality decisions.

Step-by-Step to an Exponential Mindset

Early in my career, I used the *Exponential Mindset* intuitively. I didn't realize that what I was doing was different from others. As I became aware of its power in my life, I became more conscious about when and how I used it. Awareness created power. This discovery process helped me formalize my actions and thoughts so I could share them with others. Here are the steps I use when I have a problem that puts demands on my time and resources:

Step #1: Assess your "whys" to determine the motivation for achieving the goal. If you don't have enough "whys," don't invest the time. In your *Exponential Mindset* journey, you will clearly define your why making it easier for you to wisely choose your "yes's" and feel confident with your "no's." That clarity gives you the confidence and conviction to make the tough decisions in your life easier. Your "yes" allows you to be there and enjoy it, and your "no" gives you freedom without regrets or guilt. This type of conscious decision-making is a process, not a destination.

Step #2: S.M.A.R.T. Goals are a way of life. If the motivation exists, define success with a **S.M.A.R.T. Goal** (Specific, Measurable, Achievable, Relevant, and Time-Bound). Then, frame everything you do with S.M.A.R.T. goals.

Step #3: Inventory your resources by listing/cataloging all the tasks required and time boxing them to know what you have access to for achieving the goal. What requirements must you meet?

Step #4: Analyze every task and step. Determine if it drives you toward your goal, impedes it, or distracts you from your destination. Assess whether these steps can be eliminated, delegated, combined, replaced, changed, or systematized.

Step #5: Develop a process tethered to the S.M.A.R.T. Goal, which includes a feedback loop- aka a check and balance so that if one element goes array, you know it as soon as possible and have an adaptation plan.

Step #6: Catalog the potential conflicts that may arise and what solutions may exist.

Step #7: Document & Implement the process/plan.

Step #8: Commit to ongoing improvement from the feedback loop. This action may seem like a formal process to go through when you are, for example, figuring out your family's system on how to do laundry every week. It may be overkill. The point here is that if you start to get your brain into going through this exercise, you will quickly see the problems before they arise, and yes, you can even improve your laundry process.

To create success in *Exponentiality*, it is critical to absorb the concepts in this chapter. The remainder of this book is built upon what you have learned here. I encourage you to go back to the beginning of this chapter and reread it.

Read it until you feel confident you understand the following:

- Your core beliefs.
- The Joy Triangle
- 7 Principles of an *Exponential Mindset*
- Step-by-Step *Exponential Mindset*

Chapter Summary – Chapter 1: Cultivating an Exponential Mindset

Lessons Learned

- *Exponential Mindset* Defined. The definition of an *Exponential Mindset* is a mindset of using skills, tools, and technology to make the highest and best use of an individual's time and talent. It is creating replicable processes with skills, tools, and technology. An *Exponential Mindset* means making a conscious effort to get the most out of every moment, every minute, and every interaction. *Living Exponentially* is living life to the fullest.
- Holistic *Exponential Mindset.* A decision to Live Exponentially must be made unilaterally in one's personal and professional lives to find real success.
- Joy Triangle is a graphical depiction of the relative importance of every step in the journey to *Exponentiality*. Core Beliefs – Goals – *Exponential Mindset* – *Living Exponentially* – Joy & Harmony.
- Define S.M.A.R.T Success to *Living Exponentially.*
- True harmony in one's life is from seeing his/her life as one, not as segregated entities of personal and professional lives.
- *An Exponential Mindset* contains *7 Fundamental Principles* – *(1)Triumph, (2)Level Up, (3)Goal Driven Focus, (4)Jenga, (5)Protagonist Power, (6)Slingshot, (7)Process-Driven*
- *Living Exponentially* is built on core beliefs and a decision to execute an *Exponential Mindset.*
- *Living Exponentially* requires ongoing choices to make every moment of everyday count and focused on your S.M.A.R.T goal.
- Executing processes in all aspects of one's life is a fundamental principle of *Living Exponentially.*
- Losing focus of the defined goal is a common way we sabotage ourselves in the journey to *Living Exponentially.*

- Play *Jenga. Solution-Focused flexibility* means seeing all possible solutions to a problem, not just those that appear to be feasible. *Solution-Focused flexibility* is the assumption that there *could* be flexibility in solutions that seem impossible.
- Be a Protagonist. By expecting conflict, you are better prepared to get confront it and get comfortable in conflict. Anticipating and planning for conflict is a fundamental principle of *Exponential Living.*
- Bad news doesn't get better with time. The sooner we share setbacks, the more time we have to come to a solution.
- *The Slingshot Effect* is an essential mechanic in progress toward *Living Exponentially*. Convert setbacks to pull backs.
- The Step-by-Step to an *Exponential Mindset* means that we have to (1) Assess our "whys", (2) Define SMART Goals, (3)Inventory your resources, (4) Analyze the tasks/steps, (5) Develop a process, (6)Catalog the conflict, (7) Document and (8) Commit to CPI.

Unveiled Discoveries

- Your bathroom mirror is a great place to document your core beliefs.
- We only have one life. Seeing your work life separate from your home life stages you for failure.
- Anyone can learn and eventually master *Living Exponentially*. There are no special skills, only the motivation to do so.

Action Plan

- Re-read this chapter.
- What is motivating you to take action in your life to be *Exponentia*l?
- Absorb the 4 concepts in this chapter.
    - Your Core Beliefs

- The Joy Triangle
- 7 Principles of an *Exponential Mindset*
- Step-by-Step to an *Exponential Mindset.*

- What are your core beliefs?
- Have you defined personal and professional goals? Are they S.M.A.R.T? Do they conflict?
- Are there any conflicts between your core beliefs and your goals?
- What areas of your life could benefit the most from *Living Exponentially*?
- What would be the direct outcomes of a change in these areas in your life?
- Can you prioritize the areas that could benefit the most?
- How can you share what you have learned in this section with your team or family?

Good Quotables

- *Exponentiality is a mindset using skills, tools, and technology to make the highest and best use of an individual's time and talent. In business, it is creating replicable processes with skills, tools, and technology. Exponential Mindset means making a conscious effort to get the most out of every moment, every minute, and every interaction. Living Exponentially is living life to the fullest.*
- *The human mind is our most significant inhibitor to what we can accomplish.*
- *Failure provides our most significant lessons learned.*
- *We are burning daylight with no guarantee of tomorrow. There is an urgency to today.*
- *Motivation is the only thing between you and Living Exponentially.*

- *Time is the great equalizer.*
- *Bad news doesn't get better with time. —Joe Klawiter*
- *Whether you think you can't or think you can, you are right. —Henry Ford*

Supplementary Learning Recommendations (Read/Listen/Watch)

- *The Four Agreements* by don Miguel Ruiz

CHAPTER 2

Disguised Opportunity: The Seven Biggest Leadership Challenges

Regardless of what you are leading, at some point in your role, your leadership skills will be tested. Whether you're directing a group of volunteers, struggling as a startup, or working double-time to keep up with your organization's growth, your leadership response to a dynamic marketplace will determine the success trajectory of your organization.

Over the last three decades working with entrepreneurs and business leaders, the themes that have resonated as what keeps them up at night and where they see their biggest challenges are eerily the same. In preparation for this book, I spent time with business leaders, converting my anecdotal data into a more scientific version. The results were nearly identical. *We are all struggling with the same challenges in our businesses.*

Although the challenges will appear in different shapes and sizes, they can generally fall into four primary areas of an organization:

- ***Time***: Time is the one finite asset. We can't spend the same minute twice. Business leaders and entrepreneurs face a constant struggle for their time and attention, including short-term needs versus long-term growth, internal business issues or the marketplace, family, and business.
- ***People***: The ultimate measure of an organization's success is the people who run it. Not having the right team, conflicts between owners or partners, poor relations with vendors or customers can lead to the undoing of a business. Solid relationships lead to success.

- ***Money***: 38% of businesses fail due to a lack of capital. This deficiency can be money to make payroll or capital to invest in growth. The financial strength of an organization usually determines the scope and impact they make in their marketplace.
- ***Product:***35% of all small business failures are a result of the marketplace not needing a product. Market needs and trends shift. If your business can't change with it, your business may not survive.[5]

There are thousands of examples of how these play out in organizations. For this book, I have selected seven challenges that I have personally witnessed and how they impacted our customers, as well as the success and growth of our own organization. These are challenges we faced. They are challenges we helped our customers face. They represent an *Exponential Mindset* helped create success. These are *our* solutions, not *the only* solution. I hope that these examples of challenges will give you insights and understanding to help solve your similar challenges.

The following are brief summaries of Disguised Opportunity: The Seven Biggest Leadership Challenges and what you can expect to learn from each one.

1. Exponential Life Balance by Design

Life balance and time are the unanimous struggle every leader I have encountered struggles to strategically execute. This chapter shares the challenges and how to conquer them. Personally, whenever I am happiest in all that I do, I am succeeding. Whenever my joy starts to slip away, I am not. When work-life balance my this exposed through the concept of Life Balance (vs. Work-Life Balance) and the keys to conquering the 24/7 work week! Too many people create businesses to have a better life but give up their lives to sustain the business. They succeed by the numbers but lose the joy and harmony of what they set out to do. I didn't want that for our family, and I don't want that for yours. This content is to help you learn from our journey, not because it was perfect, but because it was not. I want you to understand it faster and easier than I did. I hope that through lessons learned, you will do a better job executing it.

In this chapter, you will learn:

- The critical difference between balance and equality
- How to define your non-negotiables
- Why you must negotiate with yourself based on your highest value
- Why it is better to be **hyper-focused than multi-tasking**
- How to manage by priorities/non-negotiables, not guilt
- How to design your life; not react to circumstances
- When and how to use *The Slingshot Effect* to get what you want.

2. Be TExponential

Discover the activities and tasks that rob your personal life and your organization of time, money, and sustainable performance and what to do about it! Time creates money in business. Time is your greatest resource because it is finite. Additionally, time well-used is joy and harmony in life. It is the great equalizer. Whether you are the President of the United States or a newly employed teenage clerk at a local fast-food restaurant, the hours in our days are the same. Business status, social status, age, nor geography, gender, or race change this. This fact means that as the leader of Davisware, anything I can do to create extra efficiency in my day or in that of our employees' days will reduce stress and create a better result in our business and all of our lives. Efficiency does not mean doing more. It is not squeezing more things into a shorter period. Efficiency is eliminating repetitive tasks so that you and your organization can do less to gain better results, including more joy, both professionally and personally. If you spend less time doing chores personally, it will leave you more quality time to do the things you love to do. In business, technology can create enterprise-level business intelligence to grow individuals from task masters to individual contributors focused on the organizational mission. Data is how businesses go from surviving to thriving. It's how business leaders go from tired to inspired by what they do.

In this chapter, you will learn:

- How to use Continuous Process Improvement and technology to save time by eliminating repetitive tasks
- Why you should commit yourself and your company to establish a continuous process improvement culture
- Whenever you implement a new process, make sure it doesn't detract from the outcome quality.
- Why technology gives you time, but how you spend that time determines how exponential you are.
- Disruption is the death of productivity.
- How processes, standards, systems, and technology operationalize information so that everyone has access to The One Source of Truth.
- Why nobody in your business should be irreplaceable. If you don't have the systems in place to make them replaceable, you'll always have to be thinking about what happens if they decide to leave.
- How continuous process improvement, standards, systems, and technology improve the information companies use to run their businesses, eliminating the need to operate by **tribal knowledge**.
- Why the use of one centralized database improves communication, eliminates delays and paperwork, while taking the guesswork out of the equation.

3. Leading with My Hair on Fire.

Transitioning from doer to leader is the dilemma entrepreneurs face in growing their businesses. It is so challenging, in fact, many of them never make that transition, leading to stalled growth and ultimately entrepreneurs leaving the business, or shift out of leadership roles.

Why is this transition so difficult for many? The skillset and intrinsic motivation are vastly different for starting a business than running it as a business. Most entrepreneurs don't start a business with the idea of spending their days managing a staff of people to run their business.

This chapter describes how to convert from startup firefighting to a systemic approach to business, decision making, and problem-solving.

In this chapter, you will learn:

- Why a problem in your business that you keep dealing with but can never seem to solve – is a *fire*. If you don't spend the time to solve it for good, you will always be on fire.
- How issues that seem like different problems can be another manifestation of the same problem
- Why seeking outside council such as CPAs, lawyers, mentors, consultants, and coaches is helping in guiding leaders through uncharted waters
- How your management style impacts how well problems get solved and how fast people develop
- The difference between abdication and delegation in leadership
- Why standardized reports and regular meetings are essential for keeping employees informed and on the same page
- Why adding personnel and systems to expand the organization's capacity is a critical growth decision.
- Why the timing of hiring the right people and putting them in the right positions is important when it comes to moving from vision to reality
- How creating scalable systems supports both current and future growth
- How expanding your time horizon fuels your organization's growth

4. Confronting the Unsolvable Problem

What do you do when the unthinkable happens? As a business leader, solving problems is often the fuel that drives you. However, when a situation feels unsolvable, we tend to compromise the balance in our lives, trying to solve it the same way we have always done, with the same thought processes and tools. Confronting the **Unsolvable Problem** requires a different response. Many people call this approach to problem-solving "thinking outside of the box." I would propose that instead of this, you look to apply the Fundamentals of an *Exponential Mindset*. We are often reminded to focus on what we can control. 2020 and the global pandemic indeed told us this. We cannot control what comes at us, but we can control how we respond. Finding solutions through an *Exponential Mindset* will allow your organization to survive unsolvable problems and give you the tools to use these instances to thrive in all aspects of your life.

In this chapter, you will learn:

- Why, when you encounter failure, your reasons for taking on the problem must be compelling enough to motivate you to get up and try again.
- How unsolvable problems force you to expand your **resource inventory**.
- How to use all your resources to think outside the box
- Why there is no failure, only feedback and lessons learned
- People globally are far more similar than different; especially when it comes to their careers. Everyone wants to be a part of something bigger. They want to be valued for their contribution not commoditized.
- That outsourcing created U.S. jobs and created Americans and how this experience changed our perspective
- Why you must guard your time actively so that you spend it on what you can control and what is important

5. Culture on Purpose

Your culture provides the foundation for creating goals. Throughout the past three decades, each business I engaged with had a unique culture that was a derivative of the founder's vision and passion. Davisware, in its early stages, was no different. Every employee knew where we were headed and had the autonomy to determine how to get there. We also shared another reality for early-stage businesses, just surviving was a part of the goal. Just like most businesses I witnessed in this stage; we didn't start with the idea of building a culture. We were pursuing the vision or the opportunity, and survival drove our day-to-day activities. As a business grows, culture evolves out of random acts and decisions by the founders and early followers, often as much about what you do as what you allow. Employees take their lead from these cues and soon the cultural blueprint starts to form from what is valued.

In this chapter, we help you answer the questions of how do you build, manage, and sustain your ***culture on purpose***?

In this chapter, you will learn:

- How setting expectations and culture create certainty and lead to sustainable performance
- Why culture gives people a sense of connection – rowing team vs. golf team
- Why the process of changing culture is evolutionary, not expedient
- How codifying a culture gives it value
- How to lead with congruency by using your values and culture to hire, reward, promote and fire employees
- Aligning core values, business goals, and financial rewards creates a system that communicates what is important and what the expectation is of how people behave

6. **Harnessing the Power of Expectations and Communications**

    Discover how the clarity of your expectations and communications determine the speed at which you'll achieve your goals. These are tools business leaders use to influence reality and create desirable results.

In this chapter, you will learn:

- Why setting expectations starts and ends with your mission statement
- How to ensure that your mission statement says who you are, whom you serve, and how you serve them
- How to ensure your mission statement has a presence in every aspect of your business
- How defining a mission statement defines who you are and institutionalizing it communicates that definition
- Why closed loop communication is a discipline that changes both individual success and organizations.
- How to avoid the two biggest communications pitfalls that plague almost every business
- How to develop systems and the discipline to manage them to keep your communications on track

7. **Communications Under Crisis.**

    Setting clear expectations is essential when the sea is calm, and it is business as usual. When storms and chaos roll in, the need for clear expectations and communications is even more critical. Crises like the global pandemic make communicating difficult because of fear, uncertainty, and doubt (the **FUD Factor**) start to cloud the team and often times, the leadership. When the FUD Factor is in play, people require crystal-clear expectations of what they need to do. No matter how carefully you set expectations for your employees before a crisis, no doubt they have changed. Crisis adds considerable complexity to every level of business communication. To thrive in a crisis, your organization must develop new communications skills and technologies. **Communications under crisis** are essential leadership skills for every organization.

In this chapter, you will learn:

- How to develop new presentation skills and technical capabilities to deliver your messages.
- Why the elimination of social events was so impactful to online presence and how to react to it.
- Why the real value of a mission statement is when it is tested in a crisis.
- How to use all **four communication languages** remotely. Words, body language, emotions, and appearance are all critical to engagement
- That the value of succeeding in crisis is becoming a better organization as the outcome.
- Why your leadership team must proliferate your lessons learned throughout the organization.
- That the gift of delegating the *HOW* in a crisis is that we didn't have time to micromanage the *HOW* we wanted to do. Allowing our teams to own the *HOW* enabled them also to own the overall vision.
- Why feedback is common, but helpful feedback is rare. It is crucial in your organization, or even at a personal level, to create a communication and feedback culture. With a structured and high-quality feedback loop, organizations Level Up.
- That creating strong feedback loops in an organization requires feedback to be embedded from the mission statement and values, through the culture statements and review process, to building a solid assessment and feedback process for customers and partners.
- Leading up is the most challenging form of leadership there is, but its value is priceless.

Each of the 7 Leadership Challenges revolves around time, money, people, or product challenges. Each is a personal account of real struggles that we either experienced personally or witnessed as we partnered with our customers. In both cases, I think you will find parity between your journey and the journeys of the thousands of companies that I have witnessed where you are today. Regardless of which of these challenges strike closest to home. Regardless of how mundane or how overwhelming your challenge is, the upcoming chapters will give you guideposts to see how to apply *Exponentiality* to your own journey.

CHAPTER 3

Exponential Life Balance by Design

Inc. Magazine surveyed entrepreneurs and business leaders to understand what drives them. The responses most certainly echo what you would certainly include on your list. Some combination of opportunity, autonomy, freedom, impact, family, facilitating change, legacy, accomplishment, and control is very likely on your list of "whys." Money is famously missing. Not because money is not essential, but because it is not the motivator to execute the entrepreneurial dream.[6]

History shows the way to the Future

Once the commitment to business leadership or entrepreneurialism is well in the rear-view mirror, we as leaders need to remind ourselves of these why's and find a balance that sustains us. Too many leaders and entrepreneurs create businesses to have a better life, but they give up their lives to sustain the business. They succeed by the numbers but lose the joy and harmony of what they set out to do.

I didn't want that for our family, and I don't want that for yours. I want you to learn from my journey, not because it was perfect, but because it was not. I want you to understand it faster and easier than I did.

I want you to do a better job executing it. That will make the effort that went into writing this book worth every moment.

As the mom of a large family, I have a particular empathy for working mothers and parents of all kinds. More so than any other business leader, parents are battling life balance every moment of every day. Through our journey, I found joy in designing an *Exponential Life*. Executing an

Exponential Mindset in my life allowed me to create balance and, more so, harmony. I want that for you too.

In 2020 we saw, for the first time in global history, absent war, a complete global economic reset. Never in human history has this happened without war being the disrupter.

This perspective should help you see the magnitude of what we have seen and prepare you for the disruptive changes, both good and bad, that will continue to arise from this shift. We will continue writing this story as the vast improvements we make will generate yet-to-be-determined problems.

The timing in writing this book could not be more opportunistic. I did not plan it this way but combining the current world state with a mindset shift to an *Exponential Mindset* will allow you to leverage significant opportunities for newly found harmony, joy, and balance in your life.

When reflecting on 2020, I cannot help but think back to a less dramatic but still highly impactful parallel in history. From Colonial Times until the post-war era of the 1950s, the General Store was the icon in most towns. This store was the community's epicenter, where people did commerce, socialized, and picked up their mail. This store was typically owned by an entrepreneur whose family likely lived in the apartment above it.

Similarly, the local blacksmith lived in small quarters behind his shop, and of course, the farmers lived on their farms. Leading up to the 1950s, the concept of segregation between our personal time and our work pursuits didn't exist. The career was often a multi-generational family undertaking. With the advent of affordable transportation and improved communication systems, we invented the concept of suburban living. Not only did the suburbs create physical segregation between people's career and their home lives, but it also created psychological segregation, in which families had to make artificial equality, and the clock became the keeper of equality.

This transition made us slaves to unrealistic expectations in both our home and work worlds. During the workday, it became taboo to take a personal call or run an errand. On the flip side, when the clock hit 5 pm, we tried to make work a distant memory until it started the next day again. If you did anything to the contrary, you were a slacker or a workaholic.

Over the last decade, we have started to see a shift in this thought process and perspective, with more and more companies allowing work from home and flexible schedules. However, not until March 2020 did, we think this may be possible to be the rule rather than the exception.

So how does all of this relate to the art of being *Exponential* and *Exponential Life Balance by Design*? **Right now**, you have the opportunity to take advantage of a global pandemic and make your life better. Hard decisions and hard conversations you would have had a year ago are now much more comfortable. So, use this book and what you learn here to *seize the moment!*

Take this opportunity to apply *Exponentiality* in your life and your business. Whether we are thinking about this in terms of our employees or ourselves, we as business leaders can take this opportunity to counterbalance and create healthier organizations and personal harmony for ourselves and our teams.

As a result of the global pandemic, we have met each other's kids and pets virtually and maybe even with formal introductions. We have been in each other's private spaces and intimately know how often the doorbells ring.

Before 2020, if a dog were barking in the background, it would have been viewed as unprofessional. Today, you may even grab your dog off the floor and hold him on your lap, introducing him as Duke. In addition, the global pandemic has taken people out of their office buildings.

It has brought our personal lives and professional lives together in a much healthier way.

For me, during 2020, my favorite conference room became any of the local forest preserves. In-person meetings have converted into walks in the forest preserve with clients or employees. Before 2020, if your spouse or a co-worker were meeting a business associate in a forest preserve, it would have been perceived as gravely inappropriate.

These days, the forest preserves and parks are full! The year 2020 forced us into thinking with *Solution-Focused Flexibility*. Imagine a world where you can take this element of an *Exponential Mindset* and voluntarily apply it to your whole life?

As business leaders, we have learned that the minor inconveniences of dogs and doorbells have an offsetting value in productivity and employee satisfaction. *Solution-Focused Flexibility* has always happened as a product of history. *You now have the golden opportunity to execute it in your business and your life.* Seize the opportunity and combine it with an *Exponential Mindset*.

Build an exponential business and live a life with *Exponentiality*!

An Exponential Life by Design requires that you voluntarily apply each of the *7 Fundamental Elements of an Exponential Mindset*. Once you have an Exponential Mindset, we can begin using those principles to how we view our lives, problem-solving, company culture, communications, and continuous process improvement in all aspects of our businesses and lives.

The Great Re-Define. Life Balance—Modus Vivendi

An Exponential Life by Design starts with executing The Great Re-Define. The Great Re-Define applies several of the elements of an *Exponential Mindset* into action, including *Defined Success*, *Goal Driven Focus*, and *Expect Conflict-Protagonist Power*. Each of these mindset shifts will be applied as you start to think about The Great Re-Define.

Writing a book is an exciting journey. It's something that I have dreamed about doing for a very long time. I have been writing segments of it in my head for decades. But, unfortunately, I have spent far too many hours in front of a computer, researching and helping organize my thoughts and making sure that I have thought of every angle of the messaging I wanted to transcribe into this book.

One area that has struck me throughout this process - something that didn't quite add up was the idea of home life and work life. Unless you know something different than I do, we all have just one life.

In that one life, it is a Yin and yang or pushes and pulls between our personal and professional pursuits demands. So, as you continue through this book, I want to help re-frame the thought process of having two lives.

The idea of ***Modus Vivendi*** *is a Latin phrase that means "mode of living" or "way of life." It often is used to mean an arrangement or agreement that allows conflicting parties to co-exist in peace. Modus means "mode", "way", "method", or "manner". Vivendi means "of living."*

The phrase is often used to describe informal and temporary arrangements in political affairs. For example, suppose two sides reach a modus vivendi regarding disputed territories, despite political, historical, or cultural incompatibilities. In that case, the accommodation of their individual differences is established for the sake of contingency.[7]

Modus Vivendi is the first term that I have stumbled across that has defined the overall life relationship related to personal and professional commitments in all of my research. But, of course, professional and personal demands have cultural incompatibilities.[7]

Their relationship is always temporary because they are ever-shifting. These two segments generally conflict. Simultaneously, it is vital for these two elements of our lives to peacefully co-exist and exist in a symbiotic way. Even within the subset of our business lives, there is a push and a pull. As business leaders, we are continually balancing *Modus Vivendi* related to investing for future returns and producing current returns to ownership.

At home, we are balancing family time with spousal relationship time. Both are important and often have conflicting priorities.

Do I put the kids to bed so that they stay on a routine, or do I let them stay up to play one last game with grandpa before he leaves? Do I go to one kids' soccer game to miss the other child's bedtime routine? As it relates to the two worlds, do I spend the extra time preparing for tomorrow's meeting at the expense of family dinner, or do I sacrifice family dinner to avoid the stress of feeling unprepared?

Do I take on work to get the quality I want but miss my Saturday morning at home, or do I delegate the work and lose peace of mind in the results? Each of us can relate to these decisions and how hard they are. All of these are hard decisions with very little in the way of the correct answers. In all these cases, s*tress* on one element of our lives creates pressure on the other. A large part of the purpose of this book is to share my methods in *Modus Vivendi.*

Modus Vivendi <u>requires</u> that both parties, or elements, be addressed.[7] Moms had done this for years when their kids were fighting. When she didn't have the correct answer as to who had the toy first, she simply took the toy away from both kids. Ironically, if you were one of those kids, as much as you wanted the toy, you were nearly as satisfied with your sibling not having it. What you were experiencing was *Modus Vivendi.*

Converting Equality to Balance

What is the difference between *equality* in your life and *balance* in your life? The world defines work-life balance as equality, regardless of the terminology used. It is a general understanding that you work during business hours, typically from 8 am to 5 pm. From 5 pm on, you are committed to your family and personal life. Anything you do outside of these hours, you are either a workaholic or a slacker. You feel guilty if you take time on either side of the pendulum for the other.

Just because the world defines it that way doesn't mean it has to be for you. Balance in your life is being in the right place, at the right time, for the right reason. Balance creates harmony. Balance gives you the ability to be present and joyful in those critical moments at work and home, regardless of what time the clock says. Confusing equality with balance robs you of joy in all you do. The anxiety caused by missing a soccer game or being late and unprepared for a meeting steals that joy. Joy happens when you are totally present at the soccer game and come to the meeting ready to kill it. If you don't feel joy in what you are doing, what's the purpose? Too many entrepreneurs create a business to have a life, but they give up their lives to sustain the business. They succeed by the numbers but lose the joy of what they do. I didn't want that for me, our family, or our business. During my career, I witnessed most of the people I came across had far more anxiety stealing their joy because they had not defined the goal of harmony. If you're like me, then I want that for you too. Let me help you figure it out.

Sway in our Balance

We can achieve balance, not equality, through an *Exponential Mindset.*

Combining an *Exponential Mindset* with balance will create the joy of Exponential Living. Before we get to *Exponentiality*, let's set the right expectation on what life balance, *Modus Vivendi,* really is. We've all seen (and likely fidgeted with) a balancing sculpture like the one on the front cover of this book. You may even have one on your desk, as I do. The one pictured on the front of this book is one I found at a garage sale my freshman year of college. He's been a continuous reminder of the power of balance. What is important to note is that he rarely finds himself precisely in the middle unless he is stationary. When he leans to the left, the bar helps counter his weight and pulls him back to the right. The same is true when he leans right. This action is called *sway*. By definition, balance in biomechanics is the ability to maintain a line of gravity that includes sway. According to Wikipedia, a certain amount of sway is inevitable. It does not necessarily indicate dysfunctional balance.[8]

To find success in this book, you need to firmly buy into the understanding that a balanced life has sway. Sway is what will create joy and harmony in your life. Too much rigidity will cause you to fall or, worse yet, cause you to lose your happiness and peace both at home and at work.

Some days, weeks, or even months, I lean far to the left or the right. Acknowledging that this movement is necessary for proper balance is a reminder that sway is healthy.

Balance is not equality. Balance is dynamic and fluid, depending on the circumstances. A calculated decision to have sway in my life is my key to balance in my life. If we are moving in our lives, we will have sway. I don't worry that I'm leaning too far to one side or another. My core value to find joy and harmony in all that I do keeps me balanced. I will be pulled back by my priorities and their urgency.

Using the visual of the balancing sculpture on the cover, visualize your balance, including the sway. I learned very early that my efforts at home and my work efforts would never have anything more than momentary equality. Equality is not your friend. Balance is. Don't go any further in this book until you have solidified what real-life balance is in your mind. To design your *Exponential Life*, you need to embrace the differentiation between balance and equality. Discard your thinking about work-life balance. It is simply ***life balance***.

You can't measure equality in time. Equality can only be successful in momentary instances, and it is not sustainable. You will never, naturally, spend your time equally; forcing your time to be equal will not result in the *Modus Vivendi* you are looking for. Your personal life and your professional lives are dynamic. There were many days, weeks, months, and years where I spent far more time at work than at home. The opposite is also true. These times were the sway in my balance. So, how did I know if the sway in my balance was becoming too much? How was I sure that I didn't sway to the point of falling. I didn't always know at the time. Those are the times I fell off the wire and why I am writing this book.

I want you to learn from my successes ***and*** also learn from my falls. As I said earlier, I want you to learn *Modus Vivendi* faster and easier than I did and do a better job executing it. I hope the "sway" in my life that went into writing this book is worth every moment in you finding success.

So how *do* you know when the sway is injecting elements of a risk of losing your balance? First, you need to do a joy and harmony assessment of each side of your life. What brings you joy at work? What brings you harmony at home? What are you doing that creates conflicts between the two? Spend some time thinking about this, and when you have a list of what brings you joy and harmony, you now have the basis for your goals.

Whenever you add or take something away from your life, assess it compared to this list. Leave it on your desk, make it your screen saver or backdrop and make every conflicting decision based upon these factors. The two aspects of my life, personal and professional, are dynamic and generally un-related entities. In the real world, both elements are fighting for the same resource- my time. This dynamic is why they interrelate. I needed to assess what was negotiable and what was not. My world was a bit more complicated and more unique because our business was one that my husband and I were in together. It added a layer of complexity that most do not experience to focus on myself individually for this exercise.

First, I accepted that these two unique, dynamic entities would have conflicting demands on my time that I would have to negotiate - even with my 5-star planning skills. That way, I was prepared for conflicts as both a mother and a businesswoman. The fundamental underlying principle in these self-negotiations was that the result had to create more harmony than anxiety in both aspects of my life. My assessment of these conflicts considered the importance and urgency of both demands.

Defining Non-Negotiables

The Fundamental Element of *Exponentiality* that applies to defining non-negotiables is *Triumphing, Expecting Success*. You have to go into the definition of your non-negotiables with the understanding that you will succeed- regardless of how conflicted they may feel. In both your personal and professional pursuits, you can likely point to elements of your life that you would consider non-negotiables. These are areas of your life that you would drop everything else to attend to. But, as you sit and think about them, you can also probably think of dozens of times (or, for me, hundreds) in which you gave up what you would have deemed the non-negotiable for what was urgently in front of you. You traded in the important for the urgent.

After defining your personal and professional non-negotiables, you next need to accept that everything else *is* negotiable. Often, this is far harder than defining non-negotiables. Those we can easily name. However, we sabotage ourselves by then re-negotiating to add more non-negotiables. During my career at Davisware, some of my non-negotiables were trade shows, customer **Go-Lives**, fort customer commitments, employee reviews, our annual User Conference, and company culture-building initiatives. As a mother, my non-negotiables were to nurse my babies, coach my kids whenever possible, host classroom parties, chaperone field trips, celebrate birthdays, and be a part of every school's start and end year.

You may be able to empathize with all of these or maybe none of them at all. The important thing here is that you create your list. My non-negotiables gave me joy where I was at, just as yours should for you. You can also test your non-negotiables by asking yourself if missing out on one of them created sadness or anxiety. If so, they belong on your list of non-negotiables.

Having these very crisply defined makes resolving conflicts a positive experience, not laden with guilt. I could make tough decisions with confidence, knowing I was doing the right thing at the right time and maintaining my balance. Was this system in perfect equality? Of course not! Were there times when two non-negotiables conflicted?

Absolutely. That is where we would apply other elements of the *Exponential Mindset* to help come to a resolution. Remember, your goal is not about perfect equality. It is about balance with sway.

Before I established these guidelines, I was making decisions by managing anxiety and guilt. Every business leader/parent knows the guilt that comes with leaving a meeting early to catch a baseball game or, on the flip side, staying for the meeting and missing the game. I lived it, and when I did, it consumed my ability to be present at whichever of the alternatives I choose. I either spent the meeting checking the scores or sat in the bleachers on my device. *I was definitely not present.* After I re-defined balance to include sway and not equality, I found the ability to be fully present no matter where I was and harmony in the decision.

As a business leader, it is essential that once you have your non-negotiables defined, you have shared them with your team. If you are a team leader, you should encourage your entire team to share their non-negotiables. This process is crucial because it sets the expectation across the organization. It will also help to hold you accountable to your non-negotiables, should you allow your sway to become imbalanced.

Just the same, you should share them with your family. Setting the expectation with your family and kids that you will be at their games, *except* when your professional non-negotiables conflict. This approach creates an ally for you in your pursuit of balance.

So, what do I do when there is a conflict between two non-negotiables? That is where Life by Design comes in. This conflict may cause particular situations that require you to sacrifice one non-negotiable for another. However, once I define my non-negotiables, I started building a life that eliminated or minimized conflict and stress as much as possible. Using the *Exponential Mindset* skills to define your non-negotiables will help you progressively gain more success in meeting your non-negotiables. This system may fail occasionally, but if you can walk away from this book, creating more joy and harmony and less guilt, we have both succeeded in our goals.

My example of this came long before 2020. *Solution-Focused Flexibility* requires that we look at each circumstance as being flexible.

In many cases, I can solve conflicts by asking for flexibility around my non-negotiables. For example, two of my non-negotiables (we will hit on defining non-negotiables in an upcoming chapter) were coaching my kids' sports AND attending industry events. Those seem to directly conflict with one another, mainly because the sport was cross country, and its season conflicted directly with my busiest time of year for trade shows. By seeking flexibility, I staged my ability to do both. I assessed when most trade shows are, typically Tuesday, Wednesday, and Thursday.

Cross country practice was three days per week. Before my coaching, it was Monday, Wednesday, and Friday. By shifting my practices to Monday, Thursday, and Saturday, I fully opened up two of the three potential days. In counterbalance to this change, I contacted the industry sponsors and let them know that I would be available for any speaking Monday morning or anytime Tuesday or Wednesday. So, rather than passively waiting to see schedule conflicts, I proactively shared my passion for coaching and speaking with those associations and how both could co-exist. A by-product of this change was that several parents of my athletes also traveled. This modification to the standard schedule gave them 2 ½ solid days of business travel without disruption. Solving their travel dilemma wasn't my primary motivator but was a nice by-product of asking for flexibility proactively.

Designing an Exponential Life

To choose an *Exponential Life by Design*, most, if not all, of the Fundamentals of an *Exponential Mindset* need to be executed and often in the same situation. We chose an *Exponential Life by Design*, not one that was continually reacting to circumstances. I found joy in a lack of conflicts and being present at as many things as is possible. These processes are not just for insanely busy moms and dads. Your goal may be to have more downtime and fewer events on your calendar. This strategy can also apply to a single person who wants excellent balance in their life.

In most cases, the decision to create an *Exponential Life by Design* does not result in a life without conflicts. However, it allows you to choose the gives and gets versus the conflicts that previously arose. This choice is a critical distinction because battles remove joy and harmony. Gives and gets will enable you to consciously choose what you are offering for what you are getting.

With as many kids as we have, if I didn't make it a *conscious decision* to *Design an Exponential Life*, our joy would have been entirely different. I decided to design our lives around the life we wanted to live rather than continuously reacting to circumstances. I made a conscious decision to catalog what I could control and focus on those elements of our lives. For example, when choosing our business real estate, we selected our office building because it was within walking distance of our kids' school. That way, if needed, I could be at work early or work late, and the kids could make their way to our office. Our kids and any of our employees' kids could use desks at the office to do homework. At the same time, our workday went on relatively uninterrupted (I say relatively because anyone who has kids knows that everything is relative when kids are involved).

This decision created harmony.

The office location solved transportation issues with our kids, but the counterbalance was active participation in our kids' lives. I wasn't content to just have a successful career. I wanted to be "all in" as a successful parent.

I have coached hundreds of teams throughout my parenting, often during my busiest times at work. So how did I do this? It wasn't easy, but it also wasn't complicated. As I mentioned earlier, one of my first parent-coach positions was coaching the cross-country team. By coaching, I could control the schedule rather than just continuing to join the practices as a parent. I loved being a part of the program and being there with my kid. As the coach, I decided when practices were to make both elements of my life work.

When I started to have conflicts with meets, I simply raised my hand for more responsibility.

In a way, I used *The Slingshot Effect*.

I pulled back and added more work to my plate so that I had less conflict than before. More responsibility translated into more joy. Effectively, I could make both of my worlds symbiotic by taking on the scheduling responsibility. Doing so wasn't easy. It was hard.

It took much planning and extra effort, but I made the events and succeeded at my job. Often, I would coach a cross country race or volleyball game and fly out immediately afterward. On the return, it was often much of the same.

I would change in the bathroom at the airport from my Davisware uniform to my coaching uniform. Remember, I defined coaching as a non-negotiable.

Once I designated it as such, I found a way to make it work.

On the flip side, when I was on the road, it was intense. Often, my day started before dawn with meetings that included multiple breakfasts, lunches, and dinners. I often maximized my time by finding clients or employees to do workouts with me. It was a golden opportunity to get to know them better while getting in much-needed exercise. For most of you, this probably sounds like insanity. It was. For me, it was a decision to pack as much as I could into each day on the road, allowing me to travel less and spend more time with my family. This trade-off was 100% worth it to me. Exchanges like these allowed me to do most of my non-negotiables while still having a rewarding and successful career and business.

As I mentioned at the start of this section, the decision to have an *Exponential Life by Design* requires the ability to execute an *Exponential Mindset*. In addition, it requires being a little bit bold and challenging status quo ideas. I always try to give examples in both the personal and professional arena to emphasize that the decision to *Live Exponentially* is related to your entire life.

You cannot execute it in one or the other with success. One example of a melded solution to both a personal and a professional conflict came our way in 2013. Just eighteen months earlier, we purchased one of our competitors. As a result, for the first time in my career, I did not know every customer. Our customer base had grown by 4x. My knowledge of each customer and their businesses' personal information had always contributed to our organizational success. One of my professional non-negotiables was to be intimately connected to our customers. Now I had to figure out how to do it with our newly expanded customer base.

Conventional wisdom would have had us spend tens of thousands of dollars and many nights on the road, visiting and learning. Neither of these was feasible. We didn't have the finances to support this. Also, being away from my family that much would have been sacrificing a non-negotiable with my family. This dilemma is where a bold decision to use *Solution-Focused Flexibility* came in. This unconventional wisdom gained us the opportunity to win big, both personally and professionally.

Using Google Maps, I mapped our new customers. Then, I built a nearly 5,000-mile road trip to meet them, peppering in a vacation along the way.

We loaded up our Big Red Bus and travel trailer, along with our kids. Our road trip took our family to Canada, down the east coast, and finally to Texas and up the midwestern United States. We traveled for a total of 5 weeks, connecting with over 30 customers while exploring national parks, the ocean, downtown New York City and immersing our kids in the culture of our business. The value of this, both personally and professionally, is immeasurable.

Everyone involved learned a lot.

Our customers knew that we were real people, and we were very committed to them as customers. So, our kids learned a bit of what we do and got exposed to all sorts of influential people they may never have even met. And by the way, this was hard, not easy, but it was worth every moment.

We left our kids and camper at the R.V. park during our first few customer stops while meeting our customers. Out of necessity, we eventually would drive our crew to the customer's parking lot and leave the kids and the au pair in the R.V. while we met. I must admit, this definitely created anxiety. How were these customers going to take us seriously, rolling up in a 15-passenger van full of kids, towing a camper? But I decided that the risk was worth taking and that what it demonstrated was that we were real people with a real family and that we were very invested in their business. The global pandemic has emphasized what we learned in these situations.

Sometimes we get so hung up on the professionalism of what we are doing that we forgot to remind ourselves that it is just as important to be human. This trip humanized us!

Interestingly, as we traveled, our customers started getting word that we were traveling with our family. Soon, we were getting requests to meet the kids. With lots of nervous energy, we decided to start to bring them in. With lots of mom threats, I lined them up and brought them along. Slowly, they began to gain a rhythm, watching what we were doing.

By the time we got down to the D.C. area, they were getting comfortable with the entire drill. They knew what to wear and how to behave. The story that comes to mind is with a customer named Michael and our eleven-year-old daughter, Gabrielle. Dan and I approached the office and introduced ourselves. The receptionist showed us into the office, where Michael met us mid-way through the office. We greeted one another (this customer happened to be one I knew at a distance from professional trade shows) and exchanged greetings. Finally, he asked about our kids. Gabrielle took this as her moment to demonstrate what she had been watching. She stood up straight, smiled, and then said, "*Hi, Mr. Michael, my name is Gabrielle Davis. I am 11 years old. I am #4 (referring to birth order). I play soccer, basketball, and volleyball. My favorite color is purple, and I am good at school.*" A smile quickly filled Michael's face, both amused and impressed with her introduction. She had effectively given him her little eleven-year-old resume.

I share this story not because I need some accolades in my thinking. Instead, I share it because a large part of being *Exponential* is sharing.

The easiest way to teach people is by persuasive example. Packing your family in a van and camper for five weeks to visit your customers may not be feasible and may not even be applicable for you. However, I am confident that you will begin to find similar opportunities if you start to see the world with an *Exponential Mindset*. Where leaders go, teams will follow. When you start to see the possibilities and execute, your staff will too. That is how your life, and your organization will become *Exponential*. In this case, our family became *Exponential* also. While we were working, we were demonstrating to our kids how their future might look. Our kids became exposed to places and faces they would have never had the opportunity to experience in any classroom. They were able to see what it meant to be a business leader and an *Exponential* problem solver via their front row seats.

These bold decisions to take the risk for our family and our business quickly demonstrated themselves to have an exponential reward. Imagine what this could have looked like if we used textbook decision-making and just scheduled a series of business trips and a standard family vacation? Instead, we saved money, created quality family time and business interactions, and *Exponentially* used our time in everyone's best interest. Not every story is a success story, but each of these stories demonstrates the highest level of application of the *Exponential Mindset* and *Living Exponentially*. How can you apply this thinking in your life today?

Solving Problems with an Exponential Mindset

As I hope you are learning, *Exponential Life by Design* cannot happen with a single methodology, nor is there a standard checklist that you go through. However, if you apply any of the *7 Fundamental Elements*, you will create a life you design. These Fundamentals are tools in a toolbox. Just like not every job needs a hammer, every element does not apply to every situation. A job that requires holding two boards together with nails will be served flawlessly by that hammer versus the wrench or pliers in the bag. An *Exponential Mindset*'s art is the art of framing every situation with a possible vs. impossible mindset and using the right tools to solve the problem. To demonstrate this, I have two examples. One example is from my personal life and the other from my professional life. Both explore non-negotiable that were solved through *Solution-Focused Flexibility* in my re-defined *Modus Vivendi.* Both required that I re-defined our lives as a singular journey, not one that required equality between two conflicting entities.

As I am sure you are learning, our family is essential to me. You may not have gathered yet that the definition of family extends beyond the ten we call our own. In addition to our brood, Dan and I have 20 brothers and sisters (yes, 20 and all biological from a single set of parents) who have produced 110 of the most amazing nieces and nephews.

This factor makes our immediate family inclusive of more than 140 people! So now you probably understand more than ever why an *Exponential Mindset* became a survival technique in my world!

My niece and goddaughter, Brooklyn, is part of this big, beautiful family. I take my role in her life very seriously. Unfortunately, her senior volleyball season was restricted to only parents in the stands due to the global pandemic. This restriction meant that I would not be able to support her in her last season of competitive sports. I defined changing this as a non-negotiable. Now, I just needed to figure out how to do it.

There were many obstacles in the way, including extensive work commitments, the games being played far away at a very inconducive time of day, and a houseful of kids of my own. Rather than seeing all of these together as impossible, I decided to take them down one at a time. First, I had to get in the door. Through a series of calls, inquiries, and requests, I got access to attend in place of my brother (sorry, Jason!). My next challenge was getting to the game without disrupting my work commitments with a ticket in hand. By rearranging my day to put calls to the end of the day, I could work in the car until the minute I pulled up, with minimal interruption to my workday. Finally, I solved my commitments at home with a crockpot dinner and scheduled playdates for the kids. Overcoming these obstacles was worth the effort to see Brooklyn's face when I showed up. The joy I gained in seeing her face powered a very sleepy drive home.

In this example of problem-solving, I applied several of the *7 Fundamental Elements of an Exponential Mindset*. First, I *Expected the Possibility/probability of Defined Success.* When I set out to make the arrangements, I expected nothing other than to be at that game. I expected everyone involved to *Level Up/Meet me at my level.* I was not distracted from my *Goal-Driven Focus* by details such as not seeing her in her home gym and a compromised family dinner. It would have been easy to allow my brain to change my goal. From all of the changes that I invoked, I focused on *Solution-Focused Flexibility.* There were a dozen parts of the world that I did not control. I had to ask for flexibility on many of them. I also set my expectation that this would be hard.

Six hours of driving at the end of a long day was hard. It was worth it because I succeeded in my goal- to see her play. I did not allow myself to redefine success so that I could fail. I applied *The Slingshot Effect* to my workday re-organization. That day, I had to work long and juggle appointments, in essence, pulling back. I had to serve our family a mediocre dinner, function on a little less sleep, skip my workout, and put in an exceptionally long day to succeed in creating the memory and the joy. I saw my goddaughter play her senior year when the world said I couldn't. Many people don't find this success because they are distracted by the obstacles.

Obstacles are just the pullback on the Slingshot. They aren't sacrifices. They are pieces that you must invest in getting what you want.

A Systemic Approach to an Exponential Life

It's easy to think about systems and processes when you are at the office. That makes perfect sense and is how businesses generally grow and succeed. However, as you begin to use an *Exponential Mindset,* hopefully, you will start to identify opportunities in which repetitive tasks can be improved or eliminated with technology.

An organizational focus making the highest and best use of time and talent will yield *Exponential* results.

Upcoming chapters will focus on how to see and seize these opportunities in your business.

For this section, I want to focus on the systemic approach in your personal life. Successful business leaders are often seeing these opportunities and execute systems and processes in their businesses. Yet, at home, they simply react to what comes at them. They forget to look for opportunities for *Exponentiality* and process improvement. I mentioned earlier my coaching career and how I could have it peacefully co-exist with the rest of my life. I want to use this section to expand on this journey and demonstrate the value of a systemic approach to an *Exponential Life***.**

I mentioned earlier my decision of *Defined Success* as a cross country coach. Let's explore more on my thought process to make it happen.

A big part of this process required that I do an **inventory of resources.** In this case, and most cases, the primary resource is time:

- I compared the time demands of coaching to my current time commitments.
- I interviewed the previous coach about what was involved and how many hours it required.
- I compared the demands to my availability (basically zero).

This step is called **Timeboxing**. It is a technique to manage time and become more productive. It involves allocating time to an activity in advance and then completing the action within that time frame.

I estimated the amount of time for each responsibility. As a reminder, the great equalizer in life is our time. I had to figure out how to make sure my time resource matched up to my newly added responsibility. Without this process, there would be undue stress and certainly less joy in all I was doing.

My timeboxing was somewhere between a math equation and a personal negotiation. I did simple math to figure out that the 12-week season required an in-person commitment of 9.5 hours/week (8 hours practices/meets + 1.5 hours commuting) and another 6.5 hours (1 hour workout prep + 0.5 hours registration/attendance + 0.5 uniforms/ equipment + 2.0 hours stats/awards + 1-hour schedules + 1.5 hours newsletter/ communication/ motivation) of administrative commitment. In total, I needed 16 hours per week *IF* I didn't apply an *Exponential Mindset*.

Even with my *Possibility* Mindset, this was impossible. However, by applying the other principles, I could find magic. What could I do to reduce these hours and still gain the total experience? I had some ideas.

I started by segregating the demands between in-person and administrative time requirements. I didn't want to miss any in-person commitments personally or professionally, so I had to look for where I could find the time or another solution.

In-Person Timeboxing Negotiation. I was committed to the whole 8 hours/week of in-person coaching, so I was looking anywhere that I could find in-person commitments that I could negotiate in my schedule. Here is what I came up with:

Personal Concessions. Since coaching was a personal non-negotiable, I started searching my personal commitments to find trade-offs.

- **Trade workouts for practices.** Typically, I did a running session 3x/week for about an hour. If I designed my practices for me to participate and run with the kids, everyone won. I instantly gained 3 hours/week, and the kids loved it.
- **Location, location, location.** By using the park next to the office, I reduced travel time by 50%, saving an additional 45 minutes.

Professional Concessions. It seemed like this was as much time as I could find personally. So now, I shifted my sights to discover the additional 5.75 hours/week from my work hours.

1. **Rearranging Non-Negotiable Commitments.**

Our annual leadership summit (a non-negotiable) fell right at the end of the season. By moving it back by one month, I could gain~2 hours per week of prep time I spent to the post-season.

Total Physical Time Required	**9.50 Hours**
Less Gained Workout Time (Personal)	*-3.00 Hours*
Less Reduced Travel Time (Personal)	*-0.75 Hours*
Less Moving Leadership Prep (Professional)	*-2.00 Hours*
In-Person Weekly Time Commitment	**3.75 Hours**

2. Administrative Timeboxing Negotiation.

I went through the previous coach's notes to determine how I could reduce the level of effort, move the tasks systemically outside of the season, or delegate the work entirely. I began applying the Fundamental Principle of *Process-Driven. Always Drive Toward Process.* I began to assess what we could do to make this coaching role as systematic as possible and still be exceptional.

As a reminder, I was estimating 6.5 administrative hours/per week. I began to organize the tasks. I segregated what had to be done in-season vs. pre-season. I separated at what I could systematize and delegate vs. what was the coach's responsibility.

I delegated attendance, uniforms, stats, and parts of the scheduling and communications. I knew I wanted to make these volunteer positions, but before I did, I had to spend time creating a systemic process for each of these items to ensure their success. Just like in business, I made position descriptions and a process for successfully delivering high-quality results.

By handing volunteers a well-organized system, they were grateful to find a way to participate in the program. In short, I started to create a systemic culture similar to what you would expect in a business.

I segregated the content from the publication of communications, delegating everything other than content. As a result, we became ***TExponential*** by eliminating our newsletter and incorporating it into the school's online communication tools. Applying this to business, all too often, we go looking for a new app or a new tool when there is one already in the toolbox.

Introducing tools that serve similar purposes to the same organization creates chaos. We used the tools we already had and spent no additional money to simplify communications for everyone.

During the summer, my work travel schedule was significantly less than the rest of the year.

During pre-season, I did the prep work, found inspirational quotes for the entire season, created all forms, and set up sharing platforms. We moved everything we could to the school website to save time.

Researching and building workouts were the last significant portions of time I tackled. Previously, the former coach spent 1-2 hours per week researching and documenting new drills, keeping the practices fresh. I created a spreadsheet that added formulas and measured distances and workouts. The initial investment of time to build the spreadsheet was significant. Once completed, this document became my annual coaching Bible. I would insert the new dates for the start of the season, and the work was done. I shared with many other coaches, making the entire cross-country programs in our region more systemic and more *Exponential*. The other accidental win by doing this was that if practices got moved or changed, or athletes had to miss a practice, it was easy to adjust and not lose our momentum. If I had to miss a practice due to a competing priority, any volunteer could step in and confidently know what to do.

The **Knowledge Ubiquity** gained by creating processes, standardizing data, and creating clear expectations has allowed this program to thrive during my 17-year tenure with the program.

Finally, I realized that by switching my kid responsibilities, driving the early crowd to school each day, gaining me an additional ~1.5 hours per week.

Once I had outlined, systematized, prioritized, eliminated, and changed what I could control, I tested it by asking, *"Will this process deliver the outcome I want?"* I reduced the total hours needed from 16 (impossible) to just over 5 hours/week. I had found success!

Creating multiple options for removing the roadblock helped me access all the external resources I hadn't considered earlier. I forced myself to think/visualize broader and include options until I had what I needed. For example, when I didn't have childcare, I could bring my younger kids with me. I could prevent schedule conflicts by working in advance around whichever schedule was the most rigid. When I had something that I couldn't move, such as a trade show or speaking engagement on a practice day, I could change practice that week or have a parent-volunteer run practice. The most important lesson learned here is that I kept my solution tethered to my goal by continually asking, *"Will this lead me to Goal-Driven Focus?"* I did this until I was confident that my plan would deliver the goal without sacrificing my *Defined Success* to be an exceptional cross-country coach.

Total Administrative Time Estimated	**6.5 Hours**
Less fully delegated Registration/Attendance	*-0.5 Hours*
Less fully delegated uniforms/equipment	*-0.5 Hours*
Less partially delegated stats/awards	*-1.5 Hours*
Less partially delegated communication	*-1.0 Hours*
Less moving motivation outside of season	*-0.5 Hours*
Less process improvement via systems	*-1.0 Hours*
Administrative Time Investment/Week	**1.5 Hours**

For me, this process wasn't only about finding time to show up and coach. I had to find ways to make a great program even more impressive than the one I inherited. I wanted to prepare the program for the next coach. I invested in this program to pay dividends for the coaches and runners long after my tenure. Reflecting on Core beliefs of making the world a better place, I am reminded of the importance of these small contributions by Mother Theresa's famous words. *I alone cannot change the world, but I can cast a stone across the waters to create many ripples.*[9]

Identifying Exponential Opportunities

Once you have studied and learned the Fundamental Elements of an *Exponential Mindset* and consumed the Step-by-Step methods for executing, the final critical element is identifying Exponential opportunities. So, how do you find these opportunities in your business and life?

Exponentiality starts with awareness.

Rather than partaking in your life, begin to spend some time as an observer within your life and business.

These observations will give you the ability to inventory your opportunities to apply *Exponentiality*.

You will begin to train your brain to see all the repetitive tasks in your life. Start by picturing your life as one life. Do not segregate personal from professional because this artificial segregation causes the loss of *Exponentiality*. There are unlimited opportunities for *Exponentiality*.

You are limited by your ability to see them. The more you do it, the better you will get at finding opportunities. Keep reminding yourself; this is a journey, not a destination.

- Identify activities that give you the most satisfaction/joy and determine how often you engage in them. Your goal is to find ways to do them more often.

Take your defined non-negotiables and start assessing your business and life. What activities are impeding these from happening?

- Start working on this list.
- Make a list of your personal and professional pursuits that cause the most conflict and anxiety. These will be the most significant early wins if you can focus on them and begin to solve them.

Be an observer.

1. Clear your calendar and spend a few days observing. What activities are repetitive and do not create movement toward your goals? If they do not directly correlate to your company goals or personal goals, work on eliminating them.

2. Pay attention to what you do repetitively on a personal level. What can you replace or improve with technology so that you can do more of what you love? What can you delegate or eliminate?

Chapter Summary – Chapter 3: Exponential Life Balance by Design

Lessons Learned

- Creating *Exponential Life Balance* requires Modus Vivendi.
- Know the difference between balance and equality.
- By defining your non-negotiables, you unlock the ability to be *Exponential.*
- You cannot have two non-negotiables that are in conflict with one another.
- It is better to be hyper-focused than multi-tasking.
- Manage by priorities/non-negotiables, not guilt.
- Design your life; don't react to circumstances.

- With *The Slingshot Effect*, to get what you want, you must first pull back and invest.
- Real balance means that it is in perpetual motion, with sway being the result.
- Sway is a healthy part of balance.

Unveiled Discoveries

- For the first time in global history, absent a war, we have experienced a complete global reset.
- The advent of suburban living created the idea that we have a segregated life, personally and professionally. Not only did the suburbs create physical segregation between people's career and their home lives, but it also created psychological segregation, in which families had to create artificial equality and the clock became the keeper of equality.

Statistics to Ponder

- According to Inc. Magazine, money is not on the list of motivators to execute the entrepreneurial dream.

Action Plan

- What are your non-negotiables?
- Is there conflict between your non-negotiables? If so, how can you modify them to resolve the conflict?
- If you have conflicting non-negotiables, have you applied *Solution-Focused Flexibility* in looking at possible solutions?
- How would you assess the balance in your life? Do you have equality or balance?
- What are the sources of joy in your life? Inventory your activities. Whatever is taking you closer to joy, focus on. Whatever is moving you further away, delegate.

- Are there ways to intertwine your personal and professional pursuits that will give you more balance?
- What resources do you have to solve your problems with balance?
- Have you delegated everything that does not get you closer to your goals?
- Are your personal and professional goals in conflict with one another?
- Where can you design more *Exponentiality* into your life?
- Does your business support an *Exponential Life* for you? What about for your team?
- What creates the sway in your balance? How are you ensuring it doesn't fall off of the wire?
- You need to do a joy and harmony assessment of each side of your life. Is it on your screen saver?
- Do you use the same time management skills and timeboxing at home and at work? If not, how can you apply what you do at work at home?
- Have you taken time to be an observer of your organization? Inventory every task as to whether it is getting you closer to your corporate goals or further away.

Good Quotables

- *Time is the great equalizer. Spend it like you can never get it back.*
- *Find joy in designing an Exponential Life.*

Supplementary Learning Recommendations (Read/Listen/Watch)

- *Start With Why: How Great Leaders Inspire Everyone To Take Action* by Simon Sinek.

- *The Obstacle Is the Way: The Timeless Art of Turning Trials into Triumph* by Ryan Holiday.
- *Greenlights* by Matthew McConaughey

CHAPTER 4

Be TExponential

In a recent Bank of America study, business leaders said that the biggest roadblock to_work-life balance (alternatively referred to in this book as life balance or *Modus Vivendi*) was the administrative tasks involved in keeping their business afloat.[7] Process improvement and technology can address those mundane administrative tasks, so you spend time on strategic and entrepreneurial activities that drive the business. However, technology needs to be coupled with an *Exponential Mindset* to impact your business truly.

Time is money in business. Time well-used is joy and harmony in life. As I mentioned earlier, time is also the great equalizer.

Whether you are the President of the United States or a newly employed teenage clerk at a local fast-food restaurant, we all have the same quantity of hours in our day. Business status, social status, age, nor geography, gender, or race change this. This fact means that as the leader of Davisware, anything I can do to create extra efficiency in my day or in that of our employees' days will reduce stress and create a better result in our business and their lives. We don't define efficiency as doing more. This efficiency is not squeezing more things into a shorter time. Instead, it eliminates repetitive tasks so that you and your organization can do less to gain better results. This approach is valid both professionally and personally.

If you can spend less time doing chores personally, it will leave you more quality time to do the things you identified in the second *Living*

Exponentially chapter as the things you love to do that you do not find enough time to do.

Given that you are four chapters into this book, I feel confident that you are committed to an *Exponential Mindset.*

Your commitment is a journey that you will progressively get better at. It does not start with perfection but rather commitment. Once you have committed, identifying Exponential opportunities is your next challenge. No matter how committed you are to an *Exponential Mindset*, execution will be impossible if you do not focus on seeing *Exponential* opportunities. In *Exponential Life by Design*, Chapter Two, section 8 addresses *Identifying Exponential Opportunities*. If you didn't take notes, go back and do it. Pause in your reading and make notes on how you defined your non-negotiables and where you can see efficiencies gained in your life. There are two crucial and quick callouts here. First, do not segregate your personal and professional pursuits, even if your primary focus is business *Exponentiality*. Second, look at life as a whole, both for yourself and your team.

Secondly, become a spectator. The easiest way to see flaws in a system or a process is to step back. The song *Washington on Your Side* from the Broadway Musical *Hamilton* includes a line that has reverberated through my head so many times. "If there's a fire you're trying to douse, you can't put it out from inside the house." What does this mean as it relates to *Exponentiality*? It means that you cannot see the problems you are trying to solve from the inside. You need to become a passionate observer to see where you can improve your processes via technology and an *Exponential Mindset*.

Why TExponentiality?

In a QuickBooks commercial, the actor Martin Kove, from the *"Karate Kid"* and *"Cobra Kai"* movies, explains how QuickBooks saved him three hours a week in his business. When asked what he would do with the three hours, Kove replied, "Do some crane kicks, practice head butting, take a warm bath, and maybe ask Johnny if he wants to catch a movie." Kove did not use the word *Exponential*, but what he describes was the *Modus Vivendi* of professional and personal pursuits in balance.

The integration of technology into your business will create time. How you spend that time determines how *Exponential* you are.

Technology + Exponentiality = TExponential

As a passionate entrepreneur, I have watched what technology did in our business and thousands of our customers' businesses.

Leveraging technology helps entrepreneurs and business leaders create the highest and best use of their time and the organization. By mastering everything from managing their calendars to automating simple customer service inquiries, Davisware customers are creating efficiencies in their businesses and in the lives of those who fuel the company.

Efficiency is valuable, but it is only a part of the value of *TExponential*. Through technology, business leaders can create enterprise-level business intelligence.

This data is how businesses go from surviving to thriving. Through data, business leaders help individuals grow from taskmasters to individual contributors focused on the organizational mission. It's how business leaders go from tired to inspired by what they do. Davisware customers have improved business processes via technology. But, more importantly, they have created one set of truths. Collins Dictionary defines ubiquity as *existing or being everywhere, esp. at the same time, omnipresent.* Combining this with the definition of knowledge, *information, and understanding about a subject that a person has, or which all people have,* makes your business very powerful.[10]

Knowledge Ubiquity - One Source of Truth

A McKinsey study found that employees spend 1.8 hours every day or 23% of their day researching the information they need to do their job. Suppose you are in the service business, like so many of our customers. In that case, your technicians spend around 70% of their time on the job researching, diagnosing the problem, researching parts to use, repair codes, how to get materials, and only 30% of the time on-site actually doing what the customer hired you to do. Imagine the productivity gained by reducing this, even 10%? Without adding a single bit of overhead, you would create that percentage of dollars straight to the bottom line.[11]

Similarly, if you could reduce your staff's time looking for information and helping your on-site staff research parts and information, you would cut your overhead by the same amount you reduced that time.

How do you do this? The answer is simple but not easy. If there is nothing more you take from this book than this, take this. Creating a business and a life around one source of truth will change your life in the same way *Exponentiality* will. Knowledge Ubiquity is the result of one source of truth. One source of truth is a means to *Exponentiality.* One source of truth will allow your business to thrive and creates harmony in your life. Finally, one source of truth enables your organization to stop trying to figure out what the facts are and give them to you, so you have time to react to them. One source of truth is an essential foundation of your business.

How do we create one source of truth? The easiest way is expansive technology that works together to allow you to manage your business. Enterprise Resource Planning Systems, also known as "ERP" systems, have a fundamental value in creating a single source of truth.

Source transactional data should generate a single source of truth. For the layman, this means that the original transaction should make the data. It should involve no re-keying, no spreadsheets, and no manual lookups to gain access to information. Instead, ERP systems take data directly from the transaction and put it into a usable format for creating analytics.

This section is going to focus on business primarily, but this is equally relevant personally. There are so many new tools that are available to help with this in our personal lives. For example, having a family shared calendar continuously up to date by all parties is a single source of truth for your family in the plans for the day. A shared grocery shopping list app holds everyone in the household responsible for the list. So, if our daughter Amelia uses the last peanut butter, it delegates the responsibility of replacing it to her. It creates the source of truth from the transaction (in this case, our daughter eating the last of the peanut butter) and makes ubiquitous data we all have access to (via a shared app). I didn't need to "re-key" or keep track of this information. It also allows anyone shopping to get the groceries and notify everyone as they update the app. Now… if I could only get Amelia to do this!

Expeditiously replacing peanut butter will not change your lives fundamentally, but if you apply this concept to all areas of your life, it will. When we shift our conversation to business, one source of truth will change the delivered product to your customers. It will reduce the research element of your team's days. They will find more joy in their work because they efficiently spend their time doing what they were hired to do. Let's walk through an example in our own business.

Executing *The Slingshot Effect* and taking advantage of the pandemic, Davisware executed a considerable amount of technology within our own business. The adage that the shoemaker's kids have no shoes accurately describes Davisware pre-pandemic. We took this time to reset and reorganize in preparation for *Exponential* growth in the business. One of those tools was our customer service tool, ZenDesk. This product is a best-in-class technical support and ticketing system. By itself, it could make our teams more efficient with organized data and workflows. This product is excellent but does not gain us *Exponentiality*. We had to develop the discipline to create the data and use that data in our business.

Before ZenDesk, our customers could call, email, text, or create a ticket in our old system. We were allowing far too many inputs and too many points of error. We didn't want to limit our customers' communication ability, but we had to create a workflow that got them the best service by rewarding compliance with the optimal workflow. In short, we got our goals aligned. By our customer creating the ticket directly in our **SOR (System of Record)**, workflows could efficiently be executed that delegated it to the right teams or escalated without human interaction. Cultivating an *Exponential Mindset* expects others to meet you at your level (aka *7 Fundamental Elements of an Exponential Minds*et. Fundamental #2 - Level Up). We asked this of our customers and teams, and it improved efficiency and customer service. It was one more step toward *Exponentiality* in the business.

The next and probably most critical component is the integration of this information into the whole customer relationship. We needed to make sure every person in the business had access to this customer's data and looked at the entire relationship. We also needed to start developing a database of historical content to fix the same problem repeatedly. Then, we can document how to fix it, provide data to the engineering teams to potentially make changes in the software, and provide feedback to the implementation team on training issues to educate the customer better. All of these areas are part of the Step-by-Step methods to an *Exponential Mindset*.

We have aligned the customer's goals with the support team's goals and the larger organization by creating standardized processes. This tactic opens the door to develop Knowledge Ubiquity. When there is a customer request, all parties want the best information available, no matter who answers the call. These tools have features for pattern mapping and history storage to identify repetitive product or service issues. That way, when other customers call in with the same problem, they will get the same answer because techs are working with the same set of facts. What this process does is starts to equalize the truth because we have ***one source of truth***. We developed a mindset that says, "If it isn't in our System of Record (SOR), it doesn't exist!" This approach is Knowledge Ubiquity.

Knowledge Ubiquity creates continuous process improvement via shared learning. Every business has those internal experts whose tribal knowledge seems to be an integral part of most daily operations. These individuals are accidental roadblocks to *Exponentiality* and Knowledge Ubiquity. When technology creates one source of truth, the entire organization is ***Leveling Up*** and gaining knowledge while improving your knowledge source. Technology makes the information available to everyone, creates enterprise-wide data, and is not dependent on anyone. This perspective is *TExponential.*

TExponential Opportunities in your Business

The integration of technology into our businesses can feel overwhelming and expensive. We often struggle to link the costs to a definable **ROI**. Yet, once we integrate technology into our lives, we forget what it was like without it. Remember the days without a cell phone? It's hard to imagine how we functioned, but if you remember buying your first one, you likely struggled with the cost justification to buy it. In our businesses, what was it like before email? I remember the day I sent my first email. I was *blown away* by the fact I pressed send, and *within 10 minutes,* the email arrived on the other end. It was business-altering. We often take technology for granted until we look back and see how it fundamentally changed our businesses and our lives. This reflective exercise may help drive your team to the adoption of technology transformation in your company.

When exploring *Exponential* Opportunities, document management systems, whether standalone or embedded in our EPR, help create productivity workflows, security, cost savings, and mobility.

When consulting with business leaders, this is one of the first places I call out for *Exponential* Opportunities, even though most leaders would say they are paperless. For example, during the global pandemic, many companies expedited their execution of a paperless office because it gave them more mobile flexibility.

In short, out of the global pandemic crisis, businesses created a new tool for teams to be more flexible (Solution Focused Flexibility). These systems provide more efficiency and cost-saving universally. Yet, when surveyed, only 18% of companies consider themselves entirely paperless. This fact is a staggering statistic considering the average cost of a single piece of paper is more than **$20** to print, store and manage.[12]

Paper technology is nearly 2000 years old, yet it continues to perpetuate our businesses and workflows.

If you haven't contemplated paper as an immediate *TExponential* Opportunity, stop here and consider it. For Davisware, we made a business decision to "stop all paper at the door." On April 11, 2013, Davisware moved to our new office. This transition became the catalyst to execute a paperless office fully.

Our conscious business decision was_to implement an *Exponential Mindset* (although it did not have that title in 2013). To facilitate our transition to a paperless office, we implemented many initiatives, including:

- The design of our new desks did not include document storage space.
- We eliminated office mailboxes.
- We set up our reception area with a scanner and scanned all non-confidential mail upon receipt.
- We utilized summer help to transition our customers and vendors to electronic communications.

- We inconveniently moved our filing systems to the basement of the building.
- We began scanning old files. Our son Austin, who spent his first summer employment as our "Document Specialist," embarked upon that arduous task. I am sure he doesn't look at our time together with as much joy as I did; his work was a critical element in our transition to paperless. My campaign of "nothing bigger than a post-it note" was a success.

This workflow changed the historical documents and general paper workflows. We also converted workflows of paper within the systems we used. For example, previously, our accounting team would receive piles of invoices, reconcile purchase orders and credit card statements. Then they would manually work through an approval process, then process hundreds of checks that required us to stamp, mail, and later reconciled each one. Alternatively, once we could receive invoices via email, we imported them into our GlobalEdge ERP system and automatically reconciled them to the purchase order and paid through posi-pay EFT. The process was efficient, secure, and instantaneous.

According to NACHA, the check-writing alone saved businesses nearly **$25K annually** (average savings of $1/per check). Combine this with the processing cost savings of almost 90% on the remainder of the processing; companies save nearly $28/per AP invoice and $1/per check. Those dollars are real ROI in the business.[13]

Technology like this is transformative and easy to measure in actual cost savings. What is not measured are the intangibles. These workflows allowed our business to transition to a remote workforce without changing our core processes during the pandemic. Our teams could work around educating their children and all of the new stressors that the pandemic created vs. being saddled to their original working schedule. It provided security in storing these documents and Knowledge Ubiquity in our SOR, with everyone having access to the same data. . IDC data shows that "the knowledge worker spends about 2.5 hours per day, or roughly 30% of the workday, searching for information….60% [of company executives] felt that time constraints and lack of understanding of how to find information were preventing their employees from finding the information they needed."[14]

This situation is obviously not the highest and best use of anyone's time! Applying an *Exponential Mindset* and executing an entirely paperless office is the best use of human capital and financial resources.

While there are hundreds of unique examples of *Exponential* Opportunities in business, I want to give a couple of other real-life examples that can apply to nearly any business and one we faced in our company.

As of 2011, Davisware had not yet decided to accept customer credit card payments. Finally, an opportunity forced our hand, insisting that they purchase by card or not at all. The fees associated with accepting credit cards seemed cost-prohibitive and felt like added complexity. Doing business was hard enough. Why did we need to add yet another thing to manage? Here is why. This transition remarkably reduced the friction between our customers and us as it relates to payments. A recent Visa study shows that 78% of consumers ranked digital payments as their preferred payment method.[15]

Credit cards make your customers happier. We exchanged bank fees for labor costs (and complexity) that we eliminated in payment recording, collection costs, automated our workflows, and in short, improved the experience for both our customers and our teams. High-quality help is hard to find, and good quality customers are essential to keep. Using technology executables like this helped us make the highest and best use of our team's time. The ROI on integrated payments technology (vs. standalone solutions) is easy to calculate. Pay Stand estimates that a paper check's cost is ten times more costly than receiving a digital payment.

In our case, our overall costs were reduced by more than 30% in labor costs by converting to credit card payments.

The other significant gamechanger in our business for taking credit cards was the predictability in cash flow. Our DSO's (Days Sales Outstanding) decreased by almost 50%. We got our money faster and more reliably and didn't have to pay someone to do it. We also tokenized our transactions in this process. This tactic meant we securely stored our customer's card data to repeatedly charge cards without re-engaging with the customer each month.

As we invested time and effort into all of these technologies, we needed to not trade our business's personal touch for *Exponentiality*. There are plenty of examples in the marketplace where customers left companies because they only dealt with a computer. We were not going to be part of that statistic.

Embedding the human element into the process was equally crucial to embedding the technology into the process. For example, we used our accounting team's time to call customers to acknowledge and thank them for their payments instead of calling to collect payment or update credit card numbers. Technology freed up time spent solving transactional issues to address strategic company issues and improve customer relationships. It's important that when implementing a new process as we did, you ensure that you don't detract from the outcome. *Goal-Driven Focus* is part of the *Exponential Mindset.*

Keep *Goal-Driven Focus*. Results should always focus on *Exponentiality* in your business, both in cost savings and in the S.M.A.R.T. goal's outcomes.

If you accomplish efficiencies but don't improve your staff and customers' experience, you have not gained *Exponentiality*. Instead, you simply achieved bad results faster!

Enterprise Productivity

Every entrepreneurial business grows to a point where they ultimately need to scale. This challenge is the inflection point in the company where enterprise data is the foundation for future success. Aligning the timing on this move is critical. The insertion of an Enterprise Resource Planning Software (ERP) creates a single source of truth of business insights. When entrepreneurs no longer have their hand in every business operation element, the only alternative to similar insights is a single source of the truth ERP system. In addition to the detailed insights, an ERP system offers business leaders higher-level insights than they can create themselves working in the business. In short, the investment in an ERP system is the systemic decision to work on your business, not only in your company.

It is a significant financial investment and an even bigger resource commitment when moving to an ERP system. However, this move will create remarkable insights, streamlined workflows, and improved efficiencies that your business has never seen when properly executed. Unfortunately, business leaders are often hesitant in making this move, not because they don't believe it is necessary, but rather because they struggle to put an ROI on insights and improved efficiency. Let me see if I can help with that by referring back to the childhood game of telephone. As you may remember, this game involved a group of kids who whispered a phrase to one another. The goal was to see what the message became on the other end. When there are a few players, the ending message was often very similar to the beginning message. However, when there are many players, the ending message often did not even resemble the starting message.

Why is this? Because as players relay the message, it became converted by each individual's brain and hearing capabilities to their truth. In much the same way, you are playing the beginning message without a standard set of truth in an ERP system. When there were many players, the ending message often did not even resemble the starting message. Why is this? Because as they relayed the information, each person converted it based on their brain and hearing capabilities and their truth. In much the same way, without a standard set of truth in an **ERP system**, you are playing the telephone game. Each person in the process is evolving the data and message to their version of the truth. As your business grows, you spend far too much time discussing what *the truth* is instead of reacting to a single source of truth.

The real differentiator with any ERP system is execution. I have witnessed very similar businesses thrive with an ERP and fail with that same ERP system because of the organizations' varying commitment to implementation. A new ERP system fundamentally changes most business processes and at a rapid pace.

Throughout the business's existence, they installed various systems and procedures, often for decades. Over a few short months, every process will be evaluated, modified, and in many cases eliminated/replaced either with technology or different procedures. Implementing an ERP system is challenging, without a doubt. However, the fruits of that tricky process will allow your business potential to be untapped and prepare the business for unprecedented times like 2020.

To illustrate how businesses benefit from ERP software that helps them scale, adapt to change, and create *TExponentiality*, I've shared some examples of how our customers benefit during the global pandemic and beyond. Sharing these experiences will give you confidence in your journey toward making this type of commitment to technology.

Personal Productivity - TExponential isn't just for business

The journey toward *Exponentiality* is holistic, even when it comes to thinking about technology. It's easy to imagine opportunities to improve your business via technology, but many people don't consider it when they think about their personal lives. I have witnessed the most structured and disciplined business leaders manage their personal lives via crisis instead of through process because they forget to take home what they do at work. While there are many distinctions about how you approach each, don't forget to see the similarities. This book often speaks to the melded world that includes personal and professional.

You only have one life.

Personal life and a professional life segregated are a fallacy. The two elements of your life need to live together symbiotically. It's coordinated efforts that do not have artificial time-bound or geographic boundaries.

Your life is more like a tie-dyed shirt thoroughly mixed together!

A common friction point that many people have is failing to develop boundaries around the two competing priorities in your life. As a result, they allow their time at work to be distracted by personal preferences and vice versa.

This dilemma creates a situation where you are neither present nor the best version of yourself with either priority.

Choose focused tasking over multitasking. Resist that urge through some life hacks and technology that you can embed. I struggle as much as any parent or spouse to forego the temptation to be interrupted at work.

In the same way, it is very easy to answer "a few emails" instead of being focused on the soccer game you are supposed to be watching. In my world, with ten kids, 20 brothers and sisters, and a newly retired spouse, if I gave each of them 10 minutes a day, it would be another full-time job! But, of course, not everyone has this big of an immediate family circle. Still, I think even with a much smaller circle, these interruptions are not suitable for the quality of your work or personal time at home.

Distractions are the death of productivity. This statement is universal in our lives, not just in business. In this chapter, I've primarily focused on business technology. I wanted to share a few life hacks that I have executed, sometimes only personally and others across the gamut of my life. I am sharing what I feel are good ideas. However, the intent here is to open your thought processes to see opportunities to be *TExponential* in all areas of your life.

Instant messaging, or the "king of ping," is top of the distraction list. Whether texting, social media, and even office productivity tools such as TEAMS, the constant pinging is the death of productivity. For me, it is especially true because of the number of messages I send and receive.

On average, my day would be interrupted 102 times if I allowed it to happen. That is literally every 4 minutes from TEAMS messages alone! Add that to the 312 emails received/read per day and 269 text messages for an average of 683 interruptions from messages!

For these 683 reasons, I have to be hyper-aware of self-created boundaries to check messages and what notifications I use. For example, one thing that I do religiously is use delayed text messages to reduce interruptions.

By controlling the outbound message, I manage the most likely time that someone will respond. As a result, I send many text messages long before the world wakes up.

I delay their delivery to when it is appropriate to send them, and I deliver them in the timeframe leading up to my self-created boundaries around checking my phone. This tactic allows me to do them in bulk as opposed to an interruption for each message. In short, I schedule message delivery so that the respondent receives them (and probably responds at a time that is conducive to my schedule) when it works best for me. Thus, I am managing both the interruption and the follow-up. For example, if one of my kids is supposed to take a gift to a party, I will set a delayed reminder text message when I verbally tell them about needing the present. The delayed message is aligned with when that kid is preparing to leave for the party.

In the same way, if I am in a meeting and need to follow up in a week, rather than generate a reminder or make a note to send the follow-up message, I will immediately set up the delayed text message, killing two birds with one stone. I've eliminated the follow-up from what I need to remember. It's better than a reminder or a calendar item (and another ding) because the calendar reminder still requires me to take action at a specific time. My technology is both my reminder and my follow-up action! Why should I cloud my mind with something that I need to remember to do? Consider using this *TExponential* life hack for everything from reminding your spouse to pick up milk to reminding your co-worker of an upcoming commitment to following up with a client or sending requests to your assistant. No matter how this technology is applied, it creates a single-entry point to both remind and execute.

Delayed messaging can apply to email messages as well and carries the same benefits.

Combining this with *closing your email* can help you create a much more efficient email system. I always use the analogy that it would not work if the US Mail delivered a letter to you every time they received one. The same is valid with email. I try (not always successfully) to keep my email closed during any event that requires my focus, such as client meetings, collaborative events, and creative initiatives where focus is needed—starting and stopping kill productivity and effectiveness. As a long-time runner and coach, it is well-known that the first mile is the most painful. This condition takes approximately 10 minutes to transition your body from an anaerobic state to an aerobic one.[16] If you stop running before that threshold, you are repetitively going through the most painful part of running. If you stop running before that threshold, you are repetitively going through the most painful part of running. The same can be true for focus. A UC Irvin Gloria Mark's study suggests it takes about 23 minutes to return to complete focus after interruption.[17]

On average, we check email 15 times per day, while spending 2.6 hours, and therefore we never get back to maximum focus personally or professionally![18]

The repetitive effort of initial focus increases in value by reducing the number of times you are distracted. Successfully multitasking is a myth. Yes, in the global pandemic world, you can fold laundry while on a conference call.

This condition is possible because natural activities put less demand on the prefrontal cortex (the part of the brain used in focused attention activities). Trying to do two concentrated activities simultaneously causes the prefrontal cortex to split its effectiveness, not double it. Most experts agree that even great composers like Bach, Haydn, and Handel could only compose one masterpiece at a time. The masterpieces of your mind are waiting for you to stop multitasking!

TExponential In Box

So, how do you engage technology to create *Exponentiality* in your InBox?

1. **Set up a standard routine to check your In Box.**

   Don't overcheck it! Depending upon your role, you may need to check it more often but for most positions, check it no more than hourly and more preferably 3-5 times per day. Less than 10% of senders anticipate responses in less than an hour, so there is no urgency to checking it more often than that. The average person checks their email every 37 minutes receiving 120 messages daily.[18]

   Reducing this as suggested could save as much as 45 minutes per day in wasted time. Set specific times during the day to check and manage email.

   Use Google or Alexa to set alarms and reminders.

2. **Clear out your InBox and use folders.**

   A full InBox results in losing another 30 minutes in your day. Why? Because when we see an email, even if we have already read it, we get distracted and re-read it or change gears. Folders force you to focus your efforts and control what you are doing next. You can set rules to place them into these folders automatically, so you don't even need to do that. Also, order your folders in the order of most important. That way, whatever is most important is always the one you see first.

3. **Don't get carried away on folders.**

   Searching through folders will take you much longer filing and searching.[19] Instead, have a simple system based to categorize based upon your action, not the subject. So, emails that only require the filing of documents are in one folder in my InBox. I have another for scheduling and yet another for reading (emails that I need to learn from, not respond to), and another for critical tasks.

That way, I am organizing my InBox in my work method, not in the topic matter. I can quickly file the attachments to 20 emails if they are all located in the same folder.

4. **Control your reminders so that they can control you.**

Don't use any reminders that you don't manage. Set a reminder to check your email. Do not let email notifications interrupt you at will.

Shut off all automated notifications unless they are guaranteed to be critical to your role or success.

5. **Timing is Everything!**

Use delayed emails in the same way; I recommended delayed text messages.

Rather than setting a reminder, write the email and delay the SEND. This tactic will prevent you from needing to go back and get your focus re-engaged later. (Remember the time it takes to gain focus? You will gain those 23 minutes back by doing both the task and the follow-up at the same time).

6. **Keep Spam out of your daily diet.**

Choose your distractions! Get aggressive with spam blockers, so you aren't distracted by anything that is not important. Deleting an unopened, unread email takes, on average, 3-4 seconds. You can do this in one of two ways. Either make a habit of blocking them with each delete or set aside time each day (10 minutes on the calendar) that you go through your deleted box and block them in mass that has no value.

7. **Email rules are for everyone.**

Get diligent across your whole organization on the use of CC, BCC, and To fields properly. If your name is in the "To" field, that means there is an action item. "CC" means it is for your information. To reduce the number of people on an email, as they are no longer relevant to the conversation, move them to "BCC" to see they have been moved (closed-loop) and are off future responses.

8. **Become an observer in your In Box.**

   Pay attention to emails you get repetitively or ones you can classify and handle in mass, for example, a meeting invite acceptance. Either create a rule or, at minimum, put these in a folder and address them daily instead of multiple times per day.

9. **Organize First. Do Second.**

   When you open your email, start by briefly re-sorting your emails by Subject and delete all multi-response emails with several responses. The last email will have the entire string.

10. **Pull the last string, or you will come unraveled.**

    Get into an organizational habit of responding to the last email in a string (which should be easy if you use the trick above as it will be the only one there).

11. **Scan for urgency.**

    Sort your InBox for only UNREAD and then sort by newest (if there are several responses in a string, you see only the most current). Next, briefly scan all of your new emails from the top of the email box down. This tactic will allow you to see anything urgent and use the FLAG option to flag those to address first.

12. **Bottoms Up!**

    Finally, after doing all of the above, respond, but start from the bottom of your email box up. This approach **only** works, however, if you have deleted the extra emails from the same string.

13. Shortcuts are a way of life.

Learn keyboard shortcuts. This strategy is not unique to email but to all applications. They are 50% faster than using a mouse and will save you 64 hours per year of transition between the two (not to mention the reduction in wrist injuries from the mouse's overuse).[20]

Evolutionary Mindset through Team Productivity

Adding technology to improve team productivity is a little more complicated because it involves other people. First, you have to assess if the technology's disruption is worth the productivity gains you'll get.

When we assess where to apply technology, we look for repetitive replicable processes, quality of data, and the ability to utilize it. If I want to be *Exponential*, I must find ways to use the data enterprise-wide.

For example, let's say someone is monitoring a project with a spreadsheet. It doesn't help the team because nobody can use the data, so it becomes a silo. We can increase the spreadsheet's value to the team by putting it on a network drive shared with everybody interested in it. Putting it on a shared drive is a step many organizations take to increase productivity. But it doesn't solve the other issues. Is it repetitive and replicable? And is it accurate? One of the things I do is validate everyone's spreadsheet. I'm a little crazy when it comes to validations. I put it on almost every field because it limits the tendency to make a mistake.

Although we have increased the spreadsheet's value by making it shareable and validating it, its utilization is limited. The data is not replicable because it's not in our ERP System. If the information isn't there, then it has no value to me. I need everything brought to a central data source so that it acts as a system of record.

I learned that you couldn't have a system of record using spreadsheets because it is not a sustainable process. Unfortunately, that is one of the most common mistakes organizational leaders make. Yet, they rely on spreadsheets as their system of record.

Continuous process improvement, standards, systems, and technology improve the information companies use to run their business, eliminating the need to operate by tribal knowledge. Tribal knowledge is the unwritten law of getting things done in an organization. When you need to know how to get something done, you ask "Mary" or "John" because they've been with the company the longest. The trouble with tribal knowledge is that nobody can get anything done when Mary or John leaves or isn't around!

Processes, standards, systems, and technology operationalize information so that everyone has access to The One Source of Truth.

Each area that you find will lead you to the next step, continuous process improvement.

Process-Driven Focus through Continuous Process Improvement

Process-Driven focus is the 7th of the Fundamental Elements of Cultivating an *Exponential Mindset*. Part of this journey is not only identifying Exponential opportunities but being willing to act on them. Unlike many other areas, being *Process-Driven* also means that these areas are typically an evolution, not a final product. **Continuous Process Improvement** (also known as the acronym **CPI)** is critical to being *Process-Driven*. There are many theories and methodologies in CPI. My goal is to help you gain your commitment to CPI as a part of *Living Exponentially*, not necessarily which method you use. Training your mind to continually assess processes and identify repetitive tasks and efficiency opportunities is part of this journey. Many books can walk you through Continuous Process Improvement (CPI).

These are important but are a far second to developing a *Process-Driven* Mindset. As your organization's leader or a leader in your home, others quickly follow your lead regarding how they think about the operations of the business or your personal life. Removing *"the way we've always done it"* mentality and replacing it with an **evolutionary mindset** is key to evolution and improvement.

If CPI is part of your culture, you will find success in *Exponentiality*. As a runner, the most challenging part of running a race is signing up. The decision to press the "I ACCEPT" button on the online form is the commitment to run. So too, the CPI commitment is the first step. As a leader, CPI needs to start at the top to penetrate the entire organization. It requires you to foster an environment that encourages lessons learned from failures and focus on preventing future repetitive failures. Use every mistake or repetitive task as an *Exponential Opportunity*, vs. a mistake or a status quo. CPI and *Exponentiality* are incrementally small and not foundationally altering- initially. Continually developing processes that focus on improving quality, productivity, and efficiency through slight shifts in daily work activities or corporate culture will begin to yield significant results in your organization. This shift will empower every employee to impact the big picture truly. It also gives them the freedom to start to think *Exponentially* in their own lives. This commitment is where the true freedom and value of an *Exponential Mindset* are created. Creating *Exponentiality* in your business is fantastic. Creating *Exponentiality* at home will change your life. Teaching *Exponentiality* to your staff and your kids will genuinely make your culture and home places of joy and harmony.

Proactive Industry Reactions to the Global Pandemic

The epicenter of Davisware's customer base is commercial contracting in HVAC and food equipment service.

Pre-pandemic, these recession-proof, stable industries had high demand and slight economic fluctuation.

2020 changed this. Proactive companies reacted to create long-term value in their business and unique customer experiences.

Our longstanding partnership with these industries has resulted in tailored solutions, creating a single source of truth ERP system as the System of Record (SOR). Transaction volumes are high, and complexity is significant, even for the smallest companies. Via technology, the operational elements of their businesses create insights to better manage operations of installation, scheduling, dispatching, job cost, and inventory transactions. In addition, data centralization improves business intelligence, communication and eliminates paperwork and guesswork.

The global pandemic brought these bulletproof industries to a standstill, closing restaurants and vacating expansive commercial spaces. According to the National Restaurant Assoc., 110,000 establishments closed in 2020, eliminating 2.5M food service jobs.[21]

Commercial office space saw large increases in vacancies, shifting in needs to portable units, backup power, and air quality performance in outdoor spaces.

Proactive businesses took advantage of the shift in traditional contracting business models by reacting aggressively. SOR data began being used to make dramatic shifts in inventory stocking, labor resources, and routing—helping them become more efficient to manage client needs and do remote repairs. The pandemic shifted data & technology to be a part of the product, not just as an internal tool and overhead cost. The industry transformation moved from break-fix to preventative downtime. Pre-pandemic, our customers considered their product to be a successful service call. Today, the product is a partnership with restaurants to create efficient kitchens optimized for downtime and maintenance. In commercial space, the emphasis has shifted to building automation and intelligent use of energy.

These companies are converting data into their deliverable products, including life cycle equipment costs.

Changes have opened the door to quicker adoption of IoT, AI, and smart kitchen technology. It has shifted business models to subscription, created predictive cost models for the end customer, and a higher valuation of the overall contracting business. Pre-pandemic, very few servicers saw recurring revenue as a possibility.

Today, our teams are working with clients to create the final product their end-customer is craving.

From two of the pandemic's most disrupted industries comes companies outperforming the market and their competitors by using the Slingshot to create *Exponentiality* in their businesses. They were able to make shifts and react to the industry faster and more accurately than other businesses.

Data has been used to create opportunistic engagement for both the contractor and their end-customer through ROI on equipment and expand their product from simply repair services to data services. This tactic allows end customers to make better decisions derived from business intelligence. The value proposition changed from break-fix to prevention and partnership with end-customers. The impact that technology played in the evolution of these businesses was their success story from 2020.

Basic Continuous Process Improvement

While I didn't intend for this book to be a guide on CPI (Continuous Process Improvement) methods and theories, it is good to have a basic CPI framework from which to refer.

There are hundreds of nuances to these programs. This section will serve as a placeholder to understand the general process. The process of CPI is just a tool in *Exponentiality*. This process is applicable in personal or professional workflows. In the face of crisis, a business (or individual) has three options:

- Business as usual. Focus on defending our current position, ignoring the economic minefields, and continuing "business as usual."
- Hunker Down. Take a defensive approach by cutting costs and reducing spending until the crisis is over.
- Seek Evolution. Take advantage of the uncertainty in the marketplace, potentially pivoting your company's mission statement and focus on aggressive growth.

You may have done all three of these things in 2020. However, when you are ready for CPI, here is a basic outline to serve as infrastructure.

First: Identify the problem (plan) as a part of your process of identifying *Exponential Opportunities*. As a reminder, this includes:

- Determining what is impeding your non-negotiables from being met
- Seeing repetitive tasks in your daily routine or your business not contributing value to your life or organization
- Identifying where the most conflict is in your business or anxiety in your personal life?

Second: Create and implement a solution (do).

- How can technology play a part in the solution to either simplify or eliminate repetitive tasks?
- How are you leveraging your resources to create and implement a solution?
- Have you thought about the solution with a Possibility Mindset?

Next: Evaluate data for effectiveness (check).

1. How does the solution contribute to the mitigation of the original problem?
2. Have you stayed true to your *Goal-Driven Focus*? Once you have re-aligned your goals to the current conditions, don't change the goal again unless you are attempting to sabotage yourself.

Finally: Document the final results and implement the plan if it's successful (act).

Documentation of processes is critical in a business's ability to be successful.

Chapter Summary – Chapter 4: Be TExponential

Lessons Learned

- Use Continuous Process Improvement and technology to save time by eliminating repetitive tasks.
- Whenever you implement a new process, make sure it doesn't detract from the outcome quality.
- Disruption is the death of productivity.
- Processes, standards, systems, and technology operationalize information so that everyone has access to The One Source of Truth.

- One of your most valuable assets in your business is a single source of information or one source of truth. Having one centralized database for the entire company improves communication, eliminates delays, removes the need for paperwork, and takes the guesswork out of the equation.
- Nobody in your business should be irreplaceable. If you don't have the systems in place to make them replaceable, you'll always have to be thinking about what happens if they decide to leave.
- Continuous process improvement, standards, systems, and technology improve the information companies use to run their businesses, eliminating the need to operate by tribal knowledge.
- Invest in using the tools you already own to their highest potential. Much of the technology you already own could be better executed to create efficiency.
- Spreadsheets are for sharing information, not to be the source of information.
- Simple changes to email processes will create valued margin in your entire organization.
- Many companies look to replace tools, without first looking to improve processes in their business.
- No technology will fix bad processes or poor discipline in a business.
- The new world of business requires that you begin to think about your data as a valuable commodity in your business and a product for your customers.

Unveiled Discoveries

- Knowledge ubiquity means that information is omnipresent. Ubiquity allows your organization to stop arguing about what is true and allows you to react to the truth.
- Centralized data through an ERP system provides scalable value by having a single source of truth.

- Businesses should protect their System of Record as fiercely as their brand, their reputation, and their customers.
- Paper is a technology that is nearly 2000 years old, yet still remains central to many business processes.
- We check our email on average 74 times per day.
- Keyboard shortcuts are 50% faster than mouse reactions, which will save you 64 hours per year in transition.
- Multi-tasking does not make us more efficient.

Statistics to Ponder

- The biggest roadblock to work-life balance is the administrative tasks that keep the business afloat. What administrative tasks are you doing that are keeping you away from both joy and success?
- Employees spend 1.8 hours every day or 23% of their day researching the information they need to do their job. Imagine what your organization could look like by eliminating even half of this time by using knowledge ubiquity and technology?
- Researchers at Price Waterhouse Coopers estimate that employees spend up to half of their time looking for information each year.
- Only 18% of companies consider themselves entirely paperless. This fact is a staggering statistic considering the aver-age cost of a single piece of paper is more than $20 to print, store and manage
- Check-writing alone costs businesses nearly annually (average $1/per check).
- Pay Stand estimates that a paper check's cost is more than ten times more costly than receiving a digital payment.
- Recovery from interruption takes approximately 23 minutes to return to pre-interruption focus.

Action Plan

- Take time to be an observer. List the repetitive tasks in your business and personal life that can be leveraged with technology.
- What technology do you currently own that you do not use to its fullest? (HINT- most likely all of it). Make a list of all of your technology tools and assign a champion to further engage in its use.
- Protect your System of Record (SOR) like you protect your brand, your reputation, and your customers. All of them have equal value.
- Assess how many spreadsheets and Word documents your teams use. Verify that they are not the system of record. Look at your central database to determine how this data can be stored in it.
- Develop a mindset that says, "If it isn't in our central data system, it doesn't exist!"
- Do you still have areas of your business that operate with tribal knowledge? If so, how can you replace it with standards, processes, and systems?
- Do you have a centralized data system? If not, how is not having one impacting your business?
- Are you using data as a product in the marketplace with your customers? If not, how can you incorporate it into your product offering.
- Are you a roadblock to scaling your business? Make a list and write next to each roadblock and walk through the 7 Elements of an *Exponential Mindset* with each of them.
- How can you design your work space and workflow to support paperless office and deter paper?
- How can you use temporary resources to leapfrog the process to paperless?
- How have you engaged in a habit of continuous process improvement in your business?

- How will you apply the time you save to your joy triangle?
- What have you done to share the *7 Elements of an Exponential Mindset* with your organization?

Good Quotables

- *Be TExponential.*
- *Data is as powerful and valuable as your reputation, your brand, and your customers. Treat it that way.*
- *Too many companies spend their time talking about what is true and instead talk about how to react to truth because they have not invested in a System of Record and protected it as the most valuable asset their business owns.*

Supplementary Learning Recommendations (Read/Listen/Watch)

- *Storytelling with Data: A Data Visualization Guide for Business Professionals* by Cole Nussbaumer Knaflic

CHAPTER 5

Leading with My Hair on Fire

The dilemma of growing a small business is that entrepreneurs and managers eventually need to transition from *the* doer to *a* leader. Failure to do so leads to stalled growth, the entrepreneur leaving the business, or a shift from a leadership role. Sometimes even all of the above.

Why is this transition so difficult for many? I can answer this personally because we experienced it. The natural skillsets and intrinsic motivation that gets you to the start line are vastly different from those required to grow a business. Startup and small business leaders enjoy day-to-day firefighting (yes, we see it as joy). Touching and knowing nearly every detail of everything that happens in the business is satisfying, especially when you are usually the ultimate decision-maker. If you are reading this book, some parts of you can relate to this phenomenon. Most entrepreneurs don't start a business with the idea of spending their days managing a staff of people to run their business. Their dreams are about the company itself. These early days are long and end with exhausted accomplishment.

For me, at the end of the day, I checked off many boxes, and that felt really good.

The Davisware way

Davisware was a typical entrepreneurial company. As founders, Dan and I grew to become technical and sales leaders and professional managers. We started our business to solve a personal problem. Our family HVAC business needed a software solution, and out of that personal need, the company was born. Our communication style was informal, and employees were figuratively and often literally, family. We talked to them often, usually focusing on current performance or problems. What we considered to be long-term planning rarely looked beyond a 90-day window of time.

We spent very little time on policies, procedures, or long-term planning. Instead, we monitored our sales, customer satisfaction, and business health by the number of customer complaints we got that day, how many bugs we hit, and how much cash we had in the bank.

Everything was anecdotal because we were so tied to every detail of the business; the anecdotal nature served its purpose in many ways.

Our culture was fast, loose, and fun. Collectively, we loved what we did so much; it was as much of a hobby as it was a job. We enjoyed being together during the workday, and our workdays often never ended. If we had free time, it usually included many or all people we spent the day working next to. Transparency in the business came from everyone being involved in everything, not systemic transparency. Financial statements and the business process took a far back seat to day-to-day customer interactions and operations. There were no regular meetings. When we did decide to meet, it was called at a moment's notice. Usually, with the rap at the door and the "*got a minute*" ask. That would turn into pinging multiple others to drop everything they were doing and join, suddenly shifting our organizational focus. On the other hand, these meetings were operationally very productive.

Every decision-maker was in the room.

We assessed, disagreed, and finally agreed, sometimes in a dictatorial fashion, because there was no responsibility or organizational chart.

Anyone who has lived these days in a business can attest that they were filled with stress, but generally, they are excellent days in the company. We were doing what we loved, and even if it was all-consuming in our lives, we loved doing it.

As I look back, trying to figure out when that changed from all fun to some fun to no fun, I can visualize certain milestones that pushed the threshold. Unfortunately, however, this evolution isn't something most businesses have the luxury of saying when it happened. So instead, organizational leaders wake up one day, like many of you probably have, and realize that the fun is either escaping or entirely gone.

What created our success to this point was our commitment to our industries, employees, and customers. Our product design came out of us knowing the industry, not through data and process.

Our industry alignment was strong.

Our customers were generally happy with the products we delivered because we were living in their world.

They looked past our lack of quality control because they were so invested in what we were building. Customers settled for unstable product releases because they knew that they would have a well-engineered product that served their businesses very well with a little bit of their own investment of time into helping us create stability.

Beyond our customers, we were good employers. We were friends with our employees, and they knew that we had their back no matter what they needed. These teams repaid that loyalty with a commitment to our business and our customers that was bullet-proof. They went above and beyond in parallel to what we did for them. When our business needs for cash, sales, or customer service developed a heightened level of urgency, our rally cry to the troops caused everyone to rise to the occasion. Likewise, our customers went above and beyond for their relationship with all of us.

The trifecta of having a committed organization, committed customers, and an industry-centric product created industry leadership that was unparalleled in many ways. Even on our bad days, it was a committed partnership on all levels.

These early days were some of the most fun we had throughout our thirty years. Unfortunately, we coupled that fun with stress and a lack of life balance, but in a silo, it was a lot of fun. We loved what we did and why we did it.

That fun began to weigh heavily as personal commitments to relationships, health, hobbies, and family were neglected. The concept of life balance was putting pressure on the business. The business success also began to put pressure on us.

Our process of activating every person for every fire made us all firefighters. But, as the business grew, we were less prepared to fight those fires in knowledge and resources. We were slowly converting from successful firefighters to managing our days with our hair on fire. We had come to a convergence where something had to change.

Our growth dilemma

Many leaders can pinpoint the events that led them to the pinnacle in time, where they converted from being fruitful firefighters to leading with their hair on fire. Kristen, a long-time client, first used this term to describe her days as she dealt with explosive growth in their business.

It was the first term that accurately described the feeling I had. I quickly adopted it. "Hair on fire is" an odd phrase that many believe originated among Navy aviators. It conveys a sense of hair-raising urgency that translated to the business world as something that urgently catches our attention, causing us to instinctively react. For me, the visualization that comes to mind is me, frantically running and overwhelmed with what to do. I was **leading with my hair on fire**. My hair is in flames, and my face is stressed with the situation, causing an irrepressible sense of urgency. Suppose you are an entrepreneur, a leader managing explosive growth, a leader transforming a business, or even a parent trying to manage all of the insanity that goes with managing a family. In that case, you know exactly how this feels.

It feels like your hair is on fire.

The days that started to feel like hair on fire came shortly after making our second acquisition. The first company we purchased was in duress, but their customer base and go-to-market were very similar, making it easy to assimilate them into our business.

We brought stability to that business, and as a result, the assimilation into our business was manageable.

However, our second acquisition was a slightly different target customer; they had a stable product and stable business. For the first time in our business, we managed multiple product lines and a somewhat new target market. We had considerably underestimated the disruption to our business that this acquisition would cause, and soon this acquisition resulted in us transitioning from firefighters to our hair on fire.

Dan and I are natural problem solvers, so the challenge before us was exhilarating. Each day we were bombarded with new challenges and a steady stream of problems to solve. We approached the situation by doubling down on what we had been doing in the past. Soon, we were in firefighting mode 24/7 and were struggling to find ways to get things done. We ran from one crisis to another so often that it really did seem like our hair was on fire. Rather than looking for a broader solution, we saw ourselves as *the* solution.

We were working harder, not smarter.

We had yet to realize that the added complexity in our business was permanent, and we had a change to make in how we ran the company. But, unfortunately, that change was still somewhat far down the horizon.

At the same time, our young family was growing. We now had seven kids in three different schools and contending with all the associated activities and sports. We coached everything we could, often running from one practice to the next. Our au pair was frantically putting out the fires we could not manage, usually with the youngest in the brood. Her days were long and exhausting, just like ours. It felt a lot like her hair had caught on fire from ours. The fires were starting to spread to our personal lives. This realization was yet another catalyst for change.

Unintended Consequences

One of the unintended consequences of our leadership style was that it made our employees dependent on us. Like most entrepreneurs, we were used to making the most critical decisions.

Like most small businesses and startups, our employees waited for us to make those decisions. We had always been the single points of failure, but what was new is that our business had grown in complexity and that no longer worked.

The complexity of the business combined with our management style was creating unintended strains in our company and our managers. We started to become further disconnected from our customers. Our newly acquired customer base didn't have the history or relationship we had with our legacy customers. It became harder to satisfy them and more overwhelming. The exhilaration of problem-solving and firefighting was coming much less often.

The bad days began to be far too often.

We used to put our personal touch on issues to resolve them and satisfy our customers. Unfortunately, the pace of problems with all new customers was a pace we could not meet. The level of personalization that built our customer loyalty was not sustainable. Our customer satisfaction was beginning to wane. An unintended consequence of our hard work and long hours was that our business was stagnating. We were starting to see customer churn for the first time in our company, our profit margins were flattening, and although we were investing in the business, it wasn't turning into an R.O.I. The fun had become a rarity and the days were exceedingly long.

We had to find a new solution that didn't include us at the epicenter. If you are reading this book, you know where I am coming from or, likely, are there. *Exponentiality* helped us find our way.

Taking our Slingshot Back

As small business owners, we had the luxury of having no one but our employees and customers with whom to answer. But, unfortunately, as a small business owner, our Achilles Heel was the same— we had no one to answer to.

In addition, because we had never done long-term planning, never consistently relied upon financial statements to manage results, and had not groomed our managers to become business leaders, we had created an unsustainable leadership model.

Our business was evolving in ways we did not like. We needed to take a step back and assess how we could better respond to the complexity we had created. I hadn't yet articulated the Fundamentals of an *Exponential Mindset*, but we most certainly needed to Slingshot.

We took the advice from Albert Einstein, who said, "We cannot solve a problem with the same level of thinking that created it." Like many businesses, we had to face the harsh reality that our managers didn't have the time or the expertise to uncover the root causes of our problems. Our managers didn't have the authority to devise and implement viable solutions because we didn't empower them. We had been the experts that our customers relied upon to drive the vision of their businesses, but for the first time in our company's history, we had to turn our efforts inside. We needed to work on our business, not in it. Our desire to hold the fort was causing us to lose the war.

After some soul searching, Dan and I agreed that we needed more outside perspective in our business. I had attended hundreds of seminars throughout the years, learning how to be successful in business, yet had not taken some of the larger tasks to heart in our own business. We had helped thousands of customers grow their businesses by hiring us, consultative outsiders, to help them. Yes, ironically, for us to do the same was terrifying. I knew most successful leaders turn to outside resources to help them organize their business and delegate its management.

Even with this knowledge, investing in outside help was scary, expensive, and didn't have the return on investment we were accustomed to in our business. We had always been 100% self-reliant, and for the first time in our organization, we needed to lead by letting go. We needed to Level Up.

As we began to seek advice, we started with our customer base. They had been our informal business consultants for years.

Because Dan and I were only 22 & 17 when we started working together, many of our customers mentored us throughout the years. They acted as an informal board of directors to guide us with business advice, reporting structures, and metrics.

The hardest part of this process was admitting that we couldn't do it all. There are no prizes for reinventing the wheel, and you cannot correct what you do not face—finding a mentor for me has always been a struggle. Most seventeen-year-old girls don't start a technology business focused on the trades with their boyfriend that results in a successful global organization.

I did. Years ago, when I heard about Sheryl Sandberg, C.E.O. of Facebook, I remembered reaching out to her, asking her to be my mentor. I realized it was more than a long shot, but our daughter Hannah once told me that you couldn't score if you don't shoot. I took my shot. In case you are wondering, I didn't score a response.

Because our journey was so unique, we decided that the type of consultants within our budget and could garner the most value was from our industries. Several of our customers were willing to take on the role, and we eventually selected two to help us through this initial exercise.

Both had a substantial track record for success and brought different skills to our organization. One was an entrepreneur and operator—the other focused on consulting. So, we started our process with our first-ever off-site strategic planning meeting. Our consultants needed to learn the interior of our business, but they knew the market, the product, and the staff very well. We knew this process would involve change, but it was the only way to thrive from our growth.

Figuring out how to Extinguish Fires

Our journey with outside perspective started with a **S.W.O.T. (Strengths, Weaknesses, Opportunities, Threats)** exercise. This process grounded us in our current reality. Next, the consultants challenged us to assess ourselves honestly. This process helped us inventory our results to build on what we did well, address what we lacked, minimize risks, and take advantage of the most significant opportunities.

Out of this work came our first mission statement. We had been in business for decades and had never articulated why we did what we did. After nearly an entire day, we birthed our first mission statement. Our mission statement gave us clarity and focus.

This document meant that instead of reacting every day, we could act on purpose. It was the first step toward taking off the firefighter hat and extinguishing our hair on fire. This transition became the building block for so many of the future decisions we made. Once we got good at tying everything we did back to the mission, our organization evolved.

Next, our assessment made it clear that our structure needed to change. We needed to be more strategic and adopt S.M.A.R.T. (Specific-Measurable-Attainable-Realistic-Timely) goals that would drive the business. Our initial plans weren't perfect, but they were directionally correct.

Fire Fighter to Hair on Fire to Dinner by the Fire

As a reader of this book, this all may seem very simple. It may be something you have done since the day you started in business.

It may be a process in which you see no value. As an entrepreneur, taking the time to Level Up, Slingshot, and invest the time was the most challenging part of the reality. It felt like a frivolous waste of time that we could not afford. In hindsight, having invested this time years earlier would have fundamentally changed our business. If you haven't done this, don't wait. If you have, stay focused on what you learned. In all cases, *Exponentiality* in your business starts with this process.

- ***Triumph. Expect the possibility/probability of* Defined *Success.*** If you don't define it, how can you expect it? *Leveling Up*. Expect others to meet you at your level. This process forced us to professionalize our business, stop meandering and *Level Up* to what our customers need from us.
- ***Goal-Driven Focus****. We had no defined goal. We were like a football team, with every special team doing what they individually defined as success. We needed to all focus on the end-zone and whatever it took us to get there.*
- ***Jenga. Solution-Focused Flexibility****. We had always played Jenga. This activity was probably our specialty. What we didn't do was focus. This process forced our focus.*
- ***Protagonist Power. Expect Conflict****. Confront Conflict. Get Comfortable in Chaos. Expect Solutions. These processes were HARD. There were lots of conflicts, and it was not comfortable. Many parts of this journey took months and maybe even years, but we began to expect more solutions as we started to see results. All of this happened because we confronted the conflict we had in the business.*
- ***The Slingshot Effect****. There is no doubt; this was a Slingshot. We all had to set aside the fires we were fighting. We had to ignore our hair on fire and focus on creating a mission and the goals that would get us there.*

- ***Process-Driven. Always Drive Toward Process.*** *Building processes across our entire organization, not just in our silos, was the way toward success. Once we had a unified mission, processes became easier to assimilate across the whole business.*

During this process, I had yet to define the Fundamentals of an *Exponential Mindset*, but with crystal clear hindsight, it is easy to see, these days were beginning to form these Fundamentals. My personal journey to writing this book started alongside this process.

Converting the Culture of Urgent

One thing that we all knew at Davisware is that we lived in a culture of urgent. That culture was what made our hair feel like it was on fire day in and day out. We understood that urgent wasn't always the most important, but we couldn't figure out how to ignore what felt like hair on fire to plan for the future.

We knew urgent is the enemy of important, but how do we tell the difference?

To stop managing with our hair on fire, we had to understand the difference between urgent and important in very practical terms. Customer needs were urgent. Processes and discipline were important. In the journey of writing this book, I can reflect on these days and confidently admit that there was not significant joy in my work or my personal life while my hair was on fire. I was working far too many hours. I had imbalance and no sway with major mommy guilt for missing too many evenings at home. Family dinners were the anomaly, not the norm. I was not keeping my commitments to coaching and community service with the excellence I had always prided myself in. We were extinguishing fires by working longer hours.

Our top managers were doing the work instead of delegating through the organization because they followed our example. We did this because, well, it was urgent. We could do it better and faster than the others, so we just kept doing it.

These days were the farthest thing from *Living Exponentially*.

One revelation I had early in my career was that many of the people who significantly influenced my direction rarely knew the impact they had. Usually, the effect comes in small passing conversations that changed me.

I can pinpoint three conversations that motivated me to extinguish my hair, stop firefighting, and focus on what was important in life and our business. One was with my assistant cross-country coach and dear friend, Dan Smith. Coach Smith made a passing comment that one of the reasons he loves coaching with me is that he sees the stress of my day melt away during our practices. His exact words were, "J.D., by the end of practice, I always see that smile come back." He meant it as a compliment. He may as well have pierced my heart. *I didn't know my smile was missing.* The second was a long-time, loyal customer who simply asked me, "What are you doing?"

He didn't need to say anything more. I knew what he meant. The last was our daughter, Amelia, asking me when I would quit working all night because she liked sneaking in our bed, and now when she sneaks in, it's empty.

Ouch. None of these people likely remember the words they said.

Their words changed my direction.

I needed to change my focus from urgent to important.

In the 1967 booklet, *Tyranny*, Charles Hummel warned that "your greatest danger is letting the urgent things crowd out the important."[22] Our evolution wasn't overnight, but I was committed to something different. Just like the journey to *Exponential Living*, it had to start with commitment. The journey began with many of the tips that I've shared in this book.

Timeboxing, calendar mastery, scheduled meetings, technology tools, documented processes, and many others started to urgently evolve out of the words that stung me.

President Eisenhower said it this way, "I have two kinds of problems, the urgent and the important. The urgent things are not important, and the important are never urgent."[23] Later, using Eisenhower's principles, Stephen Covey created a decision matrix in his famous book, "The 7 Habits of Highly Effective People." This decision matrix consists of four quadrants:[23]

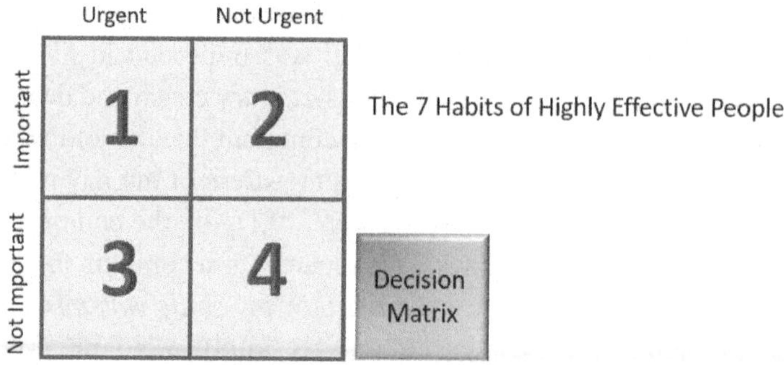

We experienced first-hand how repetitive problems drain our business and, more importantly, our people. We had to remind ourselves that insanity is doing the same thing repeatedly and expecting different results. The explosive growth we had experienced created urgent problems that were not important. But, in a much smaller, less complicated business, they were the same. Once we had committed to this process, the results started to happen. For me, my known Achilles heel is a failure to look in the rearview mirror. I had to remind myself that we *were* making progress. It wasn't life-altering, initially.

Several months into this journey, our weekly leadership meeting ended with several positive signs that we were moving in the right direction. It was out of that meeting that the next journey impacting revelation occurred. Doing important things brings me confidence and joy. My joy at work was returning.

That Tuesday morning was the first day at work in quite some time; I felt joy.

That meeting and this revelation helped me push back urgent and insert more time for the important. I began carving out days, not hours, to do the important. I realized that in this process, urgent issues create anxiety. My goals needed to change to delegate the urgent so that I could stay focused on the important. Our next challenge was now visible. Our organizational chart needed to change.

Too many hats still didn't put out the hair on fire

A significant factor in our chaos was that people were wearing far too many hats. I led sales, education, go-to-market strategy, customer success, and some accounting, and H.R. Dan covered different business areas but with the same problem. He was the single focal point of all products, engineering, Q.A., and FP&A, and equally involved in customer success, accounting, and wherever else he needed to lend a hand. Sadly, the same was true of everyone on our senior team in addition to both of us. We were the most qualified people in the business, working insanely long hours, doing 40 million things and very few of them well. I had betrayed my commitment to excellence. The results of the exceptional teams we had in place were not fantastic work. We had an incredible team, but we were failing them because we didn't have an organization that allowed them to be exceptional.

Just like most small businesses, a formal organizational chart wasn't necessary for many years. Our teams just did what needed to be done. That no longer worked with the business complexity we had and the size of our teams. The litmus test was my joy. The ah-ha moment was when I realized I had 41 direct reports, and Dan had double this.

What we were doing wasn't working for the business, and it indeed wasn't working for me. Those brief comments by a few essential people got me laser-focused on getting my joy back. This process was painful. We worked on a formal organizational chart, we had many iterations, and each got us closer to our goals. Each iteration got us closer to being delegators, from being doers. Much of what I learned about *Exponential Communications* came during this time in our journey. I knew that setting the expectation for change fixed much of the problem with change overall.

Change is successful when people are a part of it, and we are not trying to change them.

The results of a mission statement, goal setting, and an organizational chart were that our teams started to feel empowered to make decisions. We began to see work happening within the business in which we were not directly engaged. What began as anxiousness for us soon became glimmers of joy. We were starting to mitigate the dependencies on us.

Ever so slowly, we started seeing results in the business. Finally, our mission statement wasn't just printed everywhere; we began to live it.

S.M.A.R.T. goals started to be the focus of meetings, and the evolution toward professionalizing our business began to enable leaders to take on the urgent so that we could do what was important.

We were finally beginning to extinguish the fire in our hair. My joy was coming back. I could come to practice with my smile, not just end practice with it. I could be there at night for dinner and when Amelia snuck in our bed. And finally, I knew what I was doing. With my joy, I could inspire others.

Chapter Summary – Chapter 5: Leading with My Hair on Fire

Lessons Learned

- Transitioning from do-er to leader is one of the most challenging growth inhibitors business leaders face.
- If there is a problem in your business that you keep dealing with but can never seem to solve – that's a **fire**. Spend the time to solve for good, or your hair will always be on fire.
- Outside resources give outside perspective.
- Become aware of your management style. It impacts how well problems get solved and how fast people develop.
- Being a fire fighter is often a part of the early days in business. When the business converts from firefighting to hair on fire is when you have to look to move from doer to leader.
- Hair on fire is an odd phrase that is believed to have originated among Navy aviators. It was intended to convey a sense of hair-raising urgency that can be translated to the business world as something that urgently catches our attention, causing us to instinctively react.
- Don't allow the crises' of others become your crisis unless it is laser aligned with your mission statement and goals.
- If you respond to an urgent issue, make sure you conduct an after-action review to ensure that you don't repeat it in the future.
- Standardized reports and regular meetings are essential for keeping employees informed and on the same page. Commit to the process and improve it continuously.

- As you grow, it is important to expand your time horizon. You will still spend time on the day-to-day issues but must begin to dedicate time addressing issues 3-9 months out and begin to consider issues 1-5 years off.
- Unintended consequences can be detrimental to the growth of your business.
- Many of the people who significantly influenced our direction rarely knew the impact they had.
- Every one of the Fundamentals of an *Exponential Mindset* are critical in this business transition.
- S.W.O.T. exercises are fundamental to extinguishing fires.
- The decision matrix has four quadrants segregating urgent and non-urgent and important and not important.
- A bullet-proof mission statement is at the core of your business.

Unveiled Discoveries

- Most entrepreneurs don't start a business with the idea of spending their days managing a staff of people to run their business. Their dreams are about the business itself.
- When people are a part of change, and we are not trying to change them, change is successful.
- What are you doing that is staging your teams for failure?

Action Plan

- What would be the most valuable outside perspective for your business? How can you invest in consulting to achieve this?
- Do you have a bullet-proof mission statement?
- Does every employee know it?
- Is your mission statement outward facing and would your customers agree that is your mission?

- How do you narrow the focus of your business to only customers aligned with your mission statement?
- What SMART goals does your organization have and are they strategically aligned with your mission statement?
- How can you build a structure around your day that allows you to invest time in your mission and SMART goals?
- Who are the influencers in your business? Do they know it?

Good Quotables

- *Always use your rearview mirror and your windshield in life in direct relationship to their size. The rearview mirror reminds you where you've been and gives you perspective on the future. The windshield is a large opportunity to see where you are headed. Never get caught looking back too long. You run the risk of crashing and missing the opportunity to go forward.*
- *We cannot solve a problem with the same level of thinking that created it. —Albert Einstein*
- *You can't score if you don't shoot.—(Hannah Pearl Davis*
- *Your greatest danger is letting the urgent things crowd out the important.—Charles Hummel*
- *I have two kinds of problems, the urgent and the important. The urgent things are not important, and the important are never urgent.—President Dwight D. Eisenhower*

Supplementary Learning Recommendations (Read/Listen/Watch)

- *The 7 Habits of Highly Effective People* by Stephen R. Covey
- *Thinking, Fast and Slow* by Daniel Kahneman

CHAPTER 6

Confronting an Unsolvable Problem

Solving problems is why we love leadership positions. It is often the fuel that drives you. But, often, problem-solving creates sway in our lives, sometimes compromising balance.

When we get to problems that feel more challenging than others after trying our usual tools and processes, they feel unsolvable. Unsolvable Problems can create sway, but they can also be the ones that motivate us to Level Up.

Confronting the Unsolvable Problem needs to be done through a different perspective, seen through a different lens and often with other tools and maybe even different people. Many people call this approach "thinking outside of the box." I would propose that instead of this, you look to apply the Fundamentals of an *Exponential Mindset.* All of the Unsolvable Problems that we faced are how I developed the Fundamental Principals of an *Exponential Mindset.*

We are often reminded to focus on what we can control. 2020 and the global pandemic certainly told us this. We cannot control what comes at us, but what we can control is how we respond. Finding solutions through an *Exponential Mindset* will allow your business to survive Unsolvable Problems and give you the tools to use these instances to thrive in all aspects of your life.

Many once-successful companies are littering the business landscape because they did not anticipate or see Unsolvable Problems in time.

Borders Books was a 40-year-old retailer and grew to become the 2nd largest book retailer in America by 2001. It boasted profits in 2005 of $101 million.

By 2011, its 1,249 retail stores and their 10,000+ employees were all gone due to their bankruptcy, just 13 years after their peak revenue of $1.74 billion (about $5 per person in the U.S.). The failure of leadership to see the value of selling books online took them from a market leader to out of business in just over a decade.[24]

Like Borders, Blackberry was an undisputed leader in their space. In 2008, Blackberry was valued at over **$80 Billion**, with a 70% market share. However, in 7 years, it dropped to a 5% market share and by 2016 had ceased designing their own phones— just eight years after its peak.[25] A decision from the top that devices without keyboards would not catch on caused the massive collapse.

Like Borders and Blackberry, Blockbuster made critical mistakes by assuming that consumers would prefer getting their entertainment (DVDs and games) physically instead of on the internet. At its peak in the late '90s, Blockbuster owned over 9,000 video-rental U.S. stores, employed 84,000 people (about the seating capacity of the Los Angeles Memorial Coliseum) worldwide, and had 65 million registered customers. It was once valued as a $3 billion company (about $9 per person in the U.S.). Fast-forward a decade, Blockbuster ceased to exist, having filed for bankruptcy with over **$900 million** in debt.[26]

In each of these cases, industry leaders met their ultimate demise in a brief period because their leadership was not aware of the Unsolvable Problems in front of them. The industries had changed, and so had their customers.

As business leaders, stories like these make us cringe, partly because we remember their glory days and partly because we wonder where our blind spots are and can relate. Yet, our organizations and families depend upon us to continually evolve our thinking. The Fundamental Principals of an *Exponential Mindset* can do just that.

The Netflix Story

Netflix is an inspirational example of a company that successfully shifted its business model several times and grew *Exponentially* because of that. At their onset, they rented boxed products only in the U.S. through a mail service. Then, they shifted to delivering on-demand entertainment, catering to diverse needs globally. Finally, their "all you can eat" subscription service changed consumer viewing habits, allowing them to watch their favorite shows anywhere and whenever they wanted to.[27] They have grown by repeatedly confronting the Unsolvable Problem with new thinking and emerging a different, better company each time.

Netflix faced its first Unsolvable Problem when the market for their product started to shrink. After two years of stagnating sales, the DVD market shrank by 4.5% in 2007. This decline in sales was the first year-over-year retreat in the format's 10-year history. So rather than cut costs or focus on improving physical DVDs delivery, Netflix decided to future-proof their business. They decided to reinvent entertainment delivery by providing subscribers with instant access to thousands of titles that they could binge-watch on any device. Unfortunately, there was just one tiny flaw in Netflix's plan – the technology required to build their bold new vision of home entertainment did not exist. Undeterred, the company invested more than $40M in developing new streaming technologies, including a $6M investment in the new Palo Alto, California company, Roku.[28]

In 2007, Netflix launched its streaming service, Watch Now. While cable companies focused on traditional business models and quarterly revenue targets, Netflix was already looking years into the future and beyond.

By 2012, Netflix faced the next Unsolvable Problem…the cost of its product was about to skyrocket. In addition, Netflix's relationships with several studios and media publishers had become strained. Starz wanted a bigger slice of the Netflix pie, so they canceled its licensing agreement with Netflix, which resulted in thousands of movies disappearing from Netflix's streaming service overnight. Licensing other networks' content was becoming increasingly costly and complicated for Netflix – and so the company was forced to reinvent itself yet again.

2013 saw Netflix dive headfirst by investing in the world of original programming with its high-profile political drama, *House of Cards*. Netflix's investment was reported to be the largest ever at the time as they continued to think with an *Exponential Mindset*. In February 2013, Ted Sarandos, Netflix's chief content officer, told G.Q., "the goal is to become HBO faster than HBO can become us." With shows like *House of Cards* and *Arrested Development*, their original programming's success enabled the company to increase subscribers from 33 million in 2013 to 50 million in April 2014. By 2020, Netflix's annual revenue of over $25 billion (about $77 per person in the U.S.) includes 204 million subscribers and represents the highest global streaming platforms at 34%.[29]

Other examples of "out of the box" thinking included innovation for creating local content to travel globally, building a kid's content hub, and being a first mover into the cloud.

Their *Exponential* approach to business has made them the undisputed leader in streaming platforms.

Netflix leadership has demonstrated an *Exponential Mindset* at each Unsolvable Problem. Their repeated decisions to think *Exponentially* allowed them to see opportunities before those around them, make calculated risks in investment and continue to dominate innovation in their market.

The pandemic has become an Unsolvable Problem for many businesses. While few could have foreseen the pandemic coming, organizations that did not react quickly enough or who were not in a position to defend their stake have already closed their doors. Industry-leading brands such as Neiman Marcus, Toys R Us, 24 Hour Fitness, Hertz Rental Car, and Briggs & Stratton, not to mention countless bars and restaurants, filed for bankruptcy in 2020. Yet, while facing the same problems, other similar retailers have survived and even thrived. The Unsolvable Problem created new markets and opportunities for companies in these industries who learned to thrive in a delivery world, transitioned to fitness equipment and online group fitness, and took the void in the marketplace these leaders left and filled it with their growth and profitability. As a result, the pandemic's outcome has not been as focused on the size of the business but the leaders' *Exponential Mindset* in what felt like an Unsolvable Problem.

The Davisware Unsolvable Problem

In the late '90s and long before the global pandemic, Dan and I faced our Unsolvable Problem. That problem and how we responded changed our business and our lives forever. Our family was growing, and so was Davisware. Our product had become expansive, and our user base stable. We were sole-proprietors and debt-free in our business. The technology industry was rapidly growing from green screens and mainframes to desktop computing. The *Exponential* value of the internet was starting to show its power. These changes created new technology we had never seen before, including the need for a graphical user interface (G.U.I.). That is when Dan first discovered our Unsolvable Problem.

On New Year's Eve, 1997, we were doing what so many entrepreneurs do. We were using the holiday to play catch up. At that time, we developed our products on a Progress database and language platform. Dan had downloaded the next-generation version of that product to show me some of the new power and technology. He wrote a little script that involved multiple layers and several steps. Dan then showed me that in the previous version, it was only two lines of code. He sat there reflectively for a minute and said, "What I did here took me ten times longer than what I used to do. How are we going to do *that*?"

My naivety at that moment quickly became educated on our Unsolvable Problem. Dan was doing the math that added up to the impossible. Experts in technology estimated that it required 7-10 times the resources to develop in this new environment versus the old way. What this meant for Davisware is that there weren't enough hours in the day. Dan knew he was already working 80+ hours a week and obviously could not put in an 800-hour workweek! He also knew we could not afford the help to perform the extra 540 hours. Being the rainmaker at Davisware, I tried to solve the problem commercially and still came up with no answers. I could not sell the software for 7-10 times as much or sell 7-10 times as many systems. So, we had an Unsolvable Problem, and we had no choice but to set out to solve it. We had a problem that required an *Exponential Mindset.*

At that moment, we realized that our current work methods and design systems could not produce a commercially viable version of our next-generation products. This dilemma was a scary realization because it threatened our company's future and threatened the security and stability of our growing family of 5. If we did not find an answer, we would need to find another way to support our family. This conclusion may feel a bit dramatic, but Davisware and these products were our only assets and our only source of income. Therefore, we had no option but to come up with a solution.

Dan has always been the king of creative problem-solving and began analyzing the problem and looking for solutions. But, unfortunately, none of his multiple solutions succeeded on paper.

However, each failure was a valuable learning opportunity that was the foundation for our future success. Our initial instincts were to double down and just keep doing what we were doing. Then, we would work harder and figure out how to charge more. But, unfortunately, that was short-lived and unrealistic.

We had attempted to hire students locally, but the bandwidth was not making a dent. In addition, it was cost-prohibitive to execute in the U.S. With barely enough money to perform in the current environment, we started with the traditional routes of looking for financial backing through conventional banking or potentially in getting investors. It is hard to imagine a world where private equity, angel investing, and venture capital are prevalent. Still, at that time, technology was not an investment that the traditional financial world was interested in investing in!

Being an early adopter in technology had many advantages, but one of the significant disadvantages was that traditional banking mechanisms were far out of our reach. In addition, the concept of intellectual property was new, especially to local banking.

Banks could not lien our brains and therefore saw nothing valuable in our business or ideas! So, we had to find an alternative, non-traditional means of funding the decisions ahead of us. Financing our next-generation product was critical, but first, we had to develop a product solution before coming up with a financial solution.

Our Solution

As we sorted out our options, we knew we could not raise our prices enough to make an impact. We knew working harder was unrealistic with the new level of effort required. We had to find less expensive labor and much more of it.

In finding less expensive labor, our *Resource Inventory* was limited. We knew we had to think outside the box. In this case, outside of the box meant outside of our continental borders. Our solution was in outsourcing.

The decision to outsource was a heart-wrenching one. It was full of risk, tons of unknowns, and an undefined roadmap. Emotionally, it felt very un-American.

The biggest tech companies were barely dipping their toes in outsourcing abroad, so it was scary to think we were attempting to join or beat them to the race. On top of this, the foundational element of our midwestern farm roots fiercely protected the ideology of the American Dream.

The concept of moving jobs abroad, in truth, felt like a betrayal. It took us quite some time to make this decision because of our American loyalty.

After much debate and knocking on every traditional door, we realized that *because of* the decision to outsource, we were saving and creating American jobs, not the opposite. We took the leap. Thankfully, Dan is far more of a risktaker than I am. This decision was *hazardous*. I know that I would have never made this decision without his boldness. All we had to risk was everything we had. Finally, we were all in and headed abroad.

Our Challenge Abroad

Entering into the unknown world of outsourcing was not a simple one. Fortunately, Dan's brother was in the midst of the same process as a part of the Fortune 500 company he worked for. So, we had an expert within our family to look toward for what to do.

However, outsourcing was brand new, even to Fortune 500 companies. Everyone was still learning, and the results were still unknown. Learning so-called expertise was happening in real-time. Every organization that was doing it was learning by doing it. We were all changing the tires on a moving race car. The opportunity for failure was high, and the risks were many.

The first international failure came quick

As we looked at the landscape of options, we quickly narrowed our choices to China and India. We selected India because we had connections there, and the resource pool seemed limitless. Finally, we connected with a person who seemed perfect for what we needed. Using a large chunk of our personal savings, we put together a server and shipped it to our contact for our newly formed venture!

With Dan's guidance, that server would operate as the infrastructure for him to develop the software. Dan was going to need to learn how to manage remotely using the tools available at the time- mail, email, and phone (keep in mind that the internet was barely in commercial existence and was nowhere a fundamental part of our infrastructure).

The challenge of remotely managing our new venture was, unfortunately, not the problem we faced. Instead, the challenge of trying to do business halfway around the globe quickly became all too real. Our contact, our server, and our savings all disappeared. We were robbed of our resources, our time, and our precious money.

Our maiden attempt at outsourcing failed dismally.

With what I would say is nothing short of Divine intervention, we overcome this setback by short-term stateside business prosperity.

I had managed to gain a couple of key new customer accounts to help us fund our next move. Although we lost time and money, our understanding of what we were taking on increased dramatically. We were better prepared to take our next swing for the fences.

Strike Two

From there, with the advice of Dan's brother, we decided to give China a try. China was ahead of India in infrastructure and the ability to support such ideas. They had a stable power grid, internet, and an educated workforce. Unfortunately, the language, business environment, and communication challenges soon proved impossible for us to overcome. After less than six months, we pulled out and went back to the drawing board.

Our second experiment failed, but our learns learned continued to grow. Although we were still committed to outsourcing, time and energy were not on our side. As a result, our products were becoming quickly outdated, and our revenue numbers were stagnating.

This Unsolvable Problem was starting to feel genuinely unsolvable.

Many days felt that way. However, because we saw this as a do-or-die life decision, we had no choice but to continue to find the fortitude to push forward. I am highlighting the significant examples of *The Slingshot Effect*, but in truth, most days, it felt like we were only pulling back, wondering when the rubber band may give up from the stress of it all. We struggled to stick with the Fundamentals of the *Exponential Mindset*, particularly #1, *Triumph. Expecting the Possibility/Probability of Defined Success.*

Our pullback this time had to take an original approach and new perspective to our *Goal-Driven Focus*. We could not solve this problem with any of our same strategies or tools.

We needed to play *Jenga*, Confront the Conflict we expected and get ready for the Slingshot forward.

I wish I had the cognitive awareness then that I do now.

I wish I had understood the Possibility Mindset and Thinking *Exponentially*. I wish that I could have taken a thirty-thousand-foot view of my life at that time. But, unfortunately, I could not, and I did not.

The journey of authoring this book has been to help each reader find their own thirty-thousand-foot view, find their own Possibility Mindset, and find their own ability to think *Exponentially*.

Fortunately, because our options were that we had no options, we were forced to find our way. We were disappointed but could not afford to be deterred. There has never been a time in our lives when the Possibility Mindset was more critical. We had to know that success was probable, and it was just a matter of finding it. I thank God loudly that Dan had the drive not to be deterred by the risk and that I had the fortitude to trust him in the process. We were about to hit sway massively.

We were still committed to outsourcing as we forged forward, but we decided to change our strategy. After much consideration, we decided to go back to India. We now needed to learn how to play *Jenga*. Executing Solution Focused Flexibility, we focused on the parts of India that would be successful. They shared our common language, English. Their workforce was highly educated. It was a U.S.-friendly business environment, and they offered a favorable exchange rate. These *Jenga* blocks moved easily.

Our focus now needed to shift to the blocks that did not seem as obvious or move easily. We needed to become experts in the *Exponential Jenga* game. We needed to solve project management, cost management, capital, time zones, and reliable power. One by one, we found solutions.

The first realization critical to our success and livelihood was that we couldn't manage this venture remotely. Outsourcing agencies were both cost-prohibitive and didn't fit our culture, nor could our U.S.-based infrastructure support an outsourcing agency.

Doing what very few people would do (at the time, I could think of no one who would do what he did), we decided that Dan would go there himself to build a team. Take a moment and challenge yourself to think about what went into this decision. From his perspective, he was traveling alone to a foreign country with no significant means of communication or a plan. For me, I was sending my husband eight thousand miles around the globe, not sure he would be safe or when he would be coming back.

The financial fear of what it would cost and whether it would be successful were completely unknown.

This realization was hard for both of us. It would have been hard if that were all we were facing. Besides Dan spending most of 2004 alone in a third-world country, I stayed behind parenting our six children (giving birth that year to our 4th daughter that fortunately Dan was stateside for), manage our household, and run the U.S. business operations.

My nephews and I personally moved us to our new, downsized office. We wrapped up moving into our new house, and I managed both the home-front and the office while Dan was away. It was a test of our fortitude and grit. There was nothing about this year that was in balance. These days were excruciating, challenging, and long. The level of exhaustion at every level was often overwhelming. This year was the one that the sway knocked us off of our wires frequently! When Dan packed his bags and left for India with a commitment to do whatever it took to "figure it out!" that meant I had to do the same here. Together, we executed the *Exponential Mindset*.

Dan headed out to solve outsourcing on a one-way ticket to India as part of a 30-hour door-to-door journey. In today's world (or at least pre-2020), leaving for a 3rd world country may not have seemed too extraordinary. However, the landscape of India and the world was vastly different in 2004.

Internet was expensive and hard to come by. VoIP phones were just beginning to become mainstream and certainly were not in the Davisware budget at that time (We joined the VoIP revolution in 2008). The power grid in India was unreliable, at best. Phone calls were expensive if they worked at all. There was no Life360, Snapchat, or Google tracking to follow where he was physically at. I barely knew how to spell the city he landed in. In 2020, we often talked about uncertain times. The level of uncertainty we both faced in those days should create a proper perspective around today's version of uncertainty!

I think that neither of us appreciated how difficult it was on the other side. It was a make-or-break time. We had the gift of not having time to reflect upon all the challenges we were facing.

We stayed focused on that goal and claimed that success. While it was one of the most challenging years of my life (and I am sure Dan would say the same), I can also say that it was personally rewarding. I'm proud that we defied the odds and opened our doors long before many big tech organizations successfully opened theirs. His journey was filled with conflict, problems, and chaos that his unparalleled grit found a way through. He was the protagonist in the Davisware action movie! We persevered because we headed into the decision-making with the expectation of *Defined Success*. Success was establishing a wholly owned and operated Indian development office, and that is what we did.

It may sound like the yellow brick road was paved. But it was far from that. Instead, hindsight demonstrated that we were both fixated on our goal.

This fixation allowed us to find success in getting to India. However, the road to broader business success was hardly complete at this point. We had only scaled one hurdle. We had many more we had to accomplish to transform our products and livelihoods. We had many complications to figure out. While we anticipated complexity with language, culture, different time zones, and lack of reliable power and internet, we underestimated how hard they would all be. In addition, we had many unforeseen challenges. We had to learn about the accounting and legal world, not to mention geography, societal structure, culture, and poverty, to a level that we had no sense of.

Our connections to Kolkata (previously known until 2001 as Calcutta) caused Dan's one-way ticket to land him in this mega-metropolitan city. Our second attempt to outsource to India would result in Kolkata officially being our first Davisware office. Through many long hours, Dan navigated incorporating, renting office space, and becoming an Indian corporation.

With the initial intent to outsource via a firm, Dan discovered that we were entirely wrong in our original approach. We were looking for labor to produce product.

Truthfully, we were looking at that labor without a face. We failed these attempts because we hadn't realized that people are people no matter where they are (sounds a bit like a Dr. Suess book). Indians wanted to be a valued part of an organization, not purchased labor hours, just like Americans. They also wanted to be valued, appreciated, and build something bigger than themselves, not just be hired to do something.

This realization refined our goal not just to outsource but to become an Indian corporation. This decision also meant that Dan could not just fly in, delegate, and walk away. We needed to be boots on the ground and own the process. Many companies were trying to outsource at that time, and a considerable number of them were failing or facing the same challenges.

Traditional outsourcing would not work for our organization because we could not afford the turnover rates plaguing American companies struggling with their outsourcing.

American companies were scooping up labor to do a wide variety of work, but the turnover rates were as high as 40%. Davisware could not afford this drain of resources and training. We had to urgently impart our 15+ years of tribal knowledge on a team, build Knowledge Ubiquity, and move forward. According to Ari Bixhorn, VP of Marketing at Panopto in the H.R. Daily Advisor, the average U.S. enterprise-size business wastes $4.5 million in productivity annually due to failing to preserve and share knowledge.[30]

Davisware could not afford $4.50, much less thousands or millions. Most American firms arrived in India and saw the labor pool like lumber. Getting ten programmers was like going to Home Depot and ordering ten 2x4s.

The simple oversight they were all making is that the Indian workforce was no different from any other workforce globally.

Indians wanted to be a part of a community; they wanted to learn and to grow. They did not want to be *hired by* Davisware; they wanted to be *a part of* Davisware. This insight led us to set up an office in Kolkata and become an Indian employer. We hired directly rather than hiring through an outsourcing firm. Although this decision would ultimately prove to be the right one, it presented us with more problems and challenges around labor law, banking, currencies, renting office space, and building infrastructure. In addition, the hiring of our initial three employees meant that

Dan extended his time in India, and we further challenged the sway in our lives. We were definitely off of the wire.

Our next failure was upon us.

An opportunity to initiate *The Slingshot Effect* came our way very quickly. After several months, our lack of progress tested our tolerance for another failure.

We soon learned a very stark lesson in the importance and value of reliable power and infrastructure. India was a third-world country, and we significantly underestimated how this would impact our ability to do business.

The lack of infrastructure was impeding our success.

Frequent power outages caused swelteringly hot work conditions and a lack of power for computers. Only seven short months later, we conceded. It was time to pull back our Slingshot. Unfortunately, we chose the wrong city. Kolkata's uncertain power and internet and a challengingly competitive labor pool made it impossible to maintain traction in our efforts. We stepped backward and admitted failure by taking our accelerated learning curve 1500 kilometers (nearly 1000 miles (about the distance from Florida to New York City)) to what became our final destination—Jubilee Hills, H.I.T.E.C. City, Hyderabad, India.

This shift required that we had to start over with our establishment. It meant we would risk the small staff of five that we had assembled. Indians did not typically relocate for jobs and especially not for a tiny no-name startup.

Through Dan's grit and my unwavering commitment to his leadership, we found the means to start again. We were also fortunate that 2 of our five employees remarkably followed our vision and followed Dan on our move. As a result, we established our new presence and our official Davis Software Solutions, Pvt. home in Hyderabad.

For some perspective, Jubilee Hills was a part of a multi-phase H.I.T.E.C. (Hyderabad Information Technology Engineering Consultancy City) development initiated in 1995 (less than nine years earlier). With this type of emphasis and governmental support, the outsourcing industry had grown its revenues in India tenfold from 1997 to 2007. It went from

$4.8B USD to nearly $48B by 2007. By 2008 more than 20,000 workers fully occupied the Raheja Mindspace, IT Park.[31]

In 2009 the Westin hotel, the first hotel focused on American business travelers, had opened. Notable companies were flooding in. Hyderabad became Microsoft's first outsourced development center outside of Redmond, Washington. The Indian government strongly supported the vision of becoming a technical powerhouse. "Cyberabad," as it became known, was quickly becoming the place to be.

With its sustainable internet and (more) reliable power, the improvements were immediate. Infrastructure reliability was still tricky, but they planned and managed the outages so we could work around them. In addition, the strategic location of Cyberabad was chosen to support the plethora of talent coming out of the local technology-focused universities, improving our odds of finding talent who was willing to take the risk in our small organization.

The added cost of our move was certainly not in our budget, nor was losing three of the five original team members. We had to remind ourselves that failing wasn't in our budget either.

We had solved the first of many of the *Jenga* blocks in our Unsolvable Problem.

The challenge in paying for It

Once we had established a roadmap to technological success, the next hurdle was paying for it. As I mentioned earlier, traditional banking had no mechanism for financing technology at this scale. So, we had *Defined Success* as being outsourced to India and had set out to achieve it.

Now, we had to figure out how to pay for it.

The image in the rearview mirror is clear. One of my lessons learned in the journey to *Exponentiality* has been that it has value if you use the rearview mirror for perspective.

The rearview mirror is much smaller than the windshield because we should use it in that proportion. I don't think I spent enough time looking in the rearview mirror to use the history, success, and perspective to find confidence in future success. Once I started using it is when the Slingshot started going forward more often. The critical detail here is to use it *in relativity to* the windshield. If you spend too much time looking backward, you are traveling forward toward impending disaster without eyes on your destination.

We focused our eyes on success abroad, and now we had to figure out how to pay for it. By most estimations, the cost to do what we were setting out to do was millions, not hundreds. Dan and I knew that as a bootstrap company with a rapidly growing family, there was little that we could contribute from our efforts. We *had to* be *Exponential*. This insight came via our ability to do an inventory of our resources and identify *Exponential Opportunities*.

One of the resources that we saw in the immediate future was the value of our real estate. In 2004, the real estate market in the U.S. was hot, with an all-time high of U.S. homeownership of nearly 70%.[32] This fueled record price increases across the entire country of as much as 25%. This number is dramatically higher than the national appreciation average between 3-4% annually. As a result, we had gained significant value in our office building.

As much as we loved the building that we had invested tremendous sweat equity in after purchasing it in 1998, we knew it was a resource we could liquidate. We listed and quickly sold the building for a significant profit that we immediately funneled into our outsourcing efforts. We moved into a much smaller, less desirable but functional office building that required sweat equity to make it work for us. The move was strategically within walking distance of our kids' school, making it both a give and a get and part of *The Slingshot Effect*. Our real estate capital gains were the initial funding for our India operations.

This easy win is certainly worth celebrating, but the truth is that we were nowhere near our goal. We had our seed money to start. Without additional funds to invest and grow, our outsourcing effort would be very short-lived.

The out-of-the-box thinking that comes next, I can only attribute to Dan. I have long said that when there is a crisis, he is the guy you want in charge. We had a financial problem on his hands, and his creative problem-solving pointed us in the right direction to finding the solution.

This challenge was our best example of us working together to solve a problem.

(I want to use this opportunity to sidebar this upcoming story with the commentary that this is in no way a recommendation to any entrepreneur to do what we did. The story's purpose is not to endorse leveraging your home to find success but rather to see every opportunity for success and define your own risk propensity. Everything I am about to share with you was risky and scary. For us, if we had seen other options, we may not have gone this route. However, because it was successful, it is often easy to forget to recognize the risk that went with it.)

Solving this problem is our best example of *Solution-Focused Flexibility*. Outside of our business ventures, we were in the midst of designing our new house to accommodate our rapidly growing family. We had long since outgrown our tiny suburban home for our family of 8. Using my eye for opportunistic real estate, we had been able to execute advantageous trade-ups in our real estate. Combining this skill with our willingness to invest heavily in sweat equity, we were in an unleveraged position on our personal real estate. As a result, we were in a favorable position to build our new home with as much of our own equity as possible— both in cash and sweat.

Banks were offering home equity lines of credit were at 105% of the home's value. Our capital investment would only be ~50% of our new home's value by doing much of the physical labor ourselves. This factor meant the completed home would have a 55% differential between what we could leverage and invested dollars. We work feverously to build as much as possible on our own and do it as quickly as possible.

With the decision to go the HELOC route for financing, Dan also realized that by expanding the size of our house in less costly areas (common areas and bedrooms), we would be able to extend that margin from 55% to 60-70%.

I often joked that expanding the size of our house allowed me to expand the size of our family! Fortunately for us, home values at that time were based only upon calculated square footage, not on a home inspection. They corrected many of these failures in the valuation systems, but they worked to our advantage at that time. The race to move our office and complete our house was underway! Both fell squarely into 2004, where I was also preparing to give birth to our 4th daughter.

On April 4th, 2004, Eva Irene joined our family at a solid 9lbs, 9oz with her shining red hair. We went straight from the hospital to the construction site, where we were feverously working on completing our home. *(By the way, I do not recommend this as balance in any way! Instead, this book is about our successes in Exponentiality and our failures in what we did to get here. There is no doubt in my mind that this was sway was off the wire, but we applied lessons learned by the time our next daughter arrived in 2007).*

Four grueling months later, still within 2004, we moved into our new home. At Thanksgiving that same year, we welcomed Dan home from his excruciating year of work in India, where he had successfully begun our outsourcing journey and secured a way to pay for it.

All of this was nothing short of a miracle.

Our challenges at home

We had (mostly) solved the geography of outsourcing, but the solutions that we needed to find to gain overall business success were far from solved. It is easy to look back at all that transpired and underestimate what went into finding a solution. It is easy to forget the failures and uncertainty that were a part of the many Unsolvable Problems and Slingshots that we incurred. Dan's early days in India in 2004 were solutions that we often got to via an exceptionally long and winding road. Dan faced all the international business challenges while he left his very pregnant wife at home to finish the house, move the office and be a single parent to our huge brood.

These were some of the hardest days of my life. Thank God for the support network of au pairs which helped us raise our family, the employees who were far from just employees, and the relatives and friends who knew we needed our "village" more than ever.

They worked tirelessly alongside us during these days. The daily exhaustion provided the gift of distraction over the financial and physical worry of what Dan was attempting to accomplish abroad.

Our little offshore experiment required Dan to spend more than 200 days (about six and a half months) that year in India. His time abroad placed some unique challenges for us as a business and as a family. Since Dan was our sole technical leader in our company, he had to run both the US-based and India development teams. As a result, long days and little sleep became his norm. In tandem, I managed our U.S. go-to-market strategy and infrastructure to support it, which required substantial travel.

The parental responsibilities complicated the demand on my time. With kids in school, preschoolers, and nursing infants, the complexity could become daunting.

However, I never looked at it as *if,* I looked at it has *how.* In an earlier chapter, I shared how I thought about core beliefs and my goals. Achieving my goals and staying true to my core beliefs became successful via an *Exponential Mindset.*

I think it is valuable to re-share my core beliefs.

- Nothing is impossible.
- The human mind is our most significant inhibitor to what we can accomplish.
- Failure provides our most important lessons learned.
- I seek continuous improvement and learning.
- Doing a repetitive task that offers no value beyond the job is a waste of time.
- I need to know that I made a difference in the world.
- I value my time and the time of those around me.
- Wasting time robs me of being able to do something more important.
- Doing what is important gives me the confidence that I made a difference in the world.
- We are burning daylight and have no guarantee of tomorrow. There is an urgency to today.

With these core beliefs, I never questioned if I could do it all. Of course, that does not mean that the challenges were not daunting, but I never doubted that it was all possible. The question was *how?*

I knew I could not be there for everything, but I could be there for the right things. In the Step-by-Step to an *Exponential Mindset*, I reference the importance of S.M.A.R.T. (Specific, Measurable, Achievable, Relevant, and Time-Bound) goals. My S.M.A.R.T. goal was t*o effectively fulfill my essential business responsibilities without sacrificing my duties as a mother.*

I focused on what I could control. I could not control the conferences and trade shows I had to attend. I could not control the fact that Dan was in India (however, we could control when he traveled to some extent, eliminating the conflict in our schedules). I could not create a typical nine-to-five lifestyle for myself or my kids. I categorized these things between what I could and could not control, so I knew where I needed to focus.

I could create a "normal" routine for my school-aged kids. I could make an environment where I could still breastfeed my babies while working full time. I could create a childcare situation that was as flexible as I needed it to be. I could control when my meetings were scheduled and usually where they took place. I could control when my workday started and when it ended. I could control my long workdays to be before my crew arose or after they were in bed. Finally, I could control many of our financial expenses to spend as little money as possible.

I could control that my travel schedule corresponded with school holidays so that my kids could be in tow without missing school. In addition, I could control my kids' extra-curricular activities by coaching as much as possible to control the schedule.

Each of these callouts is not to demonstrate that they are the only means possible to a solution. Each one is shared to share that there are many ways to find success, but you must start with a Possibility Mindset. I had decided my professional success would not be at the expense of my personal success. I decided I was going to be an engaged parent and a great business partner. Once I set these as my goals, my Possibility Mindset allowed me to achieve them.

There are so many specific examples of how I solved these challenges that they could be a book by themselves! Maybe that will be my next book, but in the meantime, here are a few examples:

Our childcare options did not include family. Dan and I have 20 brothers and sisters, and outside of occasional help, we were on our own for day-to-day care. In 1997, we discovered the au pair program, which fundamentally changed our lives. Converting to in-home childcare, I significantly reduced the complexity of childcare with customized flexibility.

I virtually eliminated the plague of ear infections and other illnesses Austin and Hannah were bringing home from daycare and lowered our overall childcare costs. The au pair program was critical to our success because it gave me the flexibility to be successful. When I traveled, the babies and au pair traveled with me. While Dan was out of the country, I had an extra set of hands in the house and the companionship to make long, hard days feel easier.

- These young women also created unparalleled childcare quality because they shared their culture and natural curiosity to explore and learn with our kids. We can see these impacts on our family today.

Breastfeeding our babies was non-negotiable. Without being able to delegate it, our babies were at the office whenever they could be.

When it wasn't feasible, our au pairs would keep our babies on their breastfeeding schedules. I would schedule my arrival at work around the school drop-off and feeding schedule. The next feeding was due somewhere around lunch and school pick up.

Our au pair would drop the infant off at our office so that I could enjoy my lunch and feed the baby while she did the preschool pick-up. We would repeat this process at the end of the school day for the school-aged pick-up.

- Finally, I would either be home before the last feeding or have the baby (and whoever had sports) dropped off at the office for me to start my evening. This schedule meant that I got to be engaged with our children at every time possible in the day while still being focused on work. My au pairs will tell you they spent far more of their days in the car than they would have preferred, but their contributions allowed me to be fully engaged with our kids, and I achieved my goal.

My business travel schedule was typically architected around school schedules and games, avoiding as much conflict as possible.

- When it was not possible, Dan and I would "divide and conquer" so that he kept the older kids at home and the au pair and babies came with me. We relied upon backup help from family to get him through his days, and I knew where the safe havens to nurse and be with children were in every major city and airport.

- I have never had an office that did not have a kid's desk set up in it. This decision afforded me the critical "15 minutes" to finish my essential deadlines, and our kids could do schoolwork or entertain themselves.
- Today's world is far more accommodating to working at home than in my early career days. I positioned my home office at a place in the house where I could be engaged, yet with privacy to focus. In addition, it always included a glass door. This door allowed kids to see my red light/green light. If my light were green, they knew they could freely come in and see me. If I were doing monotonous tasks, they could come to join me, and I could steal a bit of family time. If the light were yellow, my kids knew they could tread cautiously, coming in to steal a quick hug and kiss or use my printer, but that they needed to be fast and efficient in what they needed. If the light was red, they knew that only in life-threatening situations were they to enter! This system created success for everyone in the family.
- I often would use my early mornings to make breakfast, lunch, and dinner all at once. I could leave the kitchen dishes for the au pair to clean up (there are lots of apologies here I owe to all of my au pairs!), but that way, I could make sure my family was fed, but not spend the time on set up and clean up repetitively.
- My commitment to exercise grew over time, but I often used them as some of our best family time. Runs with babies in the jogger, bike rides towing lots of kids, coaching sports that could include my workout, and working out while they were at their own sports practices allowed me to be with our kids and still stay committed to my health.

My schedule was demanding and chaotic, but I could meet our clients' needs symbiotically with our kids' needs. Clients were happy, our business grew, and our kids experienced a routine that was "normal" for us. They were also learning from our example and the experiences they had the opportunities to be a part of. Dan found success in India, and we eventually struck a balance that had a lot less sway in it than in these early years with his business travel.

Each of these experiences, both success and failures, made us more resilient as entrepreneurs and as parents. We stayed focused on our outcomes and handled every new challenge as it arose. The losses stung, but they never stopped our focus on *Defined Success*.

Ultimately, over the course of thousands of decisions and hundreds of obstacles, we found dozens of solutions to solve what we deemed as our Unsolvable Problem.

In 2008, we released our next-generation product, Global Edge.

We are all moving in the direction of our strongest thoughts.

Through our Possibility Mindsets, we were always focused on overcoming the Unsolvable Problem and finding our *Defined Success*.

Chapter Summary – Chapter 6: Confronting an Unsolvable Problem

Lesson Learned

Being an entrepreneur means you will encounter Unsolvable Problems, and it will test your tolerance for failure.

- There is no such thing as too big to fail.
- When you encounter failure, look to your reasons for taking on the problem to motivate you to get up and try again.
- Our organizations and families are depending upon us to continually evolve our thinking. The Fundamental Principals of an *Exponential Mindset* can do just that.
- Unsolvable Problems will force you to expand your resource inventory. Do not constrain your thinking to be local, logical, and linear. Force yourself to think outside the box.
- People in other countries and more like Americans than different, especially when it comes to their jobs. They would rather be a

part of something bigger than a job. They want to be valued for their contribution and not just treated as a commodity.

- Initially, outsourcing felt very un-American to us. But we soon learned that it was the best way to support the jobs we already had. We were employing more than ten people at the time. If we hadn't outsourced, we would have lost those jobs. We also created jobs for our team in India and introduced them to the American Dream.
- Your time will be under attack, so guard it actively so that you spend it on what you can control and what is important!

Unveiled Discoveries

- Nothing is impossible.
- The human mind is our most significant inhibitor to what we can accomplish.
- Failure provides our most significant lessons learned.
- I seek continuous improvement and learning.
- Doing a repetitive task that offers no value beyond the job is a waste of time.
- Wasting time robs me of being able to do something more important.

Statistics to Ponder

- Borders Books was a 40-year-old retailer and grew to become the 2nd largest book retailer in America by 2001. It boasted profits in 2005 of $101 million. By 2011, its 1,249 retail stores and their 10,000+ employees were all gone as a result of their bankruptcy, just 13 years after their peak revenue of $1.74 billion (about $5 per person in the US).
- Blackberry was an undisputed leader in their space. In 2008, Blackberry was valued at over $80 Billion, with 70% market share. In 7 years, it dropped to a 5% market share and by 2016 had ceased designing their own phones- just 8 years after its peak.

- At its peak in the late '90s, Blockbuster owned over 9,000 video-rental US stores, employed 84,000 people (about the seating capacity of the Los Angeles Memorial Coliseum) worldwide, and had 65 million registered customers. It was once valued as a $3 billion company (about $9 per person in the US). Fast-forward a decade, Blockbuster ceased to exist, having filed for bankruptcy with over $900 million in debt.
- According to Ari Bixhorn, VP of Marketing at Panopto in the HR Daily Advisor, average U.S. enterprise-size business wastes $4.5 million in productivity annually due to failing to preserve and share knowledge.
- The outsourcing industry had grown its revenues in India tenfold from 1997 to 2007. It went from $4.8B USD to nearly $48B by 2007. By 2008 the Raheja Mindspace IT park was fully occupied with more than 20,000 workers.

Action Plan

- Describe your Unsolvable Problem -
- What is your S.M.A.R.T Outcome?
- What are the Problem's Demands?
- What is Your Resource Inventory?
- What Are Possible Solutions?
- What Additional Resources Do You Need?
- What is your Plan?

Good Quotables

- *Problem-solving creates sway in our lives, sometimes compromising balance.*
- *We are burning daylight and no guarantee of tomorrow. There is an urgency to today.*
- *We are all moving in the direction of our strongest thoughts.*

Supplementary Learning Recommendations (Read/Listen/Watch)

- *That Will Never Work: The Birth of Netflix and the Amazing Life of an Idea* – Reed Hastings
- Movie: *Apollo 13* starring Tom Hanks, Bill Paxton, Kevin Bacon, and Ed Harris.
- *Thinking Fast Slow*, by Daniel Kahneman
- *Take the Stairs* by Rory Vaden
- *The Obstacle is the Way* – Ryan Holiday
- *Grit* – Angela Duckworth
- *Wine to Water* – Doc Hendley
- *Believe IT: How to Go from Underestimated to Unstoppable* – Jamie Kern Lima

CHAPTER 7

Culture on Purpose

"Culture is what people do when no one is looking."
—Herb Kelleher, C.E.O. Southwest Airlines

The Accidental Culture

For most of my career, I didn't spend much time thinking about culture. It was like gravity that kept us grounded even when we didn't acknowledge it was there. Culture in entrepreneurial businesses starts as a reflection of the values of the founders. Our culture grew out of *who* Dan, and I were, not unique to Davisware. We were not uncommon in this characteristic. We cherished people and relationships. We valued our time and that of others, continually trying to create the highest and best use of everyone's time. We treated our teams as a part of our family.

We knew we could count on them day and night, and they knew the same. There were no boundaries of the workday because we all just knew we needed to do what we needed to do, regardless of what the clock said. This experience applied both personally and professionally. Our teams knew what they needed to do to create joy personally and success professionally. Our entire organization operated with frugality, both with our money and that of our clients. With collectively 20 brothers and sisters (Dan has 12, I have 8), we knew what it meant to be fiscally responsible and took that position with our business and our customer's investments. Our teams knew this and echoed our behavior.

Admittedly, we both have an unquenchable work ethic and tended to hire and surround ourselves with people who shared this desire. We are both naturally curious people and certainly are creative problem solvers.

We are never too proud to find answers, no matter where they are hidden, giving us the power to be industry thought leaders- despite no formal training in the space. We valued humble learners with a natural curiosity to become creative problem-solvers in our relationships, so we hired people with similar values. Given the number of hours we both worked, there was no segregation between who we were and Davisware's culture. We *were* the culture.

In hindsight, I can also say that I took our culture for granted. It served us well. Just like our health, we have no appreciation for it until it fails. In our case, neither one of us had anything from which to compare it.

Neither one of us had careers before Davisware. I was from a family of entrepreneurs who held many of the same values we shared, so the example I had, and my experiences were the same as what we had. In short, I thought that was the way it was everywhere.

A culture of empathetic problem solvers who worked on behalf of the organization, not the individual, and did everything with a servant's heart was our *Modus Vivendi.* It was our mode of living, our way of life.

The realization that culture matters.

Like most other early-stage businesses, every Davisware employee knew where we were going and had the autonomy or direction to figure out how to get there. Often in early-stage companies, just surviving was a part of the goal. Just like most small businesses, we didn't start with the idea of building a culture. Instead, we were pursuing the vision or opportunity, and survival drove our day-to-day activities. As a business grows, culture evolves out of random acts and decisions by the founders and early followers. As other employees took their lead from these cues, the cultural blueprint started to form from what is valued and "how we get things done here."

When we first started Davisware, we didn't articulate our core values or describe our culture. We attracted and were attracted to people who shared our work ethic, values and believed in what we were trying to accomplish. We treated employees like family. We had their backs, and they had ours. Our connection and relationship transcended the office. We helped each other move, co-signed loans, bought houses, helped bury each other's loved ones, and brought babies home from the hospital. We celebrated life's joys and sorrows together. Even though we didn't have our mission statement and values written down, our tiny little company and the customers who entrusted us had no doubt what we valued. John C. Maxwell once said, "People may hear your words, but they feel your attitude." There is no doubt that the world felt ours.

Like this book's theory, we didn't see our employees with clear boundaries around their personal or professional lives. Remember, we only have O.N.E. life. This vision has been the single most influential perspective that created success for us. It is why Davisware was successful. As one example, in 1991, we had met a future employee through one of our customers. The customer immediately saw compatibility between what we needed on our team and what he offered. Unfortunately, he was several states away. In 1991, dial-up connectivity (not the internet as we know it) was still the norm, and there were no such thing as remote employees. For perspective, it was just one year earlier, in 1990, Archie, Alan Emtage, and McGill University had developed the first Internet search engine. Later that same year, Tim Berners-Lee began writing code for a client program, a browser/editor he called Worldwide Web, on his new computer. [33] Our *Possibility Mindset* and *Exponential* approach to everything we did, found a solution. With an expensive dial-up phone line and a basement office, he began his career at Davisware. For a small startup, we were defying reality and were far ahead of the world's business thought leaders.

The *Possibility Mindset* was critical to the success of this relationship. From the perspective of every other small business, there was no way to make this work. However, Dan and I were committed to the goal of finding the right talent. With that being our *Defined Success*, we just needed to play *Jenga* to figure out how to make all the pieces fit. Through trust and ingenuity, Bruce began working from his basement in Cincinnati, Ohio, in 1993. Over five years later, Google launched, and almost a decade later, telecommuting work models ramped up and became mainstream.

In the Unsolvable Problem chapter, I shared the journey that led us to solve our problem with outsourcing.

It would be fantastic if the difficulties we faced started and ended with that one. However, establishing our presence in India was only the beginning. Now we needed to discover how to extend their talent and culture to the U.S. and ours to them.

Dan was continuing his grueling travel schedules to India and had several other employees who shared his journeys. However, we had come to a place where we needed representation from our India team here in the U.S.

I want to pause for a moment and remind you that all of the lessons learned about our journey are retrospective. I say this because, as the reader of this book, I want you to take away the mindset, not the examples. The mindset is how you can create your own stories of success in your own journey.

I also want to call out that at the time, we didn't articulate the WHY we needed Indian leadership in the U.S.

In hindsight, we needed to bring our cultures together both physically and psychologically. That new challenge left us to figure out the U.S. immigration system. We could have worked on getting simple visitor visas. However, we knew that what was good for the business and good for the employee and their families was not to spend months away from home. We also saw this journey as one that impacted the entire family, so allowing the whole family to be a part of the American dream was what we set out to do. In what became poetic, I spent my Fourth of July holiday weekend preparing and submitting countless documents, doing my best lawyering work to figure out how to apply for residency and, ultimately, American citizenship. This grueling work was some of the worst tasks I have ever had to handle in my career. I had no skills for these tasks. We had no money to hire the experts who did. Our only option was me taking my Possibility Mindset and making it a reality.

Nevertheless, we found success. Each of these individuals and their families is now U.S. Citizens, and that reward stands alone.

I continually remind my kids that everything we are proud of was hard to achieve. This challenge was no different. This story is relevant because the goal of the exercise was to bring our international culture together. What it did was define what it meant to be a member of the Davisware team. Every person, from the top of the organization to the newest employee, was all in. Caring about the entire individual was our way of defining our culture. It wasn't anything written down or formalized. It was just who we were!

Our employees rewarded us with hard work, dedication, and loyalty. We often asked our people to work harder and longer than the job description described. We had employees raise their hands alongside us to forgo being paid for weeks and sometimes months because we didn't have the cash flow to pay them. The accurate measure of a culture is the little things people do that they don't have to do, nobody tells them to do it, but they still do it. At Davisware, the mindset was that whoever could— did it.

These were challenging but rewarding days in the business. We did considerable managing with our hair on fire and spent insanely long hours at the office, but everyone knew what they needed to do. As our growth trajectory continued, we were involved in our first business acquisition. In 2010, we acquired Service Management Group, based in Hattiesburg, MS. On July 2, I hastily executed a trip to Hattiesburg to work through the acquisition of a business in turmoil. My sister Melissa packed my suitcase and met me at the airport for the trip that first opened my eyes to the value of our culture. When I arrived at their office the following day, I felt a vibe I had never felt before. There was a sense of distrust and skepticism directed toward me that was foreign. The organization had struggled financially for some time but had a reputation as a quality organization of problem-solvers. They were a team in which we wanted to invest. That trip taught me that we had something special. That trip and acquisition were the first of several moments in our history that started my understanding of the value of a systemized culture. First, we had to define what was important.

What was already happening in our business was highlighted in this acquisition. Over time, we grew and added employees, and with each added employee, Dan and I had less contact with each of them. Our influence on employees began to diminish. A lack of clarity around who we were, what we stood for, and how things got done became blurred. Misunderstandings about goals, deadlines, roles, and accountability occurred more frequently. Although our culture was well-grounded, the bumps in the road were becoming more frequent and of a grander scale. Our growth and acquisitions started to unveil to me how valuable our culture was to customers. It was as vital as it was to hire the right people for the business. Not only were our employees attracted to our business because of our culture, but our customers were too. It was being unveiled to me how valuable our culture was to the revenue generation in our business. Our culture informed how to treat people inside and outside the company.

As the business scaled, our values and culture were what we needed to rely upon to make informed decisions, especially the tough ones. But then, I realized that we had built a culture by accident, and for us to grow and scale, we would have to create one on purpose. That's when our culture journey began.

Our culture was foundational to our success, and I realized it was also critical to our revenue. Unfortunately, many leaders, including us, are slow to tying together a great culture and a highly profitable, growth-oriented company. Gallop statistics on company culture show that managers determine the quality of your company's culture. Team leaders' talent, skill, and knowledge can improve company culture and productivity exponentially. There is a whopping 70% difference in culture quality between companies with lousy and great team leaders.[34]

Unfortunately, it took us five more years before deciding that the culture journey was important and urgent.

We had to remind ourselves that what got us here won't get us to our new goals. In our preparations for the new year, we had found our new mission. We needed to convert our accidental culture to a purposeful one.

I have long compared life to some aspect of the automotive business, given that is where I grew up.

This part of the journey is no different. When thinking about our journey in life, we should use our rearview mirror and our windshield in the relative relationship of their size. Both are critical to safely getting you where you need to go, but we don't have the opportunity to learn from where we have come without looking back. If we spend too much time looking in the rearview mirror, we are dangerously unaware of where we are headed. A quick glance backward gives perspective for what's ahead. That is what we needed to learn to do. My personal Achilles Heel, which often plagues entrepreneurs, is my unintentional forgetfulness to look back. In this moment of our growth story, we had set our goals to be a $20 million business by 2020. These were lofty aspirations. To achieve our goal, we needed to look back to see what had gotten us to this point, correct our mistakes and build on our successes. To transform our company and create our growth story, we needed our culture to align with our core values.

The Culture Keeper

We needed to transfer the responsibility of being the "culture keeper" to every person in the organization:

- Our core values had to be so clearly defined that our teams and customers knew what they were.
- We had to determine our non-negotiables to design an *Exponential* culture.
- Systems and processes were required to protect our culture.
- Our decisions to hire, promote, and fire needed to be precisely based upon the support of these values.
- This commitment was one of the most challenging steps in this process. When you build a business, starting with family and friends, this type of commitment means you are committed to the system, not necessarily to the individuals and the way it always has been.

Our journey to a codified culture

Sharing our story in codifying our culture would not be complete if I didn't call out that this was a multi-year project that we couldn't rush. When we committed to this journey, we knew it would be challenging to stay the course and see incremental improvements. The pressure within our business to execute a purposeful culture was mounting. We started seeing deviations from the culture Dan and I were so passionate about and how we were managing. While it was hard to find urgency when nothing felt dramatically broken, we also knew that the tiny fissures in the bedrock of our business could turn into rubble in a moment under the pressure of accelerated growth.

The journey to a purposeful culture will not be fast and will not feel urgent, but it is one of the most important decisions to make on your journey. For what it's worth, when we sold the majority interest in our business, one of the valuable commodities that made Davisware an acquisition candidate was our culture. Our investment was well worth the effort it took us to get there.

Hundreds of leadership books describe the importance of culture. These books talk repetitively about the importance of the right people in the right roles, and that thoughtful leadership and purposeful culture create a path to success. For example, in the book *Delivering Happiness* by Zappos Founder, Tony Hsieh notes, "Without conscious and deliberate effort, inertia always wins." [35] Without the conscious decision to create a corporate culture that didn't rely upon us, we would soon see its adverse effects.

Our extreme efforts and risk-taking had created our vibrant culture thus far. However, with the addition of our second acquisition in 2011 and Dan reducing his international business travel to India, it was only a matter of time before we started to see a shift in the vibrant culture that had made us successful so far.

We had to create a prescriptive culture around our values. Our culture wasn't broken. The challenge was to retain what made us successful while adding what we needed to evolve. Our journey transformed me as it transformed Davisware.

Unbeknownst to me, along with codifying our culture, I was codifying *Exponentiality*. The 7 Elements of an *Exponential Mindset* are fundamental to what had made us successful to date. I just didn't know it...yet.

Exponentiality and the path to a purposeful Culture

"Whether you think you can, or you think you can't- you're right," - Henry Ford.[4]

The first step in creating a purposeful culture is also the first step in an *Exponential Mindset.* Those are hard to get your brain around when you have seen success without codifying the culture before. It felt like a waste of time, which derailed the importance a dozen times. What kept drawing me back to our goal was my experiences of having been in hundreds of businesses. Throughout the years, there has been a common theme of entrepreneurs and sometimes multi-generational businesses. We collectively don't realize the need or value in defining a mission.

One of my favorite leadership books, *What Got You Here Won't Get You There: How Successful People Become Even More Successful*, was stuck in my brain because it described the exact situation we were facing. I knew we needed to invest the time in defining ourselves and our culture.[36] We needed to believe that codifying our culture was important AND it would drive our future success. We had to implore *The Slingshot Effect*. We had to pull back, take the time, and invest in ourselves.

Defining our culture meant we needed to define our values. Defining our values meant that we needed to articulate our mission statement clearly. We had to trade all the urgent crises for the most pressing need in the business. The time to do so was now.

As we created a codified culture, we learned that defining our core values was not the first step in our culture journey. Instead, Davisware needed a mission statement. After more than 25 years of business, we had never had a mission statement. We would never set out on a journey without a map, yet we operated without a clear destination. The first step in our culture journey was defining the Davisware Mission. By definition, a mission statement is a concise explanation of the organization's reason for existence. It describes the organization's purpose and its overall intention. The mission statement supports the vision and communicates purpose and direction to employees, customers, vendors, and other stakeholders. Creating the Davisware mission statement was where our culture journey needed to begin. It had to be our priority.

On February 5, 2015, during the busiest time of year in our business and during one of the highest growth periods we had seen to date, we took our entire leadership team off-site to set out on our mission. Dan and I needed to lead this process, but we would not succeed unless our entire leadership team owned the results. Asking a group of problem-solvers to leave their Inboxes full for two days felt like we were asking them to lasso and stop the earth from spinning. The urgent problems would always be there. So, we prioritized the important and set aside urgent for a couple of days to formalize our WHY.

This journey to codify our Mission, Values, and Culture included plenty of time reading and learning.

Anyone who knows me knows that I spend as much time as I can garnering knowledge from experts in whatever I am trying to conquer.

One pictorial that resonated with me was the Iceberg Model of Culture. At Davisware, we had the sub-grade components of culture.

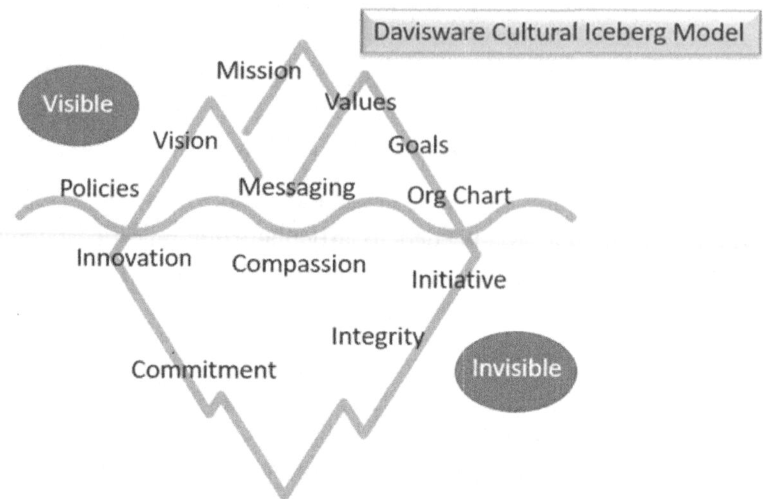

We needed to figure out how to create the visual elements of the corporate culture.

With flip charts and markers in hand, we locked ourselves away from distractions, without computers and email, and set out on this journey. Having never done this before, we knew we needed expertise from someone who had.

As I mentioned earlier, our former customer became our first-ever consultant to lead the process to begin to apply the element of *Leveling Up*. In this case, it was not us asking others to meet us at our level. It was us, alongside our team, *Leveling Up* to the expertise we had brought in. As I mentioned in the Hair on Fire chapter, the decision to do something that felt frivolous, unimportant, and un-urgent, combined with spending money on high-dollar consulting fees, demonstrated our commitment to the process. However, that didn't change that the decision was very scary. I point this out because one of the mistakes we made, and I see so many other small businesses make, is to fear self-investment. It's easy for contractors to buy trucks and tools. It was easy for us to purchase new software tools. However, it is far harder to trust the need for the Process and commit to something that wasn't entirely broken. I share this to ease some fears that we have been there. We felt similar concerns you are likely facing.

We began defining what success looked like to Davisware through two long days, lots of snacks, and alcoholic beverages. To have *Goal-Driven Focus*, we had to describe what our goal was. This next section is a summary of the Davisware Cultural Values.

Define Success

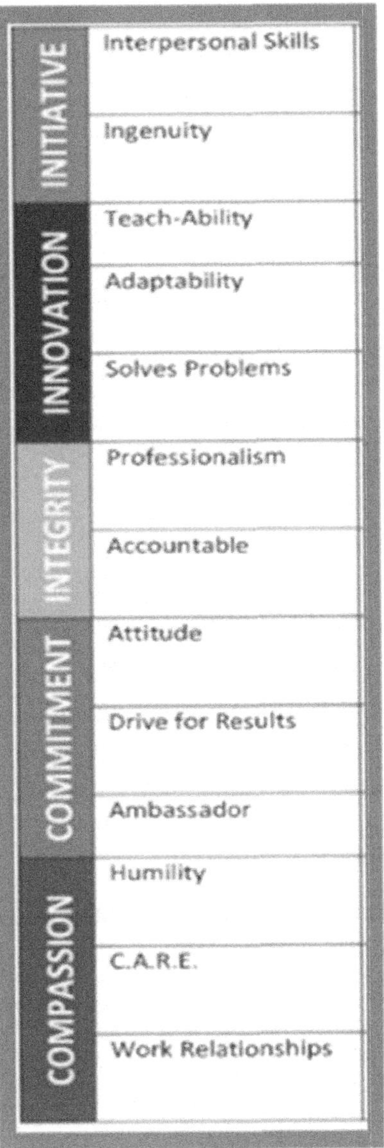

Our leadership summit's *Defined Success* was to have a clearly defined mission statement built upon articulated values. We created our mission statement. For the first time in Davisware history, we had a roadmap to what we described as success. From this work, we could begin to codify our culture.

Our mission is to leverage our industry expertise and customer relationships to create integrated and affordable technology solutions. Since 1988, we've helped service-oriented businesses, contractors, distributors, and manufacturers become industry leaders with technology solutions critical to the growth and success of their businesses.

Our mission statement told the world that we were invested in being industry experts. It said that our customer relationships were at the core of our mission. The servant's heart with which we operated was evident in our goal of always helping our customers by partnering in their success. After what felt like a hundred iterations, our mission statement stands today as the foundation for the business. We had defined our *WHY*.

The underlying Values to our Mission Statement

With our new Mission Statement, we had started to uncover what was important to us as an organization. For the first time in Davisware history, those values were not just extensions of what was important to Dan and me personally. Instead, these values were independent of us and were representative of what we as a leadership team wanted our organization to stand for. The business's mission is essential, but the business's values act as guardrails to keep everyone focused on what is critical to achieving the mission. Concise mission statement and values:

- Align employees with strategic goals.
- Enhance team collaboration.
- Empower employees.
- Attract and retain top talent.
- Improve employee communication.
- Have a direct impact on employee motivation and engagement.
- Help clients understand what Davisware stands for.
- Attract customers that share the same values.

With clearly articulated values, everyone inside and outside the organization knew what was important to our organization. Everyone has a clear expectation and understanding of what *Defined Success* looked like.

During this process, the core values that surfaced were initiative, innovation, Integrity, commitment, servantry, and compassion. Initiative was essential because everybody had to be a leader. At that time, we were a non-hierarchical and customer-focused company. Innovation continues to be the essence of what we provide to the customer.

Our focus had always been to solve our customer's problems. Integrity was non-negotiable. Our word had to mean something and was the cornerstone of our business relationships. Because we've always been relationship-driven, compassion made our list. Finally, we needed committed people because people who "just show up" would let everyone down. Part of the process of defining the values of an organization is to determine what you want.

Another critical part of this culture journey is to know what you *don't* want. None of this happens by accident. One of my favorite leadership authors, Craig Groeschel, shares in his teachings that, *"A healthy culture is a combination of what you create and what you allow."*[37] On this journey, we needed to define both. These definitions were core to our employee satisfaction and our continued success story. Without exception, people love clear expectations.

When you reflect on your life, you'll discover that most disappointment comes from the failed expectations, not necessarily the failure of an experience.

Our non-negotiables of what we allowed and what we required were critical to our success. Our non-negotiables needed to make sure we had clearly defined expectations. We couldn't leave anything to interpretation.

We began brainstorming to come up with some foundational non-negotiables and some aspirational goals.

Some of our values were things that we knew were core to our business. The most important one was Integrity. It was non-negotiable. Our customers give our teams access to most of the critical business and strategic plans of their companies. Our customers were often competitors to one another, so our success depended upon us protecting each customer's interest as though it were our own. As our organization grew, we needed to attract talent with the same mindset around Integrity. This commitment couldn't be just words on a page. It had to be something we were doing all the time and to which we held ourselves accountable. We knew that we needed to articulate whatever we defined as our values to share them outwardly. Outwardly sharing them made us accountable to each other and our customers. It ensured we were "walking the walk" because we knew a strong culture would continue to attract the right people.

The right people would get us the right actions. Businesses that lack trust often have a lot of policies and procedures. We didn't want that and knew the only way to achieve a self-sustaining culture was to hire people with the same mindset around Integrity.

Defined Core Values

Other core values for Davisware included:

- CARE (Customers Are our Reason for Everything) – Customers Are the Reason for Everything. Our customers are the epicenter for what we do.
- Expertise.
- We must continually invest in the industries we serve to stay focused on being the thought leader for technology in the markets we serve.
- We seek excellence.
- We measure our success through our customer's success.
- We are scrappy and nimble. Every person will contribute in a meaningful way.
- Every person deserves equal respect and has essential value.
- Our urgency is for customer success.
- Success is measurable, not just anecdotal.

Once we had our mission statement defined, we needed to relate our core values to our mission statement. This task then began the challenge of executing our mission and values systemically into our culture. Although articulating our mission and core values was a huge first step, the real challenge was putting them into formal action to inspire desired behaviors to achieve our business goals. You can create the words, but they don't inspire change until they become consistent actions demonstrated over time - first by your actions, then by your leadership team, and finally by your peers. This Process was, without a doubt, an exercise in *Leveling Up* by all of us.

Dan and I had to make one of the most challenging business decisions to date to ensure that our mission statement and core values weren't empty words. We had to commit to operating our business by the mission statement and values we had just defined. This decision meant that we had to commit to hiring, promoting, and firing based on Davisware's core values. We realized that the critical team that got us to where we are might not be the same team to get us to where we are going. The family at Davisware was our family - most figuratively and some in reality. The decision to create a business around our mission and values meant building a culture around these for the first time in Davisware history, regardless of tenure, relationship, or role.

The culture was the most critical driver in our future success.

It was about this time, on the flight back from a business trip, that the movie *Up in the Air* starring George Clooney and Vera Farmiga was my in-flight entertainment. Anyone close to me would be surprised by me getting entangled in a movie. Given that I haven't turned on a television in decades, I don't know how to log into our Netflix account and haven't voluntarily gone to the movies in years. Nonetheless, I became entangled in the storyline of this movie. It centers around the life of Ryan Bingham, a human resource consultant who specializes in termination assistance. Given that we had barely fired anyone to this point in Davisware history, I was intrigued by the perceived heartlessness of the main character. However, after hearing his perspective throughout the movie, my perspective altered.

What I could best describe as a three-legged stool is how I started to see employment relationships in business. It involved the relationship between an individual, your team members, and the organization. All three elements must be a good fit - good for the company, good for the team (culture), and good for the individual. Reflecting on childhood, whenever I had a coach, parent, or teacher, I disappointed, it didn't feel good, and I didn't perform my best. Applying this to your team, if you have the wrong person in the wrong role or have a team member with misaligned values, you aren't doing the organization, or the individuals involved any favors. They become similar to that childhood memory and the pain of disappointment. Changing our culture to one based upon our mission and values was not easy, but we owed it to everyone within the organization. We were ready to Level Up.

The start of our Culture Journey- Are you walking the walk?

"There's a difference between knowing the path and walking the path. —MORPHEUS, THE MATRIX"

Do your company values say something different than the actions you take? Once you clearly define the mission and values and published them to your team, customers, and partners is when the looking glass turns toward you and your leadership team. You are effectively putting a sign on your back that says, "Watch Me!". When Davisware set out on this mission, we received valuable coaching, reminding us not to shortcut the process and not to forget this. Just like in parenting, there is far more value in what we do than what we say.

Once we published our "say," our "do" had to follow. Our value statements shape our culture, but our actions said what we value. Doing this consistently and breaking old habits of what we did and what we allowed was very challenging!

In addition, keep in mind, not all values are written, spoken, or clearly articulated. The most important aspect of the value statement is how leaders live them in the business. Our teams were looking for consistency in our words and actions. Employees want to be proud to contribute to a winning organization, and Davisware was no different. As a leader, when you act congruent and consistent with your stated values, you create certainty in your employees' minds. You deliver on an expectation, which creates *Exponential* confidence in your leadership team and your employees. A confident employee makes a confident contributor to the organization. Confident contributors are not playing scared, live up to their potential, and Level Up in their *Exponentiality*. Every time your team sees you operate in conjunction with the business's core values, their confidence solidifies you as a leader. It broadens their commitment to the company's mission. On the flip side, when leaders fail to walk the walk or when leaders allow those on their team to behave out of line with the company's values and mission statement, it creates uncertainty and doubts in their minds. We've seen throughout the global pandemic how effectively individuals operate in the face of uncertainty! It is not good for anyone!

Throughout the history of Davisware, the decisions regarding employees have been some of the hardest, if not *the* hardest. There is not a single person within the history of Davisware who did not create some value in the organization. One of the *Exponential Mindset* pitfalls is that it is structured around asking others to meet us at our level. When an employee has different values, but you are consistently asking them to meet you at your level, you are effectively asking them to fail over and over again.

It took me many years to realize that doing this to an employee is not empathetic. It is not in the best interest of that individual to repetitively fail. It certainly is not in the organization's best interest or, for me, as an organizational leader. Like the three-legged stool example that I just shared, a three-legged stool only works when there is equality in the value for all. When that isn't the case, the chair topples. I can personally think of several transitions in the business where this happened. These were emotionally draining situations. I loved the people on the other end of the firing decision, and I confused what was good for them with what *felt good* for me.

In their best interest, the role they filled at Davisware needed to change or end. Most days, the titles associated with being a leader carry a lot of joy and satisfaction. However, on these days, in these situations, there is a considerable burden. Determining how to balance the individual needs with those of the organization is one of the most complicated challenges in any leadership role. It is why the mission statement, and the core values became so critical. They formed the cultural roadmap to success. Without these two elements, the decisions around staff were emotional and made with personal bias. In my journey to Level Up, this became one of the hardest lessons learned.

"A business leader's job is to create great teams that do amazing work on time. That's it. That's the job of management."
—Patty McCord

Systemic Culture

According to *Walking the Talk*, it takes 2-3 years to change a culture.[38] This guideline was accurate in Davisware's cultural evolution. This situation was different from needing to change a culture, but both require time and patience. We had spent more than twenty years building a fantastic organization with a tremendous but accidental culture. ***Our growth was a risk to that culture.***

We needed to take a defensive position to protect it. As a business grows and continues to succeed, culture can't be an after-thought, add-on, or post-it note. It is an integral part of the fabric of the company's makeup. In our case, it had always been that way. We thought about our world as a universe, inclusive of our professional and personal pursuits. We thought of our lives and those of our teams with an *Exponential Life Balance*. Our commitments to our teams we thought of in the same way. We took care of the entire person, not just when they were at work. Now, we needed to codify that.

Brittany Forsyth, S.V.P. of H.R. (Human Resources), Shopify, gave us a great insight into how they think about culture. She said, *"Determine what behaviors and beliefs you value as a company and have everyone live true to them. These behaviors and beliefs should be so essential to your core that you don't even think of it as culture."*[39] That's what we had in the beginning days at Davisware and was what we wanted at Davisware now. Our culture test was to hire, *promote*, fire, and reward based on our culture. Creating an *Exponential Culture* had to become as systemic and *Process-Driven* as how we developed software. We needed to incorporate processes, systems, and technology to ensure that our mission statement and core values had infiltrated everything we do. Our reputation for our core values needed to precede us everywhere we went.

Codifying a Great Culture

I have the following conversation for every new hire that I engage with before making an employment offer.

"As I am sure you have learned, our culture is at the core of our success, and as a cultural leader, I am the ultimate protector of our brand and our culture. In that role, I wanted to personally share who should work at Davisware. Team Davisware consists of empathetic and graceful creative problem solvers who work hard, are smart, and do everything with a servant's heart. They work with absolute humility in the quest for perfection, knowing it's unattainable. Most importantly, they should make every decision on behalf of the organization, not the individual.
Can you be that person?" *—Jennifer Davis*

One thing to be clear of in this process is, we had *much* work to do for our culture to be codified.

We had started to see a deterioration in it, but we had a vibrant organization of creative problem-solvers who were customer-centric from all accounts. So, I keep reminding you that our culture wasn't broken. I do this because that made it even more challenging to continue to prioritize this process. We started to see a degradation due to our growth, but our culture was vibrant and alive.

Our growth moved the company to an intersection where it could threaten our culture, and we had no interest in endangering what made us great so far.

Over the course of 2 years (more than three years total in our culture journey), we created a codification of the culture and set expectations at every level of what success looked like. Each step below was influential in the codification process and to us. Much of the process looked far easier in print than it was living it. Most of the process didn't seem urgent and, therefore, felt unimportant. The difficult decision to stay the course was far more challenging than any one of the single accomplishments. Famously stated, J.F.K. said that "a rising tide lifts all boats".[40]

We were lifting all boats in the organization. We were asking ourselves to lead the organization in *Leveling Up*. We had set our eyes on our *Defined Success* and now had to execute *The Slingshot Effect* to take a step back to drive forward by becoming *Process-Driven* in our culture.

"We must never lose our sense of urgency in making improvements. We must never settle for "good enough," because good is the enemy of great," — Tony Hsieh, Delivering Happiness: A Path to Profits, Passion, and Purpose[35]

1. SCREAM YOUR MISSION EVERYWHERE. We put our mission statement EVERYWHERE. We asked each employee to have it visible in their workspace as their screensaver or backdrop. We wanted it somewhere they would see it many times every day. We added it to the front page of our website and our marketing materials. We added it to our company swag and the back of our notebooks. We added it to the wall in our lobby, office displays, and every gathering space in our buildings. We reminded everyone every day what our "WHY" was. A mission statement is just words. If there are no corresponding

actions, they carry no value. These continuous reminders were that we CARE (**C**ustomers **A**re our **R**eason for **E**verything).

2. CREATE A FORMAL ORGANIZATIONAL CHART AND POSITION DESCRIPTIONS. Every person wants a clear expectation of their role and responsibility. Up until this point, we did not have clear boundaries, nor did we have clear responsibilities. Our responsibilities were an "all-hands-on-deck model." In our rapid growth, it often felt like a free-for-all. We were all servants. When others had a challenge, we loved to dive in to help.

As much as our servant's heart mentality is at the core of who we are, it often distracted our teams from their priorities and created chaos. Our customer-centric focus caused everyone to dive on every landmine instead of creating a clear path to success and an organizational chart that supported it. In this process we:

- Set out to write a position description for every role.
- Anchored each position description to our mission statement and company values.
- Created our first-ever org chart.

With this work, each contributor had a definition of their contributions and how we defined their success.

3. CREATE A FORMAL REVIEW PROCESS FOCUSED ON SELF-ASSESSMENT AND LEADING UP. Before this exercise, our review process consisted of informal meetings, with Dan or me, usually after business hours and with no agenda, input, or output. It felt more like a couple of friends getting together to share battled stories versus an employment review. We researched various review formats to come up with ones that met the needs of our organization. This Process had two essential elements. The most crucial aspect we tried to solve was creating a review process focused on self-assessment, both by the leader and the team member. In other words, we wanted the Process to focus on the relationship, not on the tasks. We also wanted to use the venue to open a dialogue of self-assessment where the team member could assess their contributions and lead up with their leader. Feedback

received in a review should never surprise an employee, and we built the process around this idea of continuous self-improvement. All review topics and goals needed to relate to the organization's cultural values and the mission statement. We continued to improve this process, never losing sight that our objective is self-assessment and the opportunity for the team member to lead up with each improvement. We knew that in a healthy organization, it was critical that everyone in the organization felt confident in their ability to lead up. I knew that our organization, or any organization for that matter, would not be what it could be without honest, upward communication. Those on the front lines of sales, support, and implementation see problems and solutions long before our leadership team even knows they exist. Solidifying and formalizing the organization's ability to lead up is essential for the review process results. Our work focused on creating an organization where the power to lead could come from the person, not the position. This commitment required that all team members could lead up (or down) wherever they are in the organization. This review process created a platform for doing so. By the end of 2019, our standard review process facilitated every employee to self-assess their contributions to the mission statement and lead up in the organization. We had several iterations yet to go, but we had taken a giant step forward toward our goal.

4. CREATE TRANSPARENT MESSAGING. The Davisware culture has always thrived around the semi-annual gatherings of our team.

We met annually for our holiday party, where we shared our goals, did a readout on our year, and enjoyed great times together. The other time together was at our annual User Conference. Any customer or member of our team would tell you this was an epic event where we highlighted our insanely hard work and the depth of our partnership with our customers and team. These two gatherings were sufficient when we were a much smaller organization, but the need to propagate a transparent and accountable culture beyond a few days a year was required. So, we added a weekly leadership team meeting. We became more *TExponential* with the help of SharePoint, organized by the team with transparency to others. This step gave us a single source of truth with documents and clarity in what other teams were solving. Most of these changes were nothing groundbreaking and ones that many other organizations do. A unique culture keeper that I initiated was the creation of the Monday Morning All Call in 2019. We used this 15-minute call at the start of the week to support the mission, solidify the values, and ensure that the entire organization heard one single source of truth. Our entire organization listened to my personal and often very informal readout on the week, both in hindsight and upcoming, that was always tied back to our mission and core values. Most weeks, I led this call either alone or with my leadership team. My mantra was that if there wasn't 15 minutes' worth of content that I thought was worth sharing across the organization, I must have been on vacation! Our vacation adventures are exciting enough to provide more than 15 minutes of content! With the title of C.E.O. comes the similar title of Chief Values Officer. In a growth-minded organization, protecting the culture is always urgent and essential, and this call was a great way to accomplish it.

1. S.M.A.R.T. GOAL SETTING. For the first time in company history, we set official corporate goals that everyone knew and were measurable and metrics-driven. The leadership team mapped the goal-setting Process, with each business unit responsible for its contributions to the goals. Rather than Dan and I set a revenue target for the business as we had historically done, we converted to business targets that supported our revenue goal, built bottom-up and top-down. Most importantly, our goals aligned with the entire company. When we were much smaller, our alignment was easy because we each wore so many hats. As we grew, each team set their individual goals, and although they were directionally similar, we did not emphasize being aligned explicitly with organizational goals. It was critical to our culture that we all knew our exact *WHY* in specific and measurable terms. *Our success had to be measurable, not just anecdotal.*

2. DRIVE EACH CONTRIBUTOR TOWARD A RESPONSIBILITY OF INDIVIDUAL GROWTH. In a technology business, personal investment is at the center of our success. Individuals need to seek expertise to be experts. After setting organizational and team goals, our teams worked to craft specific and measurable personal goals. Within those goals, each employee has a responsibility for personal and professional growth. Among the individual goals, 1-2 needed to be actionable professional learning (like classes, workshops, or seminars). In addition, one goal needed to

be about personal development. Because we founded our business valuing the entire human and saw our teams as our Davisware family, it was important that individuals felt accountable for balancing their individual development. As an aside, when the global pandemic hit and the budget was very uncertain, we weren't sure we could commit to the magnitude of training we intended to invest in. Although we did adjust our investment in what we spent on training, we still made a significant investment, demonstrating how valuable this is.

Instead of in-person training, we did webinars. Instead of outside training, we utilized our staff for individualized product training using experts already on our teams. Despite the external crisis that was out of our control, we found a means of helping our teams grow and meet their individual goals. Even though there was a global pandemic, we had to remind ourselves that our customers depended upon our expertise for their success more than ever.

Regardless of what was going on in the rest of the world, we urgently invested in each team member.

3. WAGE COMPARISON AND REVIEW. Previous to this exercise and like most entrepreneurs, we compensated our teams individually and without comparison. We made decisions around level of effort, loyalty, and tenure of service vs. results and comparison to the wages and contributions of others on the team.

For the first time in the company's history, we did an extensive compensation and team assessment. We compared their assessment with their compensation by asking each manager to rate their teams from top to bottom. We then compared the wages on those teams to verify that they aligned with the contribution value. Once we had done this for each unit individually, we compared the top positions on each team and compared those to the top positions on other teams to verify we had alignment. Sadly, we learned that this was not the case. Our values said that *Every person deserves equal respect and has significant value.* What it didn't say is that we "owed" anyone anything for their historical value. For me, this was a painful realization and a difficult leadership shift. Unfortunately, this realization was also a harsh reality for other managers.

We had biases based on emotions, not on data. If we were codifying our culture, the buy-in had to start with us. Our new culture code required data-driven decisions.

These changes were essential to our commitment.

4. BONUS POOL. In 2019 (for 2020), we created a bonus pool, another first-ever. Team members who weren't directly controlling their own inventive plans shared in a company-wide bonus pool. Previously, bonuses were determined very anecdotally and had little to do with organizational performance. Instead, they were more closely defined by how much cash was in the bank account when it was time to pay them.

Our evolutionary goals for 2020 focused primarily on the company goals. Our bonus pool was a direct mathematical correlation between company success and bonuses. Additionally, and more importantly, there was now a connection between cultural expectations and bonus incentives. Our teams clearly understood that our results and our culture were correlated. We designed the bonus pool so that there was a 75/25 split on the measurement of success. Seventy-five percent of their bonus was driven by the company successfully meeting our goals. Twenty-five percent were individual contributions and cultural expectations.

This direct correlation continued to validate the importance of the two things we valued the most- performance and culture. So, while the global pandemic shifted the 2020 plans, the spirit of the bonus pool lived through it. This structure allowed us to fulfill our commitment.

Each one of these steps was foundational to the others. So many of these were firsts in our organization, which had its own sets of challenges. It challenged us to do what was important over what was urgent to complete this journey. Defining what sets us apart allowed us to guide our decisions and inform how we interact with each other, our customers, and our partners. These were milestones on our culture journey. We codified our *Defined Success*. Now it was time to watch the results.

The calm before the storm

2019 presented many changes and challenges as we altered the foundation of Davisware permanently. As I mentioned earlier, Dan and I had sold majority ownership of the business with the introduction of our private equity partner. Dan left the day-to-day operations of the company and assumed a board role. I continued as a leader of the organization, now surrounded by new faces and significant new responsibilities. My role had expanded to include reporting to a board of directors with new bosses. We were rapidly focusing on professionalizing the business in ways we were learning to be necessary. In addition to these changes, we had just launched our most important strategic partnership with one of our key customers, to create embedded technology in our mutual businesses. Any one of these alone would have been demanding for the organization to absorb. All of these together felt overwhelming. We were looking forward to 2020 as a maturing and steady year of business. Boy, did 2020 laughed at us regarding those expectations. However, we took advantage of the time and focused on stabilizing and professionalizing many aspects of the business we would not have done without the global pandemic.

Our culture journey was entering its final stage of execution. This final stage tested if we had built a culture and a team that could embrace all of this change. There is a common misconception about change. We often think that people hate change. What people hate is the change they don't control, understand, or with which they disagree. People don't like to have change *happen* to them. They want to be *a part of* the change. Our culture journey prepared our organization for change. Our teams were active participants in the transition, not victims of it. Our newly codified culture focused on helping our teams understand the *WHY* behind the change.

We embraced the change as an enabler, not a victim. It was my job as the Chief Values Officer to help the organization balance change and culture. Change is inevitable. Our progress would be due to it, and we needed everyone's contributions to the change.

With the flip of the calendar, we saw January as our best month since we partnered with our investor. As a result, we were very optimistic leading up to our annual company meeting. On an extraordinarily snowy day in Chicago in late January, we unveiled the vision for 2020. Each leader presented their goals while I shared mine.

CEO Goals for Davisware 2020

- Create an organizational structure with all the right people in the right seats.
- Prepare the organization for growth through the implementation of tools.
- Execute the vision for our key partnerships.
- Protect, Codify, and Elevate the culture.
- Be the best investment our PE firm had ever made.

These were very lofty goals but attainable with the talent in the room. We had a creative group of problem solvers, and we had begun to assemble our new leadership team with new and newly positioned team members. We closed out 2019 with the momentum of adding nearly 30 new employees and signed almost 400 new contracts with 100 new customers. We had circled the globe with almost 30 shows & events throughout the year and created nearly 40,000 new support tickets. Davisware was used to change at a rapid pace. It was my job to share the *WHY* so that our organization could partner in our transition. We had ambitious goals that energized us to achieve them. Little did we know what was looming just a few weeks ahead. Our culture was about to be tested in unforeseen ways.

The Cultural Movement

In this same meeting, I unveiled for the first time the cultural values that we had worked so hard to codify over the last three years. They were the framework of this culture journey and were tied to performance bonuses for the first time ever. We assigned our HR leader Therese, the title of Director of Talent & Culture, officially handing the torch of "Culture Keeper" to her. We often joked that her high school resume of prom queen made her uber qualified for the duties of keeping our culture in check (and for anyone wondering what ever happened to the prom queen, now you know…).

This framework and our newly assigned cultural leadership would be what our organization relied upon through the forthcoming (still unknown) disruption.

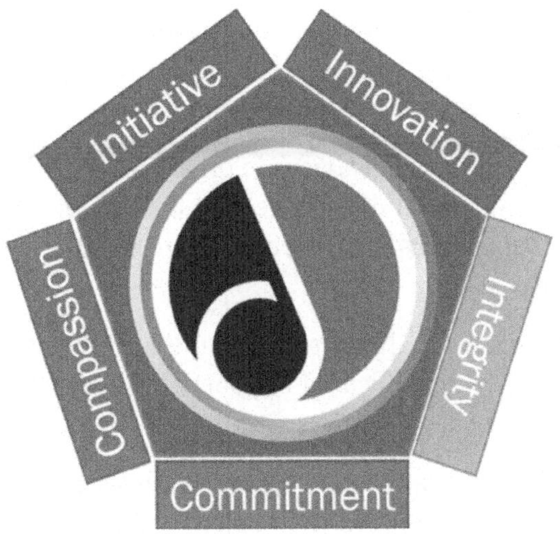

- Initiative (Interpersonal skills & ingenuity)Innovation (Teach-ability, adaptability, problem-solving)
- Integrity (Professionalism & Accountable)
- Commitment (Attitude, Drives for results & Organizational Ambassador)
- Compassion (Humility, CARE, Work Relationships)

These cultural statements balanced whom our tradition said we were and where our growth said it took us. I challenged our teams to challenge themselves as to whether they were up to this journey. We asked if they were more excited about coming to work or leaving? We questioned what their legacies would be and for what people would be remembered. Finally, we talked about **W.I.I.F.M. (What's In It For Me)** and if that is their first thought or their last thought. We knew these were the right people in the organization if they answered these questions without hesitation.

Crisis doesn't create culture; it reveals it

Best-selling author Martin Rooney said, "Crisis is a gift because it reveals to us what is most important."[41]

2020 undoubtedly tested this statement as every organization found some (or all) of 2020 a challenge. Davisware was in a unique place in its evolution. Of course, there is never a good time for crisis, but in 2019 we experienced so much change and disruption that we looked forward to stability and executing what was already in motion. Unfortunately, we were in no way ready for what was to come.

- On January 17, the Davisware organization gathered in person for our Annual Company Meeting to share the excitement and plans for a big 2020. We worked hard in 2019 to prepare for an explosive 2020.
- On February 25, 39 days later, our Board of Directors approved our 2020 budget, focused on foundational changes in the business and back-ended growth.
- Just four days later, on February 29 (ironically Leap Day), my Google history tells me I Googled *"What is a pandemic?"* for the very first time.
- On March 9, 10 days later, we had our first meeting to discuss the potential need to make some short-term budget adjustments.
- Just one day later, on March 10, our leadership team met to discuss the possibility of a precautionary office shut down and begin planning for a 2–4-week shutdown.
- On March 12, a mere two days later, Davisware's leadership team stood as thought leaders and published to other portfolio companies our thoughtfully prepared Go Home strategy.
- The next day, on March 13, we closed our U.S. offices in a precautionary response to the growing uncertainty around the pandemic, estimating this to be a 2–4-week shutdown.
- On March 16, only three days later, our leadership team debated whether to react in India. I made an executive decision that it was more critical to overact than risk underreacting and took the chance to invest in portable hardware and data cards to allow our teams to work from home if necessary. (This decision was ultimately one of the most important decisions to be made looking back. Without this decision, our company would have been paralyzed like most U.S. companies who waited to react due to the lack of availability of laptops and data cards. These events were a perfect intersection of decisiveness and good luck).

- Five days since our last dramatic decision, on March 21, we suspended all discretionary spending, invoked a hiring freeze, suspended our 401K matching, deferred payout of planned 2019 bonuses, and executed a 20% wage reduction.
- The next day, on March 22, we executed our emergency WFH plan in India long before the pandemic was impactful to that country or our organization.
- On March 26, just a month since the approval of our original budget, our board of directors approved our newly re-casted budget that we had been working on around the clock over the last 20 days.
- The next day, on March 27, we began to pivot our industry influence as we shifted our thought leadership to launch our RealTalk Series, focusing on helping our customers save their businesses.
- On April 1, we executed our first-ever company R.I.F. (Reduction in Force), less than six weeks after our invigorating all-company meeting.

Those long days in March of 2020 were when I reached deep to find the best version of myself to lead this organization through the impending crisis. In hindsight, those days were gifts, along with the leadership team who stood beside me in unchartered waters. Early decisiveness prepared us to ride out the continuing storm. Yet never was it so true that it is lonely at the top than those long, long days in March and April 2020.

"Better three hours too soon than a minute too late."
— William Shakespeare

Little did we know that unexpected world events would test our newly codified culture so quickly. We had our work cut out for us. While Davisware was my home for over 30 years, everything we were seeing was new. Never had so many things been beyond our control. I did what our culture said I had to do. Initiative, Innovation, Integrity, Commitment, and Compassion drove the decision-making. Our Monday Morning All Calls became the signature of my time as CEO. Now, our teams were waiting for each week for encouragement, support, and confidence that the organization was in good hands. Whether sharing encouragement and hope or bad news, the organization had one source of truth, creating Knowledge Ubiquity. I knew bad news never gets better with time, and as the leader, it was my job to share it as I knew it.

For two weeks, our leadership team worked alongside me in some of the longest days of my career, brainstorming through what it would take to see it to the other side of the unknown and evolving challenges we were facing.

I have repeatedly told them during and after the crisis that I would pick them to be alongside me if I were in battle. Their passion and grit were the strength in needed to lean on to see us through. One of those painful decisions was surrounding the bonus pool we had just thoughtfully executed. On March 21, 2020, I shared what became a series of bad announcements-some of the most challenging news our organization had ever received. We started by pulling back our 2019 board-approved bonuses. These were dollars many of our employees were likely already counting on.

Second, we pulled back on all wage increases committed to in our shiny-new review process. We postponed these increases until a yet-to-be-determined date. In these early days of uncertainty, postponing something felt to the recipient like it was stolen from them. Third, we asked our leadership team to take substantial wage reductions voluntarily. I asked everyone to sacrifice for the common cause (think back to my hiring statement of who works at Davisware). I demonstrated my commitment by foregoing my salary altogether. We enacted a 20% wage reduction for the remaining employees. Our finance teams began the ominous task of looking for pennies anywhere we could find them. The worst part was that these changes had to be broadcast remotely, without any opportunity to address the office culture's reactions. As far as a perfect storm, it couldn't have been more ominous.

In this call, I put a battle cry out to the organization. I described our journey as that of a battleship that had just lost its engines. We had nothing but oars. In our Davisware ship, I needed every single person, rowing in unison and with maximum effort. We were not a golf team but a rowing team. There were no points for individual success.

Teamwork was the only way our ship would endure. From the first days, when Jason, one of our brand-new team members texted me to tell me that he had stopped in at the office and noticed that no one had turned the heat down, reminding me that every penny mattered, I knew that I had the right team next to me. His action was confirmation to me that our team was on board with our vision. Nobody was watching, and nobody told him to do something that wasn't part of his job. His initiative reminded me that culture is about all the little things people do when no one is watching but create a difference every day. Our financial leadership looked at how to refine their processes to make a more significant contribution. They changed their collections process to focus on the industries that were hit the hardest and put policies in place to help our customers while protecting our future relationships.

I shared a quote from a recent conference that ships are safe in the harbor, but they weren't built to stay in the harbor. Despite what we were facing, we had to put maximum effort into delivering results. I challenged our teams to stop selling technology and start to help our customers save their businesses in any way they could.

The following week, I used my Monday Morning All Call to share this message.

As I think about our overall message this week, I ask you to continue to think of us rowing. We continue to see a lack of clarity on the future and when the current state will end.

Our customers are starting to get their P.P.P. money, which can translate into an opportunity for them to invest in their business alongside us. Now, we all have an urgency to figure out how to row together. As you talk to customers today, put yourselves in their businesses. How can you help improve their businesses? What are you personally doing to be a partner to their survival and future success? These directly translate into your support of our corporate mission, our 2020 goals, and our success. Take a personal assessment to figure out what you have to offer our customers and what you need to get better at. Are you "all in"? Become educated about the industries we service, the customers we serve, and how we can help. What have you done this week to "learn something new every day?". Our professional improvement is how you translate "rowing" and supporting our customers. We ALL can be industry experts who support the health and growth of our customer's businesses. So, as you go into your week, make that your focus.

The tallest oak in the forest was once a little nut that held its ground.

That is what we ALL need to do today on so many fronts. Within our business- we are all responsible for helping hold our ground.

The concept of us rowing our battleship means that we need every person to do more than they have ever done before and to do it smarter, faster, stronger, and better than ever before. In our personal lives, we have to hold our ground to ensure we are thinking with commonsense, not allowing the public hysteria to overcome our ability to be logical and protect our families. In our society- good must prevail. Regardless of your race, your political affiliation, your sex, your religion, good is *good.* Right is *right*, and wrong is *wrong*. We learned it in kindergarten and need to remind ourselves of what that is.

Do what is right. Back what is right. Do what is good and back what is good. Never has it been a more critical time than now for all good, regardless of race, political party, sex, or religion, to stand together. We must. We cannot back down. We have to hold our ground, just like the little nut in the forest. This country was built upon the acorns who held their ground. It's our turn. Finally, pray. Be safe and have a great week.

Our mission statement said we were "*partnering with our customers for the growth and success of their businesses.*" So, my messages had to continue resonating with new ways to partner and encourage our teams with reality.

Continuing to support our mission statement, our events team immediately pivoted to becoming online thought leaders, converting our focus on nearly 30 in-person events scheduled that year to host more than a dozen online events with thousands of participants. In times like these, we needed to Level Up our position as a partner.

In addition, in these tumultuous times, I realized our customers needed *Exponentiality* on the backside of the global pandemic. I knew how I needed to contribute personally. For Davisware and our customers, I committed to writing this book.

Leading by example, I knew that my contribution to "rowing" alongside my team included using my experience and skills to move the organization forward in its position as a thought leader while helping our customers.

With each new challenge, our team answered the call. My message was positively responded to, even though we had taken back raises and bonuses. Our partnership with our customers has never been stronger, and our impact in the industries has never been more far-reaching. Our newly formed leadership team stood alongside me, making the most challenging decisions we have ever made.

The future was growing increasingly ominous. The challenges seemed to come faster than solutions. Yet, the path forward was becoming exceedingly clear because we all took on the *Exponential Mindset*. We planned to *Triumph, Expected (our newly) Defined Success*. We Leveled Up and expected our entire team to do the same. We stayed the course with *Goal-Driven Focus*, although this was the biggest game of *Jenga* we had ever played. *Solution-Focused Flexibility* was our way through the storm. We knew to Expect Conflict and knew we had to Confront that Conflict, Get Comfortable in the Chaos, and Expect Solutions. We had to be the Protagonist. We also recognized that these days at Davisware were our *Slingshot Effect*. Everything we were building was *Process-Driven*, and by Always Driving Toward Process, we would be a better organization *because of, not despite*, the global pandemic.

I have long said that I come to work each day to protect my brand, team, and customers. That commitment has never wavered. With the help of my leadership team, that commitment led me to execute our first-ever company, Reduction in Force (R.I.F.). From a personal perspective, these decisions were some of the hardest I have ever had to make. These days, I had to have the courage to unmake promises. But, from a business perspective, I knew it was what I signed up for. Being a leader means solving problems. Being a leader meant that I had to be insightful enough to prepare for the yet-to-be-known issues we would face. I knew that every major crisis creates unprecedented opportunities. Our culture journey left us prepared to take advantage of these opportunities and for the tumultuous times that 2020 brought us.

You know, people talk about this being an uncertain time. All-time is uncertain. I mean, it was uncertain back in - in 2007 (Last Recession); we just didn't know it was uncertain. It was - uncertain on September 10, 2001 (9-11), October 18, 1987 (Day before Black Monday), and December 6, 1941 (Pearl Harbor), *you just didn't know it yet." - Warren Buffett*[42]

Investment in culture is a deposit on the solution for future problems. None of the processes we went through were in preparation for a global pandemic. Instead, they were to prepare us for future success, which is what we found.

Continuing the culture journey. Culture is never done

In 2018 we began our journey to codify our fantastic culture. In 2019, we diligently created the framework for that culture. 2020 tested our newly codified culture and revealed that our work was noteworthy. Our 2021 objective of converting our accidental culture to a performance-based, value-driven culture is currently unfolding. The core values that were so important to Dan and me 30+ years ago were protected. We had taken a fantastic culture and prepared it for growth and done so during a capital investment and through a global pandemic. Our *Goal-Driven Focus* expected to *Triumphant* in our *Defined Success* - a codified culture measured systemically. 2021 was the final stage of our execution of this journey. 2020 may have given us a Slingshot, but that allowed us to improve our culture journey.

Organizational leaders often think that this type of work feels exhausting, time-consuming, and overwhelming. *It was.* We knew that this journey was necessary for *Exponentiality* in our business. What we accomplished over the last three years laid the foundation for what we are doing in 2021 and the growth of our business moving forward.

For the first time in organizational history, we financially aligned our core values with every corporate and employee goal. Our system's simplicity and symmetry empowered every team member to contribute to the *Exponentiality* of the organization. As we continue "rowing," our teams needed to row together and in synchronization to be *Exponential.* Every rower was critical to success on every stroke. If one rower is out of sync, it impacts everyone else. For Davisware to succeed, we had to become a rowing team.

Our culture journey is nowhere near done. It will never be done if it is to remain vibrant and alive.

It is an ongoing evolutionary process that requires cultivation, much like a garden. This year, we realized that we needed to make our values more concise to be used both inside the organization and publicly facing.

What has always made Davisware a unique value for our customers has been our passion for what we do. Therefore, we needed values that were concise to share publicly. If our people and culture are our greatest asset, we wanted to make sure we could share them in a way that described who we are and why we do what we do. Craig Groeschel's leadership podcast encourages organizations to share value statements in short life-giving ways. He states:

- If you can't tweet them, they are too long.
- If they don't move you emotionally, they are too dry.
- If they don't force you to action, get new ones[38].

We wanted our values described as memorable, portable, and emotional. Our values were more informational than emotional, and information doesn't move people to action.

Emotion does. We needed to improve our value statement. We had defined our values and thought they were accurate. Still, in our *Process-Driven* culture, we recognized that they weren't publicly facing, memorable, portable, or emotional, and we needed to improve. At our 2021 All Company Meeting, we shared our new memorable, portable, and emotional company values:

WARRIOR SPIRIT

We are tenacious and don't give up. We are fighters.

RAISE THE BAR

We are curious and open-minded. We are always learning and looking to be better.

CUSTOMER OBSESSED

We are our customers' strongest advocates. We have an urgency to solve their problems, and we do what we say we are going to do.

ONE CREW

We are passionate about our ideas. But once we set our direction we row in unison as a team, and we have fun doing it!

This new and improved version of our values more crisply defines who we are and why we do what we do. We converted into words the intangible actions in our business that defined the culture. With our newly codified culture, we will continue to attract the right people, demonstrate that we value the right actions, and give our teams clear direction and a place they love to work.

The culture journey has been one that was planned for before 2020 and shaped by our experiences in 2020.

Leading the business through 2020 amplified our efforts from something good into something better. With or without our culture journey, our accidental culture would have survived the global pandemic. However, the pre-emptive work to create a purposeful culture allowed us to thrive instead of mere survival. As a leader, it became evident in this transformation and leading through the crisis that the global pandemic created; this was a unique privilege very few leaders get to do.

Chapter Summary – Chapter 7: Culture on Purpose – Making Culture Exponential

Lessons Learned

- Most young businesses' culture is a reflection of the ownership/leaders, not a purposeful decision.
- A healthy culture is created through an emphasis on *Exponential Living* for everyone in the organization.
- Your culture provides the foundation for creating goals.

- Setting expectations and culture create certainty and lead to higher-level performance.
- Good culture creates revenue. Bad culture inhibits it.
- Culture gives people the sense of connection – rowing team vs. golf team.
- The Process of changing culture is slow, evolutionary multi-year process, which makes it even more challenging to commit to.
- Codifying culture gives it value. You are congruent if you use your values and culture to hire, fire, promote, and reward your employees.
- Aligning core values, business goals, and financial reward creates a system that communicates what is important and how people must behave.
- Codifying a culture transfers the responsibility of the culture keeper to every person in an organization.
- Culture is the bedrock of the organization. It can often take many years to see the small fissures in it.
- Culture creates value in your business.
- You do not need to wait until your culture is broken to work on it.
- Creating a codified culture is achieved through a Slingshot.
- Cultural values have visible and invisible elements as demonstrated in an Iceberg Model. Visible include policies, vision, mission, values, goals, messaging, and the organizational chart. Invisible include innovation, compassion, initiative, integrity, and commitment.
- An iceberg is far larger below water than above. This means that the elements that are most impactful are those below water.
- Creating short, impactful values makes it easy to share both internally and externally.

- A strong mission statement, when supported through action, aligns employees with strategic goals, empowers employees and allows you to attract and retain top talent.
- A healthy culture is a combination of both what you create and what you allow.
- You can create the words, but they don't inspire change until they become consistent actions demonstrated over time - first by your actions, then by your leadership team, and finally by your peers. There is far more value in what you do than what you say.
- Culture requires a defensive position to protect it.
- Culture is about all the little things people do when no one is watching but create a difference every day.

Unveiled Discoveries

- Gallop statistics on company culture show that managers determine the quality of your company's culture. Team leaders' talent, skill, and knowledge can improve company culture and productivity exponentially. There is a whopping 70% difference in culture quality between companies with lousy and great team leaders.
- Five years before Google launched, Davisware created an infrastructure for a remote workforce, adding its first remote employee.
- Failed expectations are the source of most failures, not the results.
- We often think that people hate change. What people hate is the change they don't control, understand, or with which they disagree. People don't like to have change happen to them. They want to be a part of change.

Statistics to Ponder

- For perspective, it was just one year earlier, in 1990, Archie, Alan Emtage, and McGill University had developed the first Internet search engine. Later that same year, Tim Berners-Lee began writing code for a client program, a brows-er/editor he called Worldwide Web, on his new computer.

Action Plan

- How would you assess your culture on a scale where 1 is accidental and 10 is purposeful?
- What values and beliefs do you value most as an organization?
- Are your decisions to hire, promote, and fire precisely based upon the support of your company values?
- How do you communicate, reinforce, and lead with those values and beliefs?
- How can you make your culture more purposeful and effective?
- What did the pandemic reveal about your culture and how can you use those insights to move your organization and culture to the next level?
- Have you done a comprehensive wage assessment, comparing staff in similar roles, as well as staff of similar value?
- What are the data sets that you use to make decisions surrounding hiring, promoting, and firing? Are they codified? How can you make this happen?
- Are your employees more excited about coming to work or leaving?
- Culture is a perpetual journey. You are never done.

Good Quotables

- *Hard things are the things we are most proud of.*
- *When thinking about our journey in life, we should use our rearview mirror and our windshield in the relative relationship of their size. Both are critical to safely getting you where you need to go, but we don't have the opportunity to learn from where we have come without looking back. If we spend too much time looking in the rearview mirror, we are dangerously unaware of where we are headed. A quick glance backward gives perspective for what's ahead. That is what we needed to learn to do.*
- *Pouring water in the ocean rises all boats.*
- *Our culture is at the core of our success, and a cultural leader, I am the ultimate protector of our brand and our culture. In that role, I wanted to personally share who should work at Davisware. Team Davisware consists of empathetic and graceful creative problem solvers who work hard, smart, and do everything with a servant's heart. They work with absolute humility in the quest for perfection, knowing it's unattainable. Most importantly, they should make every decision on behalf of the organization, not the individual. Can you be that person? — Jennifer Davis (Asking new employees if they are ready to join our team)*
- *Ships are safe in the harbor, but ships weren't built to stay in the harbor. (Unknown - Parts Town 2020 Launch Event)*
- *The tallest Oak in the forest was once a little nut that held its ground. That is what we ALL need to do today on so many fronts. Jennifer Davis (in the first Davisware address of the Global Pandemic)*
- *Culture is what people do when no one is looking. —Herb Kelleher, CEO, Southwest Airlines*
- *People may hear your words, but they feel your attitude. —John Maxwell*

- *Without conscious and deliberate effort, inertia always wins. — Tony Hsieh*
- *Whether you think you can, or you think you can't- you're right. —Henry Ford*
- *What Got You Here Won't Get You There —Marshall Goldsmith*
- *A healthy culture is a combination of what you create and what you allow. — Craig Groeschel*
- *There's a difference between knowing the path and walking the path. —Morpheus, The Matrix*
- *A business leader's job is to create great teams that do amazing work on time. That's it. That's the job of management. —Patty McCord*
- *Determine what behaviors and beliefs you value as a company and have everyone live true to them. These behaviors and beliefs should be so essential to your core that you don't even think of it as culture. —Brittany Forsyth, SVP of Human Resources, Shopify*
- *A rising tide lifts all boats. – John F. Kennedy*
- *We must never lose our sense of urgency in making improvements. We must never settle for "good enough," because good is the enemy of great — Tony Hsieh*
- *Better three hours too soon than a minute too late.—William Shakespeare*
- *Crisis is a gift because it reveals to us what is most important.— Martin Rooney*
- *You know, people talk about this being an uncertain time. All time is uncertain. I mean, it was uncertain back in - in 2007 (Last Recession), we just didn't know it was uncertain. It was - uncertain on September 10th, 2001 (9-11), October 18th, 1987 (Day before Black Monday), and December 6, 1941 (Pearl Harbor), you just didn't know it yet. —Warren Buffett*

Supplementary Learning Recommendations (Read/Listen/Watch)

- *Delivering Happiness* by Zappos Founder, Tony Hsieh
- *Nuts! Southwest Airlines' Crazy Recipe for Business and Personal Success*, Kevin & Jackie Freiberg
- *What Got You Here Won't Get You There: How Successful People Become Even More Successful*, Marshall Goldsmith
- Movie: Up in the Air starring George Clooney and Vera Farmiga
- Podcast: Craig Groeschel' s leadership podcast
- *Blue Is the New White: The Best Path to Success No One Told You About—Until Now* – Josh Zolin

CHAPTER 8

Harnessing the Power of Expectations and Communications

"If you don't know where you are going, any road will take you there!" —Louis Carroll

Clear expectations and communications are essential for success in any business, but most impactful in entrepreneurial businesses where organizational charts are often fluid, with many people wearing many hats or in non-traditional roles. Without clearly communicated expectations and a roadmap, you leave the results your business achieves and how it happens to the decision-making of individual contributors and what they individually deem as success. Rarely does this become related to the organizational success that the leaders of the business define.

Setting expectations and communicating how to achieve them are two tools business leaders should use to influence reality and create desirable results. For example, a recent Gallup survey revealed that almost 50% of workers did not know their job requirements.[43] This finding means that half of all employees show up for work, not knowing what they are supposed to do to help them succeed or keep their jobs. How many of these employees work for you? Of course, all employees want to succeed. But that is left to chance without them knowing what the organization and their team expect. Unfortunately, there are not enough words to emphasize the importance of setting clear expectations for the organization. Yet, like most business leaders, I have struggled to remind myself how critical this is. Our job as leaders is to take the clearly defined mission of the business and set laser-focused expectations for the individual contributors in the organization. Imagine the change in productivity by driving this percentage to zero?

Both personally and professionally, one of the most important things I have learned is that failed expectation is the source of most disappointment. I want to reiterate this. *Personally and professionally, failed expectations are the source of most disappointment.* This dilemma is not a work problem. It is a life problem. Take a moment to really think about this. For example, if you expect your team to meet on a major project you are working on, and half of the team does not show up, you are obviously disappointed. If, however, you knew in advance that only half of the team would be a part of the process, your mind would solve the problem with the resources you expected. In short, there would be no disappointment because you would solve it with who showed up, or you would adjust to include the entire team.

In the same way, if your spouse expects you home for dinner at six and you show up at seven, there are failed expectations that create disappointment and a mirid of other emotions, none of which are good for either of you. If, however, your family expected you to be there at seven, even if six had been better, the emotional reaction and disappointment would be entirely different. As leaders, our job is to mitigate failed expectations by setting the most explicit expectations possible and doing so repeatedly. It is one of your most important roles.

The creation of expectations for our teams is critical. But equally important is a clear message to communicate those expectations. This juncture is where we so often fall down. We have figured out exactly what we want to do and how to achieve it in our heads. We just fail to communicate it concisely in a timely manner.

Unfortunately, often, we don't make a conscious decision to share our expectations and articulate plans to share them with every contributing member of the team. When we do this, we create opportunities for failed expectations for everyone involved and open the chance of failure itself. . George Bernard Shaw once said, "The single biggest problem in communication is the illusion that it has taken place."[44] All too often, we assume that just because we said something means that our team has heard it, believes it, or knows what to do with it. We, humans, are egocentric. As a result, we often assume that others heard and have the same understanding that we intended. Our leadership requires that we focus beyond ourselves and ensure that our communications are you-centered, not me-centered.

We achieve a you-centered perspective in the timing of setting expectations and creating the mission. When the sea is calm and its business, as usual, is the right time to develop you-centered expectations. This situation can is similar to communicating with our spouses. If I share with Dan the four things he needs to pick up from the grocery store as he is walking out the door to get them, I am far more likely to get what I wanted than if I give him the list in the last 16 seconds of the Monday Night Football game he is watching. We can't communicate expectations at a time when the recipient is not able to receive the message. Now, calm days may never feel like they exist for many leaders, especially when experiencing rapid growth. However, these are critical times that must trump urgent to achieve *Exponentiality* in your business and life.

Our organizations have just survived a global economic and social reset. This reality demonstrates that your business is resilient and that nothing is more urgent than taking the time to do something as important as this. If you did not take the time before the pandemic to define and communicate a clear mission statement and vision statement, now is the time. If you took time for this important task before the pandemic, there is a strong likelihood that your business is different now than before the pandemic. Take the time to refresh and reassess it now to ensure every team member knows what is expected of them and how it relates to its mission. Take the time. Your organization is relying upon your leadership to do it.

Other chapters go deep into mission statements, but it is so intertwined with communications and expectations that several elements are worthy of repeating or mentioning in more detail. Taking time to do this will prepare you for the next storm. And by the way, the next storm is coming. There is uncertainty about when, what, and how, but it is one hundred percent certain it is coming. When the next storm arrives and chaos rolls in, you and your team are ready. Crises like the pandemic make communicating difficult because emotions are high. Fear, uncertainty, and doubt (the FUD Factor) are in play. These are different emotions than Dan is feeling in the last 16 seconds of his Bears game, but both sets of emotions prevent people from actually hearing us. In emotional times where FUD is involved, people require crystal-clear expectations of how they need to contribute to the overall organizational goal. No matter how carefully you set expectations for your employees before the pandemic, expectations have changed. Just consider some of the changes that have occurred and the challenges most businesses are facing:

- The social contracts of what we are supposed to do, when we are supposed to do it, and how we are supposed to do it have fundamentally changed.
- Lockdowns and technology have forced many to redefine what the workday looks like and when it takes place. Now that we are beyond these mandated changes, employers and employees are trying to determine if they want to return to the old normal.
- The world has never reacted to a pandemic like this before. We cannot look in the rearview mirror at history for answers for our go-forward.
- Our forecasts and financial models lost integrity because our data in the rearview mirror is no longer relevant as a comparison.
- Every organization is adjusting, reacting, and reorganizing, and redefining its trajectories without the luxury of history and data. We have to respond and redefine with real-time data. Reaction times are no longer measured in months or years but instead days and hours.

These are just a few of the ways that the business landscape has permanently changed. Many industries have seen dramatic shifts in market dominance. Small businesses, the hospitality, entertainment, and travel industries were devasted, with many closings permanently. On the other hand, big tech, online streaming services, delivery services, online meeting platforms, and cybersecurity have boomed and created influence in business arenas never before seen. *What we do and how we do it has permanently changed.*

Two of the industries Davisware customers dominate were dramatically impacted—commercial HVAC and commercial food equipment service. With commercial buildings vacant and commercial kitchens often completely shut down, we saw innovative pivots by many companies to create their economic success. In contrast, we have seen others struggle to keep their doors open. These examples tell you success is possible (The fundamentals of the *Exponential Mindset-Triumph*), regardless of what is happening within the overall industry. An *Exponential Mindset* will create success. We are now experiencing the new normal. Business owners have had to develop a new mindset, use new tools, and set new expectations and even a new corporate mission to create their prosperity once again. Painful transitions like the one we are just now emerging from are unanimously recognized as change agents that made businesses better and more efficient at what they do.

Most business models and business planning processes were designed for more predictable times.

As a result, models failed to perform well in this chaotic environment. Instead, leaders needed to react in real-time and trust their gut more often. Change happened more frequently, more unpredictably, and with enough size to makes them "disruptive." The disruption took place in every aspect of our personal and professional lives. So, the question for business leaders became, "how do you effectively grow sales, profits, and customer loyalty in an unpredictable environment where everything changes in days and weeks rather than months or years?" During the pandemic, all businesses had to pivot.

What this proved is that a well-run business will continue to prosper in disruptive times. These well-run businesses had communication structures in place and had created a framework for expectations- even when they needed to change urgently. Now, exiting these tumultuous times, the businesses who were well-prepared going into the pandemic will take that same position coming out of the pandemic, reassessing and focusing on CPI (Continuous Process Improvement) to make good *great* or great even *greater*. Since we cannot avoid the crisis, our focus needs to be on understanding it, developing skills to help our businesses adapt to the chaos it produces, and focusing on what we can control. The first step is to provide clarity for the organization with clear expectations and consistent communications.

Why is communicating expectations so important?

In the early days of our business, we had a very tight group of people, many of whom we were related to and often working in the same room and intimately involved in every detail in the company. Personal and professional time was thoroughly blended, as were the workdays and nights. These days were rewarding and fun.

These days, our core group was interchangeable in client meetings or vendor negotiations. We all wore many hats, and those hats were traded between us whenever the need struck. As a result, we did not need much formal communication. However, as the business evolved, so too became our need for communication. Unfortunately, as is seen far too often in growing organizations, the business growth and the communication loops did not always grow in unison. Communication disconnects translated into failures with our customers and lessons learned for our organization.

Having raised as many teenagers as we have, I relate these times in our business as the teenage years. Teenagers and their parents rarely have similar expectations or communication styles. As a result, there are lots of failures in these areas in raising teenagers. In the same way, growing organizations struggle to find the balance and the best means of communicating.

Just like in sports, a confident teammate is a successful one. Communicating expectations creates a paradigm in your business that builds confidence for each contributor to do their work. Their effectiveness will wane when your teams are "playing scared" or do not know the playbook. The more prolific this is in the business, the more detrimental this will be toward overall success. Clear expectations within an organization empower your teams to think like leaders and business owners. When you get them to think like you, your expectations are met.

Effective communication channels bridge the gap between expectation and delivered reality.

How do you keep your growing team informed and focused on the right priorities? The road here leads back to the same answer. A clearly defined mission statement is the beginning. When we invested time in this process, it was one of the most challenging decisions. It felt like "fluff." It felt like an epic waste of time to write our mission statement and solidify our core values in the world of fires we were trying to fight. To date, every person in the room still instinctively knows our mission and our core values. However, we needed to prepare better for the growth before us to find more success beyond that. In hindsight, our strategic decision to make this investment was one of the most important things we did. Unfortunately, we did not do it sooner.

Bullet-proofing Your Mission Statement

Setting expectations starts and ends with your mission statement. Your mission statement says who you are, whom you serve, and how you do it. After days of deliberation and far too many iterations, we established the Davisware mission statement.

Our mission is to leverage our industry expertise and customer relationships to create integrated and affordable software solutions. Since 1988, we've helped service-oriented businesses, contractors, distributors, and manufacturers become industry leaders with technology solutions critical to the growth and success of their businesses.

We used concisely chosen, well-thought-out words that translated the mission that Dan and I set out on in 1988. These words are the foundation of who we are and from which everything we do gets its meaning. We invested considerable effort to bullet-proof this statement - an investment that became priceless in 2020. When we wrote it, we felt good about our work. When we thrived in crisis, our hard work was justified.

After creating an actionable mission statement that defined who we were, what made us unique, and whom we served, our leadership team's task was to forge forward to institutionalize and operationalize the mission statement for everyone in the organization. The execution of your mission cannot be left to chance. You can't delegate it. The institutionalization of the mission statement is how it proliferates through the organization. The leadership team can help proliferate it, but if the mission statement is not the most important thing to you, why would it be important to your teams? It wouldn't. When I initially meet business leaders, it's very quick and easy to discover whether they are focused on being leaders of their business or working in the business. I simply ask them about their mission and how aligned their goals and concerns for their business are with their mission statement. As a leader, make institutionalizing your mission statement your highest priority and make it as urgent as it is.

Institutionalizing our mission statement

Every word in Davisware's mission statement has meaning and application to how we run the business. It guides and informs all of our actions while giving us clarity. For these reasons, it has to be present in every aspect of our business. Therefore, I thought it would be valuable to break down our mission statement to demonstrate how you can achieve it. Before explaining how we institutionalized it, we will walk through the thought processes and the questions we asked ourselves as we developed our mission statement. The work you see below is the coagulation of 2 full days' worth of notes and discussion, sometimes heated, that got us to our final results.

Our mission is to leverage our industry expertise...Where and how in the business have we proven we are industry experts? How are we ensuring we remain industry experts? How are we demonstrating our industry expertise to those in the industry? We realized through this process that what made us valuable was that our industry expertise allowed us to be trusted to create exceptional solutions targeted at our customers' needs. Our customers choose us because we have consistently demonstrated our commitment to the industry. That is why it was leading our mission statement. It said we were committed to an unquantifiable investment of time into our trade associations and events. That time was priceless to our organization.

...(leveraging) and customer relationships...How are we valuing and creating customer relationships? What are we doing to leverage the relationships that we have? How do we know we have good customer relationships? Again, through this process, we quantified the value of our customer relationships. Those relationships sold more software than any marketing we had done, so investing in on-site visits, in-person boot camps, and our User Conference were fundamental investments our business required us to make.

to create integrated (solutions)...What is an integrated solution, and why is that valuable to our customers? Where does core functionality start, and partner relationships begin? We saw that one of the reasons our customers chose us and why they saw us as a partner is that we had pieced together the complexity of field services with technology.

We helped them grow their businesses by having interrelated data and protected it fiercely. A common mistake made in technology businesses is to try to build everything. Technology sprawl happens, and we fell victim to it ourselves. By going through this process, we started to see our need to make technology differently. Instead of building everything, we focused on building the core technology for our customers' businesses and partnering with other companies to build the rest. Out of this process grew our partnership programs and our APIs. Without going through this exercise, it is unlikely we would have made this conclusion at this time, if at all.

...and affordable technology solutions... What is our price-point comparatively to our competitors? How do we create value in a higher-priced solution? What should we be aware of as it relates to our costs? What technology should we be involved with that is beyond software? Through our customer partnerships, we discovered that our customers' businesses were capitalized through sweat equity and often not enough.

We needed to offer cost-sensitive solutions and a business model focused on winning with our customers' growth. Our mission statement helped us solidify our decision to move our entire business to a subscription model. We carefully selected the word "technology" vs. software. Our expertise and our influence in our customer's businesses far exceeded software. The lines between hardware, software, firmware, and integrations were rapidly blurring, and without the ability to focus on the larger scope, we would have been limiting ourselves and our customers.

...Since 1988... How do we remain true to our longevity in the industry without becoming stale? How does our longevity provide value to our customers and products?

We always wanted to demonstrate our expertise while validating it with our years of commitment. New customers needed to learn about our longevity. Calling it out also forced us to remember our history. While the pandemic caused us to all be nimble and find confidence in making decisions that history didn't provide an example of, we couldn't forget the value of that history. We had thrived before and would thrive again as long as we stayed focused on our mission.

... we've helped service-oriented businesses, contractors, distributors, and manufacturers become industry leaders... So how do we remain focused on only these business segments? How do we recognize growth-minded customer partners? How do we stay aligned with the needs of this exclusive business segment? In a business built on relationships, we historically struggled to limit which opportunities we took advantage of. Our mission statement was our reminder. We had been distracted to do business in markets and segments that we could not offer the same level of industry expertise.

*...with technology solutions critical to the growth and success of their businesses...*How do we help our growth-minded customers as a thought partner with technology? How do we stay ahead of our customer's needs? How do we become a part of the "secret sauce" that makes our customers successful? In this statement, we again focused on technology, not just software. The keyword here is *critical*. By focusing on core software and fiercely protecting their industry workflows and data, we would be a part of their essential tools, creating longevity and partnership in their business growth.

We built our mission statement to be concise about whom we wanted to be, whom we wanted to serve, and whom we wanted to employ. This mission statement was both inward-facing and outward-facing. It was relatable and measurable. Now, the demanding work was institutionalizing it with our teams and our customers. Institutionalizing it meant that we embedded it anywhere within the institution to relate what we were doing to who we are. The irony of this process is that if we felt like dedicating two days to this process was challenging, committing our time every day when urgent was consistently in our face felt almost impossible.

We did it, but not without many setbacks and many times where we forgot the important over the urgent.

The process of institutionalizing your mission statement is unique in every business. Once you gain the muscle memory of this process, you will find unique ways to accomplish this in your own business.

A few of the actions we took to institutionalize our mission statement included:

- We went to a heroic effort to find a notebook size and shape everyone loved. We printed our mission statement in a bold, visible font on the back cover. That way, regardless of where our teams were, it was with them and visible to anyone they were meeting.

- We asked that each employee displayed the mission statement somewhere obvious on their desk or computer. Then, we had contests to share their most creative ways to display it.
- We displayed our mission statement in multiple locations throughout the offices and all meeting spaces; this way, internally and externally, it was visible and present.
- We included our mission statement at the bottom of every email so that *everyone* knew what we were about regardless of their relationship with Davisware.
- We also utilized the mission statement to develop our job descriptions, ensuring they were aligned. Rather than starting with the tasks that made up a role, we started with the mission statement that depicted the vision of the role. Then we boiled it down to the responsibilities and the functions that supported the mission. Every team member needed to see how their part was connected to and supported the larger organization's mission.
- In every public presentation, our mission statement was someway embedded, either in print or word and ideally in both. Therefore, we modified our presentation template to include our mission.

We used our mission as the basis for our leadership meetings and conversation. We focused our annual meeting around our mission. We used our mission as our focal point when disagreements arose regarding what we should do tactically or strategically.

Each of these tactical decisions became foundational in the success we garnered in aligning ourselves to our mission. We can reflect on these decisions as some of the most critical decision points we had in the future growth of our business. The decision to prioritize important over urgent became a demonstratable success in our future.

Operationalizing our mission statement

Articulating a mission statement defines who you are. Institutionalizing the mission statement communicates that definition.

Operationalizing puts our mission statement into action. It was used as the guideposts for our teams to fill their roles. Each of these steps was critical to the success of living out the mission. The review and improvement of the mission statement and the supporting role of your mission are essential to operationalizing the actual content. The ongoing operationalization of the mission statement aligns itself with executing an *Exponential Mindset* that is *Process-Driven*. Our new framework forced us to operationalize its continuous review and improve what we had built. Fortunately, the work we put in over those two days yielded our success in a mission statement that has stood the test of time. Although we have made minor tweaks, the 50+ iterations we went through in those days were well worth it.

Our mission is to leverage our industry expertise. Our team needed to know the words of our mission statement translate to them to execute their roles. This commitment happened through our emphasis on hiring industry experts. As a result, those not from the industry understood the importance of becoming an expert and engaged in our industries. If our customers continue to see us as industry experts and their thought partners for the growth and success of their business, they will see us for our long-term value, not the short-term wins. This approach also increases the chance of forgiveness by clients for short-term failures.

This vision will also help your organization when you fail because that will happen too. When you communicate your mission statement and the business operations validate it, your customers and your teams will see failures in perspective and grow from them, not be diminished by them. The tenure and value of our expertise override the short-term highs and lows and allows us to continue our mission of partnership with our customers.

My usual elevator pitch about Davisware is that we are a technology company for companies with guys in trucks who fix things, build things, and deliver things. Our technology helps our customers organize their transactions and assets, communicate with them, and make data-driven decisions about their strategic mission. These functions are what the technology does, but it is not what we do. What we do is help our customers become thought leaders through the sharing of our expertise.

We help them use industry-specific technology that creates growth and success in their businesses. Having been in these industries for 30+ years and having hired teams from these industries, we have thousands of years of expertise in hundreds of companies with similar missions to those of our customers. Our most valuable asset is our expertise, and we happen to use it to sell software. Therefore, our mission statement needed to be institutionalized, operationalized, and communicated with that importance.

Operationalizing our mission statement means that our teams have a clear direction for how their roles contribute to our customer's success. So often, when I meet with new customer opportunities, and I ask them what sets them apart from their competitors, they talk about their price and the quality of service. These are *literally the same talk track* as their competitor, with whom I have had the same conversation.

Neither of these things makes them unique. At Davisware, our competitors have software that does many of the same things that we do. Some software is better than ours, and some are worse than ours, but all generally do the same thing. What makes us unique is that we developed our workflows from within the industries we serve. Our expertise has caused us to passionately focus on developing the data they need to create growth and success in their business. Our industry expertise is what makes our value proposition unique which is why it leads our mission statement.

As you think about what makes your business unique, it is crucial to differentiate yourself from your competitors. Our mission statement means that our teams understand the value of their industry expertise. Likewise, our mission statement reminds our customers that expertise differentiates us and what we offer them. We have been in hundreds and maybe even thousands of contracting businesses. What sets us apart is that our customers know how to use our tools better and those tools are better adapted to their industry needs expressly because we understand what they need.

In comparison, very few of our competitors came out of the industries we serve. In contrast, most of our customers grew up in a single business or have only been in a handful. Imagine the value of the perspective of hundreds of businesses that Davisware teams bring to our customers? THAT is the most significant value to our customers and is what our operationalization attempted to demonstrate. Some areas that we operationalized included:

- Standardized messages and communication platforms
- Troubleshooting knowledge-sharing platforms to help us get even more engaged and create even more expertise in our teams
- Cross-functional teams assigned to accounts for tactical execution of customer needs
- Standard platforms of information for our teams to share expertise
- Continuous industry expertise recruitment into the business

The commitment to communications starts with a commitment to your mission. Once you have entered *what* you need to communicate, operationalizing the message includes a commitment to anchoring every meeting, every communication, and every objective to that mission. This approach is where you will find success.

The mission under crisis

The real value of a mission statement is in crisis. Before the global pandemic, our mission statement was the unifying focus for our team and was the message that we shared with our customers. When the pandemic hit, it became the north star to our organization with rapid focus. So, what did our mission statement translate into during the pandemic? It translated into different types of activities focusing on the same mission. Davisware has always been well-known for being a team of empathetic and creative problem-solvers.

We, as an organization, have always had very personal relationships with nearly every customer. During 2020, we took every extra minute in every day to put a renewed focus on these relationships. I thought about our operational pivot in the same way as a pivot in my day-to-day personal life. Personally, if one of my friends had a crisis, my commitment to that friend wouldn't change during the crisis, but how I executed that relationship would change. I may decide to do childcare, make meals, or take a day off to spend time and listen. I would do things that are generally not in the day-to-day scope of that friendship.

Our approach with our customers was similar. During one of my early Monday Morning All Calls, I shared with our teams that we needed to double down on our role as a partner in the success of our customer's businesses. During a pandemic, success meant survival. I translated our mission to the new need of our customers. I described what we were facing in the following way.

"Davisware is facing unprecedented times, with unprecedented fears. We have no history to look at in how we react. In the grand scope, Davisware is a great business and has survived many other unprecedented challenges. What isn't unprecedented is that we will do what we have always done and focus on what we can control. There isn't a good time for a global pandemic. In the course of Davisware history, it's a terrible time. We have new investment partners. We were about to make massive investments in product and infrastructure, and we hired new staff to prepare for growth.

None of these situations are ideal. However, we won't be paralyzed by where we are.

We are going to focus on where we want to go. I would like to refer you back to our comparison of being on a battleship from last week.

Battleships take massive energy to switch directions; massive engines and a massive staff propel them. Nothing about them is nimble. And yet, they can find success in some of the fiercest battles the world has ever seen. Today, we are the battleship, and the pandemic has left us with no engines, just oars. We've always talked about being creative problem solvers and have self-described our team as #AllRockstars #NoBenchwarmers. Now, we get the opportunity to prove it. You've all been given your "oar." It's all of the preparation that you have put into today. Your preparation is the investment partners we have and the leadership of our organization. Your oar is your industry expertise, creative problem-solving, and your empathy for what your customers and teammates are going through. We need every person in this organization rowing. We need to row in unison toward nothing other than our mission. We need to turn on a dime, and it will only happen with every person on the boat rowing.

If that's not you, we don't need you.

Davisware needs you and so do our customers. After all, our ship could be safe in the harbor, but battleships weren't built for the harbor. We are going out into the stormy seas. We are going to control what we can control. We are going to execute and persevere for ourselves and our customers. We will stay true to our mission statement to partner with our customers through our industry expertise and technology. Our customer's businesses and industries are some of the hardest hit by the pandemic. Relief is nowhere in sight. You can contribute to Davisware's success by helping our customers succeed- just as you have always done. What can each of you do to contribute to our customers' success individually? Figure that out, and then do that. We are headed into battle. We are headed out to sea. We need every rower to #justkeeprowing."

The battle cry that I set out for our teams in mid-March would become our hashtag throughout 2020. The demonstration of our success in the hard work that we did on our mission statement several years earlier contributed to our success in 2020. What could we do to demonstrate our industry expertise? What could we do with technology that would support our customers and our industries? Our direct engagement with our customers expanded from our support and implementation staff to nearly every person on our payroll. From the CEO seat through accounting and even human resources, we took saving our customer's businesses personally. Our executables changed, but we never changed our laser focus on our mission to be industry experts and partners in our customers' businesses. Instead of selling customers software and teaching them how to grow their business, we used our expertise to teach them how to survive. Switching our executable is an example of our organizational *Exponential Mindset* on *Solution-Focused Flexibility*. Our mission was the same. Our tactical application was totally different.

We had teams who were not ordinarily customer-facing working with customers. We spent time talking about the most critical customer service skills and how to execute them. Even though these teams had not historically served in these roles, our organizational communications focused on strong closed-loop communication, empathy, product knowledge, problem-solving, patience, a fantastic attitude, excellent listening skills, and a willingness to go the extra mile. We talked about personal responsibility and demonstrating confidence as well as tenacity. We asked our teams to be authentic and attentive to our customers' needs. We gave our teams more flexibility in their problem-solving to respond quickly and manage the customer's needs. We reminded ourselves that our customer's urgency was not ours, and we needed to adapt. Finally, we reminded our teams to act professionally regardless of how the stress of the problem was causing our customer partners to treat us. They may not remember how they treated us, but they will remember how we treated them. These tactical adaptations in our processes strengthened our mission and our partnership throughout the pandemic and beyond.

A controversial change I asked our sales and account management teams to make was to stop selling technology and start finding solutions to help our customers save their businesses. Many companies struggled with cash management. In the wake of the pandemic, this problem urgently grew. When the federal government created the ingenious solution with Paycheck Protection Program (PPP) loans, we found our means of helping our customers. I immediately saw this program as my opportunity to help our customers by learning as much as we could about the program and sharing what we learned about how to secure PPP loans for their business operations and where the data resided in their systems to apply. We urgently became an expert on every detail of the programs that weeks earlier didn't exist.

Many business owners had no idea how to apply or the broad scope of other available programs, and they were critical to our customers' survival. So, we did an immediate pivot to become experts on how to apply for the programs successfully.

We assisted anyone who wanted help, not just our customers. We found ways to leverage our technology to help our customers apply and gain forgiveness. For example, we did an outreach calling campaign to our customers to help them get the loans sooner, better, and faster than most assumed possible. We quickly pivoted from in-person trade shows boasting about the newest technology. Instead, we shifted to becoming online experts with a new series of webinars demonstrating the use of our technology and reporting to apply for their government assistance. Customers and non-customers widely attended these webinars, and our expertise was so valued that we helped the industry and protected our position as industry experts as well.

In addition to hosting and producing our webinar series on pandemic-related topics, we put maximum effort into helping our partner associations do the same. We did what we always did. We *"...leveraged our industry expertise and customer relationships to create integrated and affordable ... solutions. Since 1988, we've helped service-oriented businesses, contractors, distributors, and manufacturers become industry leaders with technology solutions critical to the ... success of their businesses.*" Again, we did what we've always done.

The faster we could help save the industry, the quicker and better we protected our own business.

To become the PPP loan expert for our customers, we had to do a quick pivot to operationalize our expertise fully. We used the *Exponential Mindset Slingshot Effect* to accomplish this objective. Our pullback was becoming an expert on PPPs (Paycheck Protection Program). Four weeks earlier, there was not an expert in the building. Now hundreds of businesses looked to Davisware as the expert to drive some of the most critical timing their business had ever seen.

Out of necessity, our team also became experts. Our shot forward was not direct, but it was praiseworthy. We realized that to save our business, we had to help our customers save theirs. Our fortified position as a partner for our customers, not just a vendor, demonstrated its Slingshot forward in our resulting cash flow, overperformance in cash preservation, and customer attrition. We implemented our *Slingshot Effect* with clear expectations and consistent communications, all anchored to our mission statement. We wanted to make sure that our customers knew that we were partners in their business's success- regardless of what it took. Our customers already knew we were their technology partner. Through the global pandemic, we fortified our partnership in the success of their businesses, far beyond technology with new executables and newly found success.

I'm not sharing these successes to boast about our results or to brag about Davisware and its team. I am biased in the value of both the organization and the team, but that is not relevant here. I'm sharing this information for the sole mission of this book. My goal has been for you to learn from what we did and do it better and faster than we did. If you can take any valuable lessons learned here, I hope you do. There are lessons to be learned in sharing both our successes and our failures. This particular share was a fantastic accomplishment for me as the leader and, more importantly, for our team. Each of these decisions could have turned out differently. Some of the decisions we made didn't grant us the success we were looking for. Those failures are also lessons learned. The most important thing is to understand the value of the *Exponential Mindset*. Executing the *Exponential Mindset* throughout the global pandemic is *actually what* created our success.

Rewarding the organization with Closed-Loop Communications

Closing the loop on communications is both challenging and rewarding. Closing communication loops prevents most miscommunications. From one-to-one to large-scale meetings or communicating by email or text, closing communication loops is a discipline that changes individual success and organizations. Closed-loop communication means every person directed in action understands what is involved and who is responsible for communicating when it is solved.

Exponential Meetings through Closed Loop Communications

Meetings and emails create a vast majority of the communication issues in business. Yet, research suggests that 50% of meeting attendees feel it's a waste of time.[45] Think about that as it relates to your organization. What can you do to reduce that perception to 25% or even 10%? How would this impact your overall business productivity? My guess is *Exponential.*

Establish an *Exponential Mindset* as it relates to meetings, don't micromanage the process. Instead, execute critical strategies in the business to create this opportunity. First, regardless of meeting size, the communication loop is the most critical agenda item. This decision requires creating a meeting framework that supports closed-loop communications. What value does an executed agenda have if it doesn't get communicated back to those who need to know? This failure is why the meetings translate into feeling like a waste of time for those attending.

Every organization needs a standard meeting framework. Accomplish this by creating, sharing, and enforcing a *Process-Driven* (a fundament of the *Exponential Mindset*) meeting system. Feel free to use our example or adapt it to a process that works for your organization.

This list is not exhaustive, but it will get you started in executing *Exponential* Meetings.

Start each meeting by allocating time at the onset of the meeting to define the purpose and what success would look like, including who is responsible for communicating that success. It's the meeting's mini-mission statement. Defining the goal, what the definition of success is, and who is responsible for communicating it determines the success of the meeting and closes the loop of communication.

At the close of any meeting, everyone should know what action items they are responsible for and how those actions will be communicated back to others. This step is obvious but rarely is prioritized as it should be. The role of the leader is to establish the process and expectation to execute organizationally, whether or not you are in a meeting. All meetings should execute with the same parameters. Establishing this expectation aligns itself with the *Exponential Mindset* and *Leveling up*. You are defining and communicating expectations. Most organizations understand this process but too often lack the leadership discipline to enforce the need consistently. As I mentioned earlier, most disappointments come from failed expectations. Apply this truth to executing closed-loop communications for organizational success. Doing so is both urgent *and* important.

Another helpful process for meetings is only inviting those who can contribute to the outcome. Oversized meetings with attendees who are there to "listen in" without a contributing role is a waste of resources. In addition, meeting size balloons are out of proportion because the follow-up communications aren't prioritized, so listeners come to gain the implied knowledge they need for their success that should have been shared post-meeting.

Post-meeting discipline around communications increases your team's confidence that proper information sharing will occur and mitigates the need for added attendees. In addition, discipline around closed-loop communications will give your entire organization confidence to depend upon the follow-up and will self-select out of unnecessary meetings.

This insight was a lesson learned at Davisware.

When we reduce attendee lists, we noticed that individuals began to feel excluded and dismissed instead of feeling like we were assisting their productivity. Executing a successful closed-loop communication strategy starts with communicating what that means and how they each contribute. I knew what I was trying to achieve. However, I failed to share this thoroughly enough with the entire organization. This failure was unquestionably a lesson learned.

Beyond narrowing the audience, the next focus is meeting preparedness. Invitations should include a basic agenda and any expectation of any preparation needed. By consistently having all meeting invitations include both an agenda and an expectation on preparedness, you start to shift the mindset of meetings from one where you prepare and learn to the one you come ready to share information and deliver results. This shift changes the value of and the perception of the meeting. No one should walk in unprepared. As a result, meetings become shorter, and the value skyrockets.

Most companies struggle in timeboxing meetings, including Davisware. The value of a meeting dramatically improves when they start and finish on time. By reducing frequency, length, and attendees while enforcing closed-loop communications, we continue to improve. Our meetings are more productive and happen less often. There are fewer people in them, and we come more prepared and leave feeling more informed.

An essential part of timeboxing is prioritizing the agenda with the most critical items first. Just like in life, we like to start with the easy items - the low-hanging fruit. As a result, we never get to the most important things, or if we get to them, we rush through them because we have mentally moved on to our next meeting. Start with what's essential and leave the low-hanging fruit for when you are walking out the door!

Finally, assign a timekeeper for all meetings. This specific executable dramatically changed our meeting quality. The timekeeper is responsible (and has the authority) to divert the discussion back to the agenda and keep everyone focused, regardless of how critical new topics that arise may feel. Tactically, this timekeeper is responsible for ensuring that the discussion is wrapped up with enough time to summarize the results, create a plan of action, and assign responsibility for communicating results. An example of what this looks like is below:

0-5 minutes-settling, introductions

5-10 minutes-agenda setting/review previous comments

10-50 minutes-meeting topics

50-55 minutes-wrap up

55-60-minutes-review action items and communication loops

Although this feels very formal, our experience has demonstrated that this discipline creates success. When we don't, we struggle. It seems simple, but the discipline to execute can be complex.

When I calculated the headcount costs of our meetings, I quickly prioritized this process. When I began to see the results of highly functional meetings, I craved that result in all sessions. If you can take this process away from this book, you will contribute to my mission in writing this book.

This process is an evolution, just like every element of the *Exponential Mindset*. Executing *Exponentiality* in your business has more to do with continuous improvement than quick results. Both Davisware and I can be personal examples of this. We've significantly grown since we started this journey yet still work to improve by applying the Elements of the *Exponential Mindset* in all that we do.

Eliminating death by email via Closed Loop Communications

Death by excessive, unproductive meetings is only outdone by the productivity death by excessive emails. We've all contributed to or had our productivity killed by it. Hundreds of emails pile up in our inboxes. Often, we are included because there is one single thread of information relevant to us. However, the email is forwarded, and the REPLY ALL is used prolifically. Pretty soon, you have seen 100 emails that have little or nothing to do with you. Each one of those emails steals your most precious commodity-time and is a distraction from your mission.

Irrelevant communications do this to you as well as *Exponentially* within the entire organization. Creating internal communication procedures for written communication is even more critical than for meetings. Davisware teams are solving complex problems every day. This added complexity creates a perception that we need to include more people in the solution. For these reasons, micro-managing workflow on email has been core to *Exponentiality* at Davisware. This commitment was so important that we used our Monday Morning All Call to offer internal training on successfully executing these processes. We created written documentation, and we continually remind teams about the process and how to use it. Productivity improvement with email is low-hanging fruit. Our approach was to manage email communications precisely using the TO, CC, and BCC fields on an email. The BCC in most companies is to secretly include another person - a terrible practice. Instead, forward a SENT email whenever something like this is vital. We use BCC to move parties off an email string and closing the communication loop. This action will cause all future REPLY ALL actions to exclude those people. It is an excellent tool for simplifying and reducing email boxes across the organization.

For example, if I send an email out "TO" a dozen people with a question on pricing, none of those twelve people knows who is responsible because it is addressed to 12 people. So, this situation causes no one to be responsible.

Instead, if 12 people need to be in the conversation (versus knowing the result), carefully select the string members to be those who it is TO as ONLY those who require a response. The others who just need to know are on the CC. Omit anyone others who may only need to see the outcome until there is one. When I militantly executed this with my executive assistant and staff, my email traffic reduced by over 30%. After witnessing this, we documented and trained our organization to do the same. This approach allows us to apply the *Exponential Mindset* of always being *Process-Driven* to reduce death by email.

The process I referred to above was crucial to our organizational *Exponentiality*. We used our mandatory Monday Morning All Call to share the process and executed our *Process-Driven* Mindset. This process reduced overall email by nearly 20% while increasing efficiency and closing the loop communication. Imagine a world in your business where you eliminate 20% of the time spent on emails. The ROI on these savings alone would pay for you to buy this book for your entire organization (and maybe even your customers depending upon how prolific the problem is in your business)!

The tactical execution of this process is so important that I want to take the time to share one more iteration of an example of how this works. Welcome to a day in the life of Lisa, my executive assistant.

No matter how good your scheduling and organizational skills are, the complexity of ten kids, multiple businesses, and a jet-set lifestyle make my schedule challenging for the best (and Lisa is the best). However, by adding these processes, she became even more efficient and successful at what she did.

I frequently create an email request for a meeting. For our example, our request includes three Davisware team members and a customer. The email that I initiate the process with is written only to Lisa. However, I write the email so she can forward it to all parties (so they can scroll down and see the details of my request if necessary). My email will include whom I want to join (and if there are any optional parties), what the meeting is about (the agenda), the urgency, and any relevant meeting details.

Lisa receives my email and responds by addressing it in the TO field to all attendees and adding a salutation line. Then, all meeting attendees are addressed while she moves me to BCC (and acknowledges my exit on the string to the group). This practice keeps a concise line between the TO Field and an expected action.

When I sent the original email to Lisa with her name exclusively in the TO, I delegated the closed-loop communication to her. Rather than repeatedly copying everyone on the meeting as we work out the meeting details, she removes me from the transmission by moving me to BCC. Thus, we have prioritized the ownership of the closed-loop communication. I am confident that she will take on the responsibility of closing that loop by adding me back once the meeting is scheduled. A critical piece to this puzzle is that she calls out that she is (moving Jenn to BCC) when she addresses the others on the string. That way, everyone knows that I am exiting the conversation and that Lisa is covering the closed-loop. This process has successfully reduced emails while improving the close of the communication loop.

If I were to call out one of the most successful communication changes we made in the business, it was this. Not only did it reduce email traffic, but it also created clarity on responsibility for action. In the same way, when communication breakdowns happen (sadly, yes, they still occur), almost exclusively, we can see the cause. But unfortunately, our teams usually forget to execute the *Exponential Mindset* by focusing on Process and Leveling the organization up.

If you take a single action item away from this book, take this one. It will change your business *Exponentially.*

Creating strong feedback loops to become Exponential

The Element of an *Exponential Mindset* that highlights *Goal-Driven focus* requires that you focus on goals and have created a feedback loop to create your ability to Level Up. It requires a growth mindset, not a fixed mindset, and a successful feedback loop.

Feedback is essential, but it is also vital to recognize that not all feedback is good feedback. Although feedback is common, helpful feedback is hard to find. Therefore, it is crucial to create a personal and professional communication and feedback culture in your organization. With a structured and high-quality feedback loop, organizations Level Up. With a consistent culture of communication and feedback, your organization can become *Exponential.*

Both inside and outside feedback loops are essential. Often, small interactions have profound impacts upon you and your business. In my case, it was a good industry friend, customer, and business consultant, Rick White, former CEO of Tech-24. He had been a good customer for several years and was a strong user of our products. What started as a friendly problem-solving conversation soon became heated. Rick was looking for a thought partnership on an operational problem and called me to help him brainstorm. Little did Rick know that Davisware *actually* did have a solution for him. When I told him that the software, he already owned had the features he was looking for; he was livid. Rick had spent countless hours of his priceless time trying to solve his issue. Finally, he shared with me his very heated and frustrating perspective. He said in his most charming (and still utterly pissed off) southern accent, "*Jenn, we don't know what we don't know, so you have to tell us what we don't know because we don't know it.*" In keeping this book PG-13, I omitted the rest of the comments. My reaction was not ideal. I laughed, mainly because what he said sounded so redundant. My response got a response from him. He hung up on me.

Unfortunately, in our history, Davisware had a reputation for building fantastic technology that nobody knew about. Internally, we often referred to it as the **Basket Syndrome**, which is lighting candles and putting baskets over them, rendering the candle's value useless. Translated to this story, we loved to create new technology and not share the news outside our organization.

His comments were highly valuable. His company depended upon us to build great technology and communicate that it existed, and make sure he understood the value. Since that call, I have repeated this story a hundred times and referred to it many more. The truth is, what value is there in anything we do if those who benefit don't know about it? Little did Rick know his comments would get him published in this book. This point also proves a valuable lesson: you never know whom you will influence or when that influence will occur.

Our communication failures were not rooted in an intention to hold back exciting news. Instead, we lacked focus on systemic communication. Our feedback loop didn't formally exist, and we didn't systemically align it to help us communicate. An essential part of a thriving culture was successfully executing the Fundamental Elements of an *Exponential Mindset. Goal-Driven Focus* is rarely successful without systemic communications and feedback loop—both of these need to be *Process-Driven.* Helpful feedback loops in organizations solve many problems. Good feedback loops create *Solution-Focused Flexibility* (aka *Jenga*) opportunities. Without them, organizational growth is painful and slow. Davisware was better because of the profound wisdom I received that day from Rick.

Strong feedback loops are important channels for personal growth and growth for an organization. Unfortunately, most people don't know how to give or get feedback that matters. As a result, most organizations don't build a strong feedback loop. Getting feedback is common but making it helpful requires being a part of the culture and being systematic. Systemizing feedback into your culture assures you will find people within your organization who can consistently provide valuable feedback.

Doug Stone, the co-author of *Thanks for the Feedback*, notes that the value of feedback comes when the recipient of the feedback does something with it. Our focus usually is on how we give feedback, not how we receive it. In Doug's work, he notes that we create a growth-oriented mindset if our organization craves feedback vs. dreading it.[46] The culture chapter of this book emphasizes the systemic need for evaluation. An *Exponential Mindset* is successful when are driving toward CPI (Continuous Process Improvement). Strong feedback loops create outstanding process improvement.

The employee review process, also referred to in the culture chapter, is the most common area in businesses requiring improvement. The purpose of this well-intentioned process is to create feedback loops and a communication channel. A good review process should consistently be reiterating feedback that team members were already systemically hearing. The organizational goal is to close the gaps between the givers and the receivers of feedback and emphasize the receiver's improvement. This focus means we have to decern good feedback vs. irrelevant feedback and execute based upon the appropriate input. Referring again to *Thanks for the Feedback,* Doug shares the story of trying on a pair of pants in a store and then leaving the store, saying *none* of the clothing in the store fits. Just like trying on one pair of pants does not indicate the worthiness of all the clothes, so too, one piece of feedback doesn't reflect the value of all the input given.[46]

Shifting how we view feedback is essential. Our perspective is often looking at what is right in the feedback vs. what is wrong. All feedback is rarely correct. It is also safe to say that rarely is all feedback is incorrect. Learning to prevent knee-jerk reactions is vital. We can gain a tremendous amount of valuable input by listening to *all* feedback. We are eager to respond, not to absorb what we are hearing.

Unfortunately, valuable feedback is often sandwiched between what isn't, and we become defensive about the feedback that could be the most helpful. We then use the wrong or outdated feedback as our excuse for not hearing any of it.

With feedback, whatever you find yourself becoming the most defensive about is the feedback you need to listen to the most.

Asking clarifying questions separates the person who provides the feedback from the actual feedback. It's not about you or the giver. There is also a difference between getting feedback from a giver vs. getting feedback from a critic. Not all feedback is equal, and often people who lash out the hardest are hurting the most.

Throughout my career, I have always gotten most of the brunt of upset customers and team members. While most people would see this negatively, I saw this as an opportunity to grow and learn. Between all of the negativity that was often spewed at me, there was always wisdom. It was the sandwich. I had to pick out the pieces that were valuable and ignore the tomatoes, which I hate.

The job of a leader is to discern between the two.

Sometimes I came out of these conversations bruised. I learned, in most cases, there was some element of truth. By maintaining empathy for the giver (not easy), we got through the anger quicker and to what the honest and valuable feedback was. Our customers and our teams have always known my door was always open. I didn't look forward to these conversations, but I knew there was personal growth and a better organization on the other side of it. Discerning the difference between feedback and criticism is incredibly challenging. A healthy culture has systemically embedded, timely and helpful feedback. It took us many years to systematize these processes, but my open-door policy started the process by being open to the feedback to begin with.

If I was committed to *The Slingshot Effect* of continuous improvement, these conversations were necessary and valuable. Andy Stanley's famous quote, "Leaders who don't listen to others, will eventually be surrounded by people who have nothing to say."[47] From the start of our business, I knew we had a lot to learn.

We built our success upon the helpful feedback from our customers and teams. Unfortunately, your teams nor your customers sit where you sit. They do not see what you see or think how you think. Without the ability to systematically provide feedback, you will never gain the alignment between what you think you know and what you need to know.

Continuous Process Improvement through Feedback

Getting good feedback and translating that into systemic improvement in your operations requires that the feedback loop is also systematized. This step will help to discern the difference between criticism and feedback.

A critic feels vindicated, making it even more vital to discern the difference between the two. Although some criticism is correct, your job is not to convince the critic of your position. It's your job to lead your organization, fulfill your mission and uphold your values. So, while there may be truth in the criticism, we are not obligated to react to the critic.

Creating strong feedback loops in an organization requires feedback to be embedded from the mission statement and values, through the culture statements and employee review process, and by building a solid assessment and feedback process for customers and partners. The Davisware mission statement calls explicitly out and holds us accountable for creating strong customer relationships. From inception, we grew out of the industry we served, and our mission statement reflected it.

Our core values called us to be ardent team members and customer partners, both of which required feedback loops. The institutionalization of NPS (Net Promotor Score), CSAT (Customer Satisfaction Score), and eNPS (Employee Net Promoter Score) scoring systems gave us systemic data to reflect trends. Alongside this, the focus on being empathic problem solvers meant that whatever the problem was and whoever was trying to solve it, we were all willing to help. While sometimes this position created organizational confusion in roles and responsibilities, it contributed to a culture of feedback that allowed us to find success and continue to grow and improve.

When we get to the other side of feedback, we are better because of it. I cannot think of a single instance in which that has been true. Even the most unfair or untrue feedback or criticism has some element of truth or somewhere that I could improve in my reaction. If we change our mindset to think about what is right in what people share vs. what is wrong, we will value all those conversations.

Chapter Summary – Chapter 8: Harnessing the Power of Expectations and Communications

Lessons Learned

- Clear expectations and communications are essential for success in any business, but most impactful in entrepreneurial businesses where organizational charts are often fluid, with many people wearing many hats or in non-traditional roles.
- Setting expectations and communicating how to achieve them are two tools business leaders can use to influence reality and create desirable results.
- Crises like the pandemic make communicating difficult because of fear, uncertainty, and doubt (or the FUD Factor).
- When the FUD Factor is in play, people require crystal-clear expectations of what they need to do.
- Setting expectations starts and ends with your mission statement. Your mission statement says who you are, whom you serve, and how you do them.
- Make sure your mission statement has a presence in every aspect of your business.
- The real value of a mission statement is when it is tested in a crisis.
- Whether you are talking one on one, in a meeting, communicating by email or text, closing communication loops is a discipline that changes both individual success and organizations.
- There are two areas in business that cover 95% of the issues that cause communication issues - meetings and emails. You must develop systems and have the discipline to manage them to keep your communications on track.
- Customers may not remember how they treated us, but they will remember how we treated them.

- Start each meeting by allocating time at the onset of the meeting to define the purpose and what success would look like, including who is responsible for communicating that success.
- At the close of any meeting, everyone should know what action items they are responsible for and how those actions will be communicated back to others.
- Invite only those who can contribute to the outcome of meetings.
- Discipline around closed-loop communications will give your entire organization confidence to depend upon the follow-up and will self-select out of unnecessary meetings.
- An essential part of timeboxing is prioritizing the agenda with the most critical items first.
- A timekeeper is an important role in all meetings.
- Productivity improvement with email is low-hanging fruit.
- Feedback is common, helpful feedback is hard to find. Creating a culture of communication will improve the quality of the feedback.
- One piece of feedback doesn't reflect the value of all input given.
- Shifting how we view feedback is essential. Our perspective is often looking at what is right in the feedback vs. what is wrong in the feedback. All feedback is rarely correct. It is also safe to say that rarely is all feedback is incorrect.
- Asking clarifying questions separates the person who provides the feedback from the actual feedback.
- Utilize your mission statement to develop job descriptions, ensuring they are in alignment with one another.
- Articulating a mission statement defines who you are. Institutionalizing the mission statement communicates that definition. Operationalizing puts our mission statement into action.

- Communication failures are not typically rooted in an intention to hold back information. They result from a lack of focus on systemic communication.
- Creating strong feedback loops in an organization requires feedback to be embedded in the organization from the mission statement and values, through the culture statements and review process, to building a solid assessment and feedback process for customers and partners.

Unveiled Discoveries

- Personally, and professionally, failed expectations are the source of most disappointment. Think about this. Apply the things this week that have disappointed you the most. Was it a failure or a failed expectation?
- What we do and how we do it has permanently changed.
- It is important to recognize that not all feedback is good feedback.
- Discerning the difference between feedback and criticism is incredibly challenging.
- Tumultuous times are the times where there is greatest opportunity. Look at history for those to whom you deem successful. It is highly likely that they took time in the down turns to capitalize and create success.
- Painful transitions like the one we are just now emerging from are unanimously recognized as change agents that made businesses better and more efficient at what they do.
- By executing *Exponentiality*, I was able to reduce my email traffic by nearly 20%. How much could your productivity increase by doing the same or more?

Statistics to Ponder

- A recent Gallup survey revealed that almost 50% of workers did not know their job requirements.

- Meetings and emails create 95% of the communication is-sues in business.
- Research suggests that 50% of meeting attendees feel it's a waste of time.

Action Plan

- How were your communications and expectations challenged during the pandemic?
- What were your most valuable lessons learned?
- Does your mission statement say who you are, whom you serve, and how you do it?
- Is your mission statement unique as compared to your competitors? Does yours sound like there's?
- How can you improve the institutionalization of your Mission Statement?
- How can you improve how you have operationalized your mission statement into action?
- What actions can you implement to improve meetings and emails?
- Have you calculated the labor costs to hold meetings?
- What can you do to institutionalize NPS and eNPS surveys in your business?
- What can you do to reduce the perception that meetings are a waste of time in your organization?
- Inventory your employees, asking yourself honestly, how many of them know their full job description? Afterwards, start by creating a strong job description for those who know the least of what to do.
- How can you create you-centered communications so that your teams hear the message?

- What can you do to take charge of your calendar and solidify blocks of time to work on mission, communications, and position descriptions?
- What can you do to take advantage of the new opportunities that the blended world of personal and professional life brings to you and your teams?

Good Quotables

- *Confident teams are successful teams. Never ask your teams to play scared.*
- *We won't be paralyzed by where we are.*
- *If you don't know where you are going, any road will take you there! — Lewis Carroll*
- *The single biggest problem in communication is the illusion that it has taken place. —George Bernard Shaw*
- *The value of feedback comes when the recipient of the feedback does something. —Doug Stone, the co-author of Thanks for the Feedback*
- *Leaders who don't listen to others, will eventually be surrounded by people who have nothing to say. —Andy Stanley*
- *Your teams nor your customers sit where you sit. They do not see what you see or think how you think. —Craig Groschell*
- *We don't know what we don't know, so you have to tell us what we don't know because we don't know it. — Rick White*

Supplementary Learning Recommendations (Read/Listen/Watch)

- *Thanks for the Feedback: The Science and Art of Receiving Feedback Well* – Doug Stone
- *The 5 Love Languages: The Secret to Love that Lasts* – Gary Chapman
- *The 5 Languages of Appreciation in the Workplace: Empowering Organizations by Encouraging People* – Gary Chapman
- *Atomic Habits* – James Clear

CHAPTER 9

Communications Under Crisis

With the introduction of private equity into our business, we experienced an incredible injection of change. We began a total reorganization from business units to functional units. We had re-established a leadership team and a regular meeting cadence. The idea of a board of directors to report to was new to us and came with a certain level of trepidation. Dan had left the business as its technical leader and founding thought leader of Davisware. We had hired new staff, remodeled, and injected a new way of thinking into the business. I worked to change my thought process from *our* business to *the* business. We were still partners, but it was no longer wholly ours.

The changes were exciting but were still changes that created a new nervousness Davisware had never seen. These times were good times. They were nervous times. They were growing times for the organization and everyone in it. But none of that would prepare us for what was to come.

Eight short months later, we would learn what a global pandemic was and how it was about to rock our worlds.

We didn't know that the times leading up to March 2020 were uncertain. We were all about to get a rude awaking.

Joe Klawitter, a wise coworker, once told me that bad news doesn't get better with time. There is profound truth in that. We shy away from being the bearer of bad news, yet, with time, the impact of the information escalates. Bad news, in fact, gets worse.

In one of my favorite all-time YouTube videos, the Hollywood actor Will Smith shares his experience with sky diving is everything,[48] as I discovered it when I had just accepted the challenge from our son to go skydiving together. In this video, Will and his buddies agreed to go skydiving as a part of an evening out. The following day, when he was sober and far more aware of what he had committed to, he assumes that the decision was a drunken challenge, not one with any intent. Much to his dismay, his assumption was unfounded.

The group intended to follow through on the challenge. In typical Will Smith manner, his rendition of the experience is far more entertaining than I can cliff note. The night before the scheduled skydiving adventure, he has nightmares about the upcoming experience while questioning his sanity. Yet, that fear and questioning weren't enough to overcome the challenge his buddies put in front of him. He followed through on showing up and going through the training for the jump. He was fearful in the plane waiting to jump, wondering the value of jumping out of a perfectly good airplane. He was afraid on the count of 1 and then 2- and then they pushed him out. They do this to prevent you from grabbing onto the side of the plane on three. Because that would be our natural reaction to jumping out of an airplane, when he was freefalling above the earth, he was at maximum risk. At that moment, his fear should have been the highest. Instead, I can attest from personal experience that these moments are blissful. The moment of maximum risk did not correlate to maximum fear. The fear of anticipation was more potent than fear at the moment. There was nothing in his bed the night before to be fearful of, yet he was afraid in anticipation. He described the experience by saying that God put the best things in life on the other side of fear.

Similarly, and less dramatically, we do this with bad news. In a sense, we are creating bigger and worse news than if we shared it in a timely fashion. This is because our minds dwell on all the details instead of focusing on the reality of the moment.

I started drafting this book many years ago in my head. Little did I know, I would have a real-life opportunity to test the theories that I had so long held true in my leadership throughout 2020 and into 2021. Leading through the 2020 year was hard. Writing this book has been challenging. However, much of the content of this book became better and more refined through the global pandemic. Through the crisis, Davisware grew as an organization, and I grew as a leader. The pressure of the situation caused us all to be better. Crisis adds considerable complexity to every level of business communication. The pandemic forced us to make tough business decisions urgently and without data and the confidence that history brings. These decisions not only altered the course of our business but impacted the lives of every employee in a magnitude we had never experienced before. For context, in less than 21 days, the business altering decisions we made included:

- Wrote and executed a new and fully drafted WTH (Work from Home) plan with our US staff, transitioning to a fully remote US workforce
- Ceased all sales travel during our busy show season
- Converted all upcoming presentations (I was scheduled to be on stage 7 times in 6 weeks) to remote
- Executed a remote go-live plan for our customers who were actively launching a product
- Ceased all involuntary implementation travel
- Created mobile infrastructure in India (this team had no facilities, equipment, or internet to work from home before the global pandemic)
- Pre-emptively closed our India offices before a single global pandemic-related death in India, knowing how challenging working from home would be for many employees.
- Completed our first RIF (Reduction in Force) in the history of Davisware
- Executed a customer outreach by all staff, including accounting, implementation, sales, support, and leadership, to reiterate our mission and partnership with their organizations
- Established a reforecast budget with the support of our board of directors for what was an uncertain future
- Executed daily briefings with the leadership team for a feedback loop and communication path for daily updates on the unfolding crisis
- Did outreach to every employee to support and understand what unique challenges they may be facing in their work and at home

- Postponed the 2019 bonus payout planned to be paid out in March 2020
- Canceled all raises and 401K company matching
- Performed a 20% across-the-board wage reduction
- Several leadership team members executed a voluntary wage reduction of more than 20%, including some who deferred all wages, including myself.

To say there was a lot to communicate about in a short period is understated. This experience fortified my leadership in becoming confident and humble, as I was given many opportunities to practice. During our Monday Morning All Calls, I shared my struggles with kids, the internet, and uncertainty. I tried to be relatable to our teams, yet confident that we controlled everything we could control. There was plenty of bad news to be shared and waiting had no value. We shared what we knew, as we knew it. We made decisions strategically, preventing death by a thousand cuts. Best-selling author Chris Voss often speaks of using **tactical empathy** during his time as a lead hostage negotiator for the US government.[49] It is emotional intelligence on steroids and is critical in times of crisis. Crisis leadership requires that those who follow you know more information than ever, and with timeliness. They need relatability and empathy by calling out negative emotions.

Most studies agree that negative thoughts and emotions are more dominate in our brains than positive ones.[50] So, crisis leaders need to call them out to prevent our teams from creating their reality, which is generally more negative than actual reality.

In those early days, my willingness to share our organizational realities and my own personal struggles were foundational to our successful crisis management. It was true that I was terrified for my kids, worried about my mom, and trying to figure out how to live day to day. These were relatable messages to our team. It helped us all remind ourselves that we were not alone. We also talked about the negativity, doubt, uncertainty, and fear plaguing our teams. This process diminished the power of negative thoughts and started the path to solving the problem.

The urgent transition to online meetings and events

Before the pandemic, we had regularly scheduled leadership meetings, weekly standup meetings, and drop-in meetings. The pandemic caused us to convert those meetings to virtual ones. We increased the cadence and spent more time than ever on the resulting communications. Nothing could be left to chance.

Moving to online communications is far more complex than simply flipping on a camera. The challenges did not end at equipment and facilities. Outside of the technical transformation, the transition to online communications highlighted the need to recognize the basic rules of communication. We had to learn and use all four communication languages remotely. Words, body language, emotions, and appearance were critical, despite the backdrop.

Whether we had an interactive audience of one, a large-format meeting, or even a monologue without interaction, figuring out how to use all communication methods became more critical than ever.

Dr. Albert Mehrabian's 7-38-55 Rule of Communication teaches us that the words that we use only account for about 7% of the received message.[51] In virtual environments, we lose the non-verbal and body language communications if there were no conscious efforts to focus on the other communication mediums. I knew how important these mediums were from spending a career presenting on stage, but that wasn't true for the rest of the organization. Our world needed to learn how to be "on stage" for online meetings.

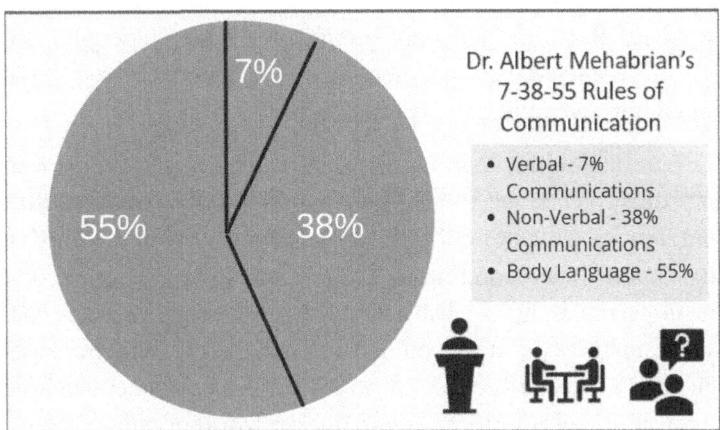

This reality meant we needed cameras on and great audio, but we also needed to consciously practice and use these tools. We spent time training employees on eye contact and positioning the audience picture close to our camera, giving the sense you are looking at them. Quick, decisive glances into the camera provide a sense for the audience of high engagement in a personal conversation. Pauses on stage often feel painfully long. On camera, they feel ten times worse. Yet, in both cases, they have tremendous engagement value.

Internally, we adopted some guidelines for the meetings to ensure engagement and transparency. Cameras were required to be on in sessions of three or more attendees and encouraged for all meetings. This guideline was a personal challenge that I hated as much as anyone. There is a stark difference between being on stage or at the podium compared to being on camera. I hated my face on camera and the continuous reminder of my age in the electronic mirror. Mostly, I hated that it stopped me from multitasking. Despite all my objections, years on stage reminded me that 55% of all communication happens via body language.[52] In times like these, we could not afford any miscommunication. Prioritizing communications in crisis is why we thrived through the pandemic. The cameras being on was our insurance policy. The value of making our meetings as transparent and accessible as possible meant cameras were a necessity, and I needed to signal the importance of quality communications.

Turning a camera on may not eliminate multitasking and distractions, but it did ensure everyone saw the body language we were communicating. The spectacular unexpected benefit is that we were all more focused. We reduced our company culture of meetings starting late and habitually running over. We were suddenly giving time back to people, and they were all more attentive in our meetings. It was an expected, rapid, and immediate improvement in our productivity.

The parallel journey to moving our internal meetings online was helping our professional associations figure out their online presence for shows and conferences. Much of our success was our ability to demonstrate our industry expertise and commitment to the industries we served on stage. Without in-person events, we had a new risk to our business. There had never been a time in history that we couldn't interact directly with our customers through shows and conferences. We built our mission statement around it. It became an urgent priority to figure out the world of online influence.

The transition to virtual events eliminated many social elements, so our online presence had to be on target.

The transition needed to include a shift to have the non-verbal and body language skills used on stage, starting with adjusting for the new audience. At conferences and trade shows, it was apparent who the audience was. They were physically gathered in front of me. Now, the audience was a fluctuating quantity of unknown participants. Publicly presenting requires engaging with the audience in front of you and that your message matches the audience. I knew that I was physically looking at a group of contracting business owners. It was easy to recognize what message to share and to adjust based on their real-time feedback.

Now, my audience was a camera with a flickering display of quantities and names of attendees, distracting me like a ticker tape. But, on a positive note, the pandemic allowed us many repetitions in a short period to figure out the most effective ways to execute online events and presentations.

This process allowed us to Level Up. Our new normal will include the flexibility of using both online and in-person meetings.

We will have the confidence to use both and have high-quality results. We are still writing history and lessons learned to see which changes become permanent improvements and what returns to business as usual over the next 12-18 months, but now we know both are possible.

A new process that formed focused on learning whom the event targeted and who was the registered audience. Historically, I knew based upon where I was and with whom I was looking. But, unfortunately, that luxury no longer existed.

What "hat" I put on as a presenter always matched the audience's perspective and the message I was delivering. Online, there wasn't body language and physical cues to tell me this information, so research and data became my eyes and ears on the audience. As a result, there was a high likelihood that attendees wouldn't stay engaged for the entire presentation. In addition, the distractions online are far more extensive and far less controllable than they are in a conference center. This condition meant that we needed to set expectations throughout the presentation repeatedly.

We changed our ask of the audience regarding engagement, time, and topic. It changed how we presented and delivered these messages. If our goal was to have each attendee engaged throughout the speech, we needed to create a more concise presentation for the conditions and members of the audience. As a result, our presentations became shorter, our topic matter became less, and our recap repeatedly happened throughout the presentation.

Online events changed many elements of the presentation. For example, we adopted many aspects of in-person meetings to online meetings. The most common example is the dress code. Online, it became even more critical than on stage.

We were now behind cameras and alone in our living rooms. We had to rewire our brains to see the camera as the audience and our living room as the stage.

There is considerable research on color-coding in presentations and the resulting message the audience takes away. According to the Institute of Color Research, people subconsciously judge a person, environment, or product within 90 seconds of initial viewing. Between 62% and 90% of that assessment is based on color alone.[53]

As with in-person meetings, I used the concept of mirroring in meetings directly with a specific customer or opportunity. Our teams would wear the company colors of the guest to whom I was presenting. This approach made us relatable and familiar and endorsed the message that I was delivering.

We would use black to be seen as an authority on a stage, for example, when I was presenting to CEOs or CIOs. However, I will choose blue if we want to be more relatable to the audience, such as when I presented to contracting staff or presented content to a group that felt hard to digest. For more casual atmospheres, a plaid or a small pattern will elicit that reaction.

Globally, some of these guidelines showed a notable fall-off when the world transitioned from in-person to online. College logos, baseball caps, and hoodies became approved attire. If our goal was to engage the audience and help them take away content (this ties back to our mission statement that anchored us as industry experts and partners to our customers), we needed to apply my knowledge universally.

Anything we did online required us to relate it to what we knew about human interaction and communication. We were always looking to share expertise in a relatable way. The audience needed to be confident that we were experts and were their partners. We had to relay that we understood their industry and where they were coming from. Without an event, our mission statement was at critical risk. These presentation elements were more important than ever.

Those early days of online meetings brought to light some of my behaviors. The virtual mirror that came our way in 2020 was harsh in its candor of our habits- especially mine! With Zooms, we were suddenly looking at ourselves all day! Early on, I was distracted by my wrinkles and a crooked smile. I also learned that my behaviors were distracting to the audience as well. I knew the onstage public speaking rules on how to use my body language to match the size of the crowd and how to talk with my hands, but little did I realize what I did when I wasn't on stage.

These revelations revealed all of the distracting movements I made that had been distracting others during in-person meetings for years. How often I smoothed my hair, touched my face, and adjusted my shirt became amusing side conversations. I never knew how often I got ice, but Derek, my coworker, sure did! Much of the communicational value that I gained during this time was to become aware of distracting behaviors that I had always had. When we were in person, there was less risk than online. However, once online, every detail mattered so much more than it did before simply because my ability to connect was so much more limited.

I made a point to eliminate these behaviors (although not totally, unfortunately!) while focusing on appropriately transforming body language. These elements focused on a concise transition to an online presence to take advantage of any physical presence possible, even remotely.

Years ago, I asked a client if he wanted to create a meeting or a moment? A meeting just relayed information that people soon forget. A moment ties information to a story or something with which the audience can relate. Obviously, if we are communicating, we want our audience to remember what we said. Therefore, our focus should always be on creating moments.

Creating moments online was as important as in person. On stage, I would often create moments in my stories through laughter and silence, often created while I was moving across the stage. Online, that opportunity does not exist, so we have to choose to make them consciously.

Laughter is one of the most powerful communication tools, so it was essential to find this online. Adding another person to your presentation (a virtual audience member or two) will give your audience the cue that it is the time to laugh or react. Even online, it is important to never speak over laughter. In the same way, it is important not to fill the silence. People often need moments to process what was said- even online. When the message is meaningful or reflective, the audience needs time to process. The use of silence emphasizes the importance of what you said (or will say).

When we are in a public forum or a large meeting, we interact and move, which helps us through these difficult transitions. When we are online, we have to create them ourselves. Since our audience online is often muted, eliminating our ability to laugh, having a commentator on the presentation can fill this void by creating banter, laughter, and commentary. We discovered this early on and started to develop panel presentations vs. a single presenter, even if the role of the other one or two people was just for feedback and reaction. They give cues to the audience as to how to react and to the presenter to leave the silence. We can't create safe silence online with movement as we do on stage. Therefore, just calling it out and asking for silence acknowledges that the point you just made was so important that you will give it a moment to resonate. Recognizing silence adds value, not awkwardness.

Finally, reflecting on my undergraduate studies in education, one of the most important things taught me during those years was the simple way we all learn. The best way to get a message across to others is to tell them what you are going to tell them (set the expectation). Tell them what you wanted them to know. Tell them what you told them. Then, give them a follow-up or a course of action (for students, this is homework) to reinforce the message or make it actionable.

For any audience to hear your message, you need to set the expectation by telling them what they will learn from the presentation. In an online environment, where engagement can wane, it is vital that 3-4 times during any talk, there is a reminder of what they will get from the presentation. You can also leave a visual on your slides where possible.

Once you have shared the message, use a clear transition to give them the lesson or lesson learned. Use closing statements like; to summarize, let me repeat myself, or one more time to make your transition. These cues tell listeners to take note and that you are almost done. These words increase audience engagement. Using word repetition is also a successful way to solidify the message.

Finally, providing your listener an action item, whether a follow-up, takeaways, or homework of some sort, creates value. This technique gives your audience the ability to take your words and put them into action.

These methods were important in live audience meetings but applying these methods to virtual meetings became how we differentiated the value of our presentations over the hundreds of other options that 2020 provided. Using these methods kept our attendance numbers high and our engagement focused. In addition, these methods supported our mission statement to remain industry experts and engaged with our customers.

I learned to apply much of what I had informally learned from being on stage for 30+ years. In addition, the pandemic helped me discover and execute systemic action in our organization.

Learning the value of the Water Cooler

As 2020 continued to unfold, keeping people focused on our priorities continued to become challenging. Lack of direct supervision and social interaction with their peers made our leadership team realize how much we had undervalued "water cooler" talk as an effective means of grounding the organization! As a result, we lost the validation of successfully relating our messages to our mission statement. Our challenge was to reinforce the connection systemically and purposefully every time I could.

As the presenter, the tie back to our mission statement and goals felt repetitive, even ad nauseam. In reality, we needed to maintain the path to our goals in the most direct way possible. It sounds cliché, but a clear vision and communications start at the top. Like dropping food coloring into the water, communications dissipate the further from the source the color extends. As it starts at the top, the color is very dark. It becomes more translucent as it filters its way towards the bottom. We tasked every leader to use every conversation and message to connect back to that mission statement.

More than ever, the use of technology would dictate how successful we were at keeping focused on our vision and mission. We had to be *TExponential*. Technology helped us share the message that we would stay true to our mission by controlling what we could control and that we were not going to recoil and wait for the storm to pass. As a result, we doubled down on our internal investment of time and money, using this time to create new communication systems and execute new tools. As a result, we improved communications during this crisis and applied them systemically for our ongoing success.

One of our early lessons learned was that we were not much different from our customers using technology despite being a technology company. For example, I read a statistic once that said the average power user of their cell phone uses about 8% of the embedded technology.

Imagine that! Davisware, like our customers, only scratches the surface using many of our tools. We had untapped efficiencies in technology we already owned.

We set out on a mission to change this. We began to execute online whiteboards, breakout rooms, lobbies, and screen sharing- all features within our existing tools. These newly discovered features improved our collaboration, invigorated our teams, and solved some social interaction issues. They stretched us to feeling closer to in-person than we had been feeling. We found new ways to collaborate in our organizational chart. We learned how to mute the noise in our business in ways we had never done before.

We began using our All Calls for knowledge sharing to solve the new problems we were mutually facing. In many ways, whether you were a new team member or a 30-year veteran, no matter what position you held in the organization, we were all mutually struggling with the same problems. These days became very rewarding in our collaborative efforts to solve mutual issues regardless of our titles. We were solving problems together.

We committed to expanding our use of tools to make collaboration better. In parallel, we addressed some of the challenges with distractions at home and the reliability of the technology. One of the outlying challenges that we had uncovered but had yet to solve was our team's need for the missing social interaction. This challenge took us longer to solve.

The more significant issue most of us faced was our new home dynamics. Unknowingly, I had been in training in the art of *Exponentiality* for 30+ years- perfecting what we now needed to do organizationally.

Unfortunately, until now, I never shared *Exponentiality* systemically with our teams. I used the ideas and strategies in this book personally but not fully shared professionally until now.

We were replacing our water cooler talk by embracing an *Exponential Life Balance by Design* in our approach to remote working. We learned to welcome our employees' personal life into our work environment. We celebrated getting to know employee's children, spouses, and pets. We embraced these elements as a part of our culture vs. something counter to it.

Our meeting cadences were adjusted so that people with families could get kids off the bus or start dinner and be present in both worlds. As a result, we became far more flexible when our days began and ended. Ironically, many of our teams worked far more hours and gained more joy. They could use sway to create balance. They were learning what I had learned a long time ago. If you can create a life in which your professional and personal pursuits are symbiotic instead of in competition, you create joy in *Living Exponentially*.

In many ways, going virtual expanded our ability to bond and extended the reach of our culture. It just took us some time to recognize it and get comfortable with sharing our personal lives in this way. While our team worked in their family room, their families became familiar with names, voices, and even faces that would have never been possible otherwise. Our work pursuits became relatable to our families, and our teams invested in our families. Indeed, the global pandemic became the case study for *Exponentiality* in Life and Business, Davisware style.

We learned to welcome flexibility and families into the virtual environment but still had our share of technology challenges. Internet bandwidth issues became common as entire families were fighting for bandwidth. We became experts at splitting our call with the audio and video, allowing us to quickly toggle between the computer and cell phone without disrupting the meeting.

No team member needed to be left behind. We elevated our organizational ability to communicate by investing in lighting, seating, and desk configurations. These were painful investments to make when looking exclusively at our budget, but these investments were mandatory in keeping our cultural commitment through exceptional communications. Before I had a board of directors and investors to answer to, Dan and I would decisively make these decisions for our people. In this case, I had to remind myself that my journey and responsibility had not changed, regardless of whether I answered different ownership. Our teams needed to feel our investment in them, irrespective of where they worked and who owned the business. Investing in people had made us successful so far. There was no reason to back down now.

The methods used for crisis communications were as critical as the messages themselves. Out of every crisis comes high-quality lessons learned- the global pandemic was no different. In-person and remote meetings have evolved to be far more effective and fiscally responsible. Our commitment to being *Process-Driven* helped us thrive in times of crisis and will continue to help us take advantage of our lessons learned and be more efficient both today and in the future.

Communicating certainty through uncertain Times

Despite the uncertainty and challenges, these days as a leader were some of the most rewarding days of my career. I have mentioned multiple times that the things in life we are most proud of are the hardest. Difficult situations are the ones that challenge us to grow and allow others to succeed. Our teams and customers faced situations that they had no history to look to, no consultants to show them how, and frankly, a world filled with fear and doubt at unseen levels.

Reminding myself that fear is the thief of joy, my priority was calming fears. I took my role seriously to allow our teams and our customers to find joy. Like an athlete who gets hurt when s/he is scared, business owners and teams cannot succeed when they are afraid. People and businesses who play scared get hurt. They get hurt in their career growth, socially, emotionally, spiritually, and financially. Leadership in these times requires that leaders support and give them confidence about the future. They were looking for honesty and relatability. They were looking to see if they had strong leadership.

The workdays in March, April, and May were endless. Still, the opportunities were a luxury (yes, I said luxury) that many leaders never get to experience. Our leadership team was unstoppable. They started as good leaders and grew out of these times, *Exponentially* alongside me to be great.

The elements of the *Exponential Mindset* became foundational to everything I was doing as a leader during these times. We focused on controlling what they could control and how that related to our corporate mission. Therefore, my messages can be outlined in the framework of the Elements of an *Exponential Mindset*.

Expect the possibility/probability of Defined Success

Davisware was going to succeed. We altered our definition of defined success as we embarked on the new version of normal, but we would succeed. Our organization had to believe this, and I had to keep the teams focused on that reality. We reminded ourselves that the person who believes they can succeed and the person who believes they cannot are both right. Our organization needed to depend on every member to create positive momentum toward our newly *Defined Success*.

Leveling Up.

Every person in the organization needed to level up. We had no other options. Some people exited the organization, and others took on new responsibilities doing things they had never done before. We had many uncharted territories to cover, and without exception, every person needed to Level Up.

Goal-Driven Focus.

Never in the company's history was it more important to focus on our goals and organizational mission. Every message needed to tie back to our mission and values, no matter how repetitive it felt.

Solution-Focused Flexibility (Jenga).

We were playing the world's biggest game of *Jenga*. All the pieces to our puzzle were in a new order, with pressure in places we never saw coming. Rather than focusing on what could have or should have, we focused on being flexible and creative about succeeding. We needed to look *every-where; there* was a solution, tapping on every virtual block to see which one moved and helped us achieve our goal- even the ones on the bottom.

Protagonist Power. Expect Conflict. Confront Conflict. Get Comfortable in Chaos. Expect Solutions.

Nevermore than now did we need to figure out a way to be comfortable in conflict. The world was full of more conflict than solutions. We needed the confidence to see through the chaos that came with it, just like our favorite protagonists.

The Slingshot Effect.

Life is full of slingshots. We had to see that the global pandemic was that and only that. It was not a failure. It was not something to be feared. On the contrary, it was an opportunity to re-assess, reorganize, and get ready for the future state of our business that would be better and more successful than ever.

Process-Driven. Always Drive Toward Process.

We needed to avoid the frantic thoughts that tempted everyone and focus on new processes and ways to improve our business. By creating processes, we were preparing for the next crisis. It was our roadmap of what to do.

Some new facts that became evident centered around new problems that we had never experienced. Although I had always cared about my people and their personal lives, their personal lives were MY problem for the first time in the business's history! For instance, our India teams had wi-fi and power issues unrecognizable to our US team. Many did not have high-speed internet or reliable power, and now, this was our problem.

The Indian teams' homes are substantially smaller and multi-generational. Helping them come up with workable solutions was now ours to solve. Our employees stateside had fewer foundational struggles, which didn't make them less because others were suffering more. They had to figure out childcare, remote learning, and other daily living arrangements. Those problems were not Davisware problems before. Now, with *Exponential Life Balance*, they became our problems. Communicating my empathy for their situations and helping each of them set their Possibility Mindset was critical to our success. Everyone needed an *Exponential Mindset*!

Of all of the fundamentals of *Exponentiality*, creating a Possibility Mindset was the most essential to initial success during the global pandemic. However, staying in that mindset was another challenge.

This objective was exceedingly tricky when there was bad news to share (as we covered, there was much bad news to share). Continuing to deliver messages with truth and transparency was critical. Bad news leads to the question of the "whys" and the "what's next." When sharing the difficult decisions around reduced staffing, our teams feel confident that it wouldn't be "death by 1000 cuts". This confidence would allow them to remain in a Possibility Mindset.

They needed the confidence to see that the decisions were strategic, not a personal reflection of skills or people. We needed to create confidence in them that we valued our newly smaller team and were our primary focus. Finally, they gained the confidence to stay in the Possibility Mindset by knowing we were all in this together.

To keep our teams focused on the Possibility Mindset, I needed to focus on mine. Never in my career was it more important not to play scared. Our teams, who were new to the *Exponential Mindset*, needed to learn how to do it from me.

During these days, I related my leadership to my passion for teaching skiing to others. I am not sure how many people I have taught to ski, but it's a lot. All of our kids were toddlers when I put them on skis for the very first time. They could all tell you that I repeated to them a single phrase ten thousand times.

"Look where you want to go, not where you don't." If you don't want to hit that tree or that rock, don't focus on it. Look where you want to head. In the global pandemic, we needed to look where we wanted to go, focus on what we could control, and translate that into successfully fulfilling our mission statement. All of our kids are skiers because they learned to look where they wanted to go! Davisware learned to do the same and thrive in the global pandemic.

Creative problem solving is a trait that Davisware always valued in our hiring process. During the global pandemic, this skillset paid off for Davisware. However, in our corporate *Jenga* game, we had to create a new means of success we could control.

Generating new revenue from sales had been thwarted. However, we did have an untapped source of revenue in our massive backlog of product implementation. Repeated failures in product launches generated a backlog that had been the bane of our existence for many years. Fortunately for us, they became one of the strategies that saved our revenue and our organization. Unfortunately, when I proposed this idea to our new private equity partners, they didn't respond with the confidence waves I had hoped. Our private equity firm told me much later that executables like this one have never been successful. Our leadership team, however, saw it another way. The combination of this being one of our only options and the fact that I was confident in our creative group of problem solvers to figure it out, we set out to *Level Up. Triumphing and Expecting Success* as our only options, given our team the resolve to see it through.

When customers want to change software, they struggle to commit or, once they commit, why they struggle to go live because of the level of effort it takes on their side to implement it. All of the people critical to the project's success are also critical to the day-to-day business. It makes it very hard to prioritize important over urgent!

The pandemic changed all of that.

For the first time in our customer's history, clients had time. Our backlog customers had already financially invested, so there wasn't the fear of investment of money. With focused efforts and the right resources dedicated to the product, I had confidence that our teams could stabilize our product and clear our backlog to generate the revenue we needed to execute. We had two hurdles to overcome if this play was going to be successful. First, we needed to stabilize the product that had been more than seven years in the making. Second, we needed to convince our customers that a global pandemic was the perfect time to execute a new software implementation. Both seemed unrealistic in hindsight. But, at the time, my Possibility Mindset spread through Davisware like that food coloring in water, and we just decided to succeed. The only thing we needed to figure out was that minor detail of "how."

As I looked around our organization, between existing responsibilities and the skillset of an uber problem-solver, there were a couple of faces that came to mind. Our CIO, Mark, had no product development or software engineering background. We often described him as the least qualified, the best guy for the job. I had confidence in him because I had witnessed nearly 50 years of his problem solving as my older brother, not to mention his decades of problem-solving at Davisware. He has found solutions to computer issues, automotive repairs, hopelessly broken household appliance, home fix it projects and even our daughter's Polly Pocket dress repairs. I have never seen a problem that Mark Friederick couldn't solve. Being "qualified" was irrelevant.

With Dan having stepped out of the day-to-day, our new CTO, Ram, somehow found it in himself to find trust in my confidence in Mark. Together we assembled a team of exceptional problem-solvers, including the newest member of our product team, Rick who moved from the sales team just 3 months earlier. None of them were "qualified" for what we were about to ask of them. They weren't classically trained in product development, much less doing so under duress. Ram was brand-new to the organization, without a depth of product knowledge that we could have used. Yet, at this point, problem-solving skills trumped all other needs. Trust and teamwork would prevail. This team's ability to solve problems would overcome anything that did not add up on paper. We partnered Mark and Rick with our newly promoted engineering lead, Madhuri and set out on a rapid journey to stabilize and launch this product. Just like in the movie Apollo 13, failure was not an option. Our entire customer base was depending upon us, including some of the most prominent in the mechanical contracting industry. This "unqualified" group would see to it that we would succeed. I knew it.

Over the next 82 days, this team redefined what success on that product looked like. Through my personal relationship with our customers, I began our Fall on the Sword Campaign, acknowledging our grave problem and cataloging a means to success. Through personal phone calls (and one impromptu family dinner I invited myself too), they heard how fiercely I protected our relationship, where failure wasn't an option. Regardless of the effort or time we needed to invest, our reputation was shaken and the hell if I would stand by and let it be broken. The Davisware family deserved better.

With the help of many others in the organization and relying upon our newly organized implementation team, we began to execute. Again, I set remarkably grand expectations for these teams. Like the global pandemic, we needed real-time solutions while facing mountains of uncertainty and challenges we had never seen before. This part of the business thrived during the pandemic because we all focused on what we could control, executed an *Exponential Mindset*. We delivered against all odds.

Proliferating communication through your organization from the Top-Down

The challenges of the pandemic included all of what we were dealing with in real-time. However, the more significant challenge was that my vision could not end with what we were currently experiencing. Our current lessons learned are needed to achieve our future culture. There was no value in succeeding through the global pandemic in the *Exponential Mindset* if our outcome didn't make Davisware became a better organization.

We continued to measure our success in our focus on our mission statement and our future results. I needed our leadership team alongside me, proliferating what we were learning and the *Exponential Mindset* throughout the organization.

When an organization goes through adversity like these times, our priorities shift. Our days became filled with more urgent responses to real-time problems than we had ever experienced. As a result, it became more critical than ever to delegate responsibility and leadership through the organization by creating ownership. Our leadership team defined the *WHAT* (people will always work for this) and the *WHY* (inspires people to dedicate themselves to a cause). The most challenging part was delegating was allowing our broader teams to choose the *HOW* (to motivate ownership).

Our broader organization needed to own our vision. It had to come by allowing them to select the *HOW*. As a leader, allowing someone to choose a different *HOW* than we would choose is the most challenging test. Delegate without abdicating is an ongoing leadership struggle. Leaders need to stay engaged to manage the *WHAT* and the *WHY* and leave the *HOW* to the person who owns it.

During this crisis, it was a gift that none of us had the time to micro-manage the *HOW* we were delegating, no matter how much we wanted to. It was also a gift that we had so much to talk about. As a result, we prioritized meetings, keeping us engaged in the *WHAT* and the *WHY*. Allowing our teams to own the *HOW* enabled them also to embrace the overall vision. This gift was one of the keys to our successful execution of bringing this product to market and using the backlog to save our P&L.

I compare this whole experience to the childhood game of "telephone" I mentioned earlier. We often sat in circles in kindergarten (back when six feet apart wasn't the standard and whispering in someone's ear was still socially acceptable). We would whisper the teacher's message from one student to another. It was a rarity that the original message resembled the original message.

Thinking back to that game, imagine the results if the teacher gave a general overview of the *WHAT* and the *WHY* of the message to the whole class before the game started. If the message were simply transferring the *HOW*, undoubtedly, the results would have been significantly different.

Similarly, if the mission statement and values in the *WHAT* and the *WHY*, the participants in our internal games of telephone (aka daily operations) would execute a *HOW* that gets our targeted results. This process empowers our teams to think like leaders and empowers them to align with their leaders. This alignment empowers team members to become leaders. When we teach people to work, they just work. When we teach people to do, they just do. When we teach people to own, they take ownership.

Eliminating micromanagement was profoundly impactful in the professional growth of our organization. This approach didn't mean that we were giving away leadership. It meant we were sharing leadership and creating leaders from every seat in the organization. There were many times in this evolution of our business that we were questioned within the organization. It didn't always go smoothly, and our results weren't instantaneous. We worked hard to keep our skepticism in check and to keep criticism constructive. We worked hard to stay rooted in our *Exponential Mindset*.

Outside of the leadership team, critics could be very loud. Therefore, our success had to be louder. I spent countless hours during these times listening to some of my favorite podcasts to underscore my focus and direction. One of those podcasts (remaining unnamed because I cannot remember which one) reminded me, "do not allow compliments in my head or criticism in my heart." Our success needed to be loud. The best way to silence critics is to outperform and outlast them. That precisely is what we did.

Our success was rooted in our focus on successful communication. We had an advantage during the pandemic that I knew we would lose post-pandemic. When people are in a heightened state of emotion, they are moved to action.

Our teams knew that their lives and livelihoods were on the line if we were not successful. Each rower on my team knew we depended upon them. It wasn't anecdotal; it was real. Performance was high, and results were outstanding.

In the post-pandemic area, converting to a less emotional environment that still created the same results meant focusing on what we wanted people to know and feel. What we wanted them to know, and feel would contribute to what we wanted them to do. Emotions move people to desired outcomes. Post-pandemic, we continue to find new ways to engage our teams through the lessons we learned.

As we closed out the pandemic phase of our business, the next big transition was looming. My days as CEO would be ending, and the era of the Davis' leading the organization would be drawing to a close. After nearly 32 years of first Dan and then me, we would be putting a new leader in the driver's seat.

In many ways, this transition may have been one of the most difficult in the history of the business had it not been for the global pandemic. As a result of this crisis, our organization had solidified our communication methods. As a result, we now had a history of surviving uncertainty and challenging times, giving our teams confidence; as we turned the page on this new chapter, they have seen uncertainty before.

In this transition, I had to lead with a deep and grounded confidence, despite my emotions. Our teams needed to see my vision of growth while managing the delicate balance of being real. This transition would be the 3rd of the trifecta of demanding changes in a short time. Dan, our long-time leader, left his full-time role in the business. Davisware survived the global pandemic, and now for the first time in Davisware's history, it would be led by someone without the last name of Davis. Relying upon all that we built during the global pandemic made this transition far better. Although it was not without bumps, the change was well-planned, our organization was well prepared, and we were ready. I led our teams to the desired outcome by using all we had built.

Bottoms up communications – managing up

Like most entrepreneurs, Dan and I did not have bosses for 30+ years. Other than our commitments to each other (and the conflict created by that dynamic), we had the luxury of never reporting to someone other than our customers and teams. That all changed in 2019 when we took on our investment partners.

Those first days were exhilarating. I felt like I was drinking from a fire hose. I am a curious and perpetual learner and suddenly had so many opportunities to learn. It was easy to see from our new partner's previous successes a roadmap to our success.

During these first nine months, I took in and learned all that I needed to professionalize and grow our business. Then, in March of 2020, that all changed when I began to understand what it means to manage up for the very first time.

I gained a new and vivid appreciation for every employee who had the courage throughout the years to step into our offices and provide feedback. While we felt our doors were always open, I now understood how it felt to find the courage to step through the door. Early in the pandemic, it felt like I was suddenly watching an instant replay of every employee who found the courage over the last 30 years to share their perspective. I had to learn, in a flash, how to manage up.

As the long days of March continued, everyone on the planet, including our investors felt increasingly anxious. I had empathy our investment partners and how helpless they must have felt with the lack of depth of knowledge about the company that we had. We had more than 30 years of history to look back on. They were not directly engaged in our business day-to-day. I could empathize with their emotions, imagining how it must have felt to watch the recession-proof, rock-solid business they had just invested face tremendous uncertainty in unparalleled ways. I would not have wanted to be in their seats, being able to control very little directly.

In addition to our business, they had an entire portfolio of "recession-proof" companies that they had to watch facing the worsening global outlook. These days gave too much credit to the word "unprecedented." I was reporting to them, and they were reporting to the investment committees who had trusted their leadership and decision-making to invest in great companies.

The pandemic proved that even great businesses could fail, despite the best due diligence. Davisware was in the midst of a perfect investment storm. They had made a significant investment early in that cycle and strongly anticipated a rapid growth trajectory this year. Unfortunately, those expectations were quickly changing.

The timing was not on anyone's side, nor was uncertainty and its incompatibility with private equity.

Our PE firm partners had made very calculated investments founded on data. Now they found themselves thrust into a new situation where they had no data, and any data they had was becoming more irrelevant by the day.

Davisware was not immune to the growing sense of panic in the world.

They asked us for data and forecasts on what felt like a daily basis and about a situation that was so fluid, we had no good data to provide. It felt like being asked how bad the damage of an earthquake would be when the earth was still quaking. They wanted certainty, and we could not give them what they wanted.

What this time taught me about that relationship was the value each of us played. The outside perspective from our investment partners gave us places to look for grenades, and our collective 1000+ years of experience operating and managing this business allowed us to react in the best way possible.

Being new to the relationship, they did not have a comfort level with what needed to happen. Likewise, being new to the relationship, I did not initially recognize the importance of leading up. So, over those first few weeks, working around the clock meant spending hundreds of hours working in the business and, often, equally reporting up.

What I was not doing was leading up.

After weeks of endless phone calls and emails asking for more data, more meetings, more reporting, and more certainty (that I couldn't give), I found the courage to lead up.

I needed my efforts to be focused on the business, not on reporting about it. We needed to stay committed to the metrics we had built but could not afford the added layers of reporting and meetings.

Our adjusted mission was to help our customers save their businesses, thus saving ours. Unfortunately, in these early days, I allowed too much of my time and our leadership team's time to be consumed by creating reporting instead of leading up. I was allowing sway in my balance that was not healthy for anyone. The leadership team needed me to row alongside them in the same way they rowed alongside their teams. One of my personal Achilles Heals is that I often trust my expertise and experience last.

I came to realize I had to trust myself first. Our teams were counting on me to do so. I knew what we needed to do. We had been through many crises during my 30+ years in this business and this industry. While the uncertainty was different this time than any other time, the challenges were the same. I knew this business, this industry, our customers, and our teams better than anyone. I could not help but think about an excerpt of one of my all-time favorite philosophers, Dr. Suess, and his profound book, *Oh the Places You'll Go. "You have brains in your head. You have feet in your shoes. You can steer yourself in any direction you choose. You're on your own. And you know what you know. And YOU are the guy who'll decide where to go."*[54]

Our PE firm did not have the depth of knowledge about our business, but I did. In one of my less proud moments in my professionalism, I shared my perspective. I shared my viewpoint with our investment team in a world where I was probably more real than right. After one of our many collective CEO calls giving their updated perspective (from what felt like four hours earlier), I reached back out.

While the context of my message was accurate, my delivery was not as professional as it should have been. Our team needed me in the business, not spending more time reporting up. There was not enough data in the world to find the contentment and certainty they wanted. I shared that "it felt as though we were all acting like a bunch of 4th-grade girls who had just seen a spider." I was an operator and knew this business well, just like many of the other CEOs. We were the most expert people at managing crises at the table. We knew what to do. Our jobs were to execute, and our PE firm's job was to support us. We all needed to pause and realign to what we needed to do.

Despite my delivery, our PE firm partners were the same stewards to our business as they had been from the beginning. Once I had the confidence to lead up, we all reset expectations and plans for reporting, meeting, and cadences. All that it took was leading up for us to create a much better path forward.

Never in the history of my work at Davisware was it lonelier at the top than these days. Never in the organization's history did I feel more needed or engaged in the mission I was setting out to do. Never in the history of Davisware did I feel more confident in the leadership team that we had assembled. We did not have butts in every seat, but I knew I had battle generals with whom I could go to war. There may have been better resumes that could have filled those seats, but I would choose that team again because they had helped us build this business. They knew what hard felt like, and they knew how to create success, regardless of what we asked of them. This team and these days were gifts.

That night, I reflected upon the events of the past few weeks and what had contributed to the day's conversation. I knew if I felt this way, it was highly likely that my newly befriended portfolio CEOs did too. I was a business founder. I knew every skeleton in the business and every customer. Many of them did not have that luxury. I needed to "lead up" to our private equity partner *and* the other CEOs. I was a freshman portfolio CEO, but I had to do the same if I asked my teams to Level Up and lead up.

I took some precious time, took the risk, and shared my perspective with this amazing CEO group.

CEO Team,

My name is Jennifer Davis, co-founder and CEO of Davisware. I am writing to follow through on my commitment to thinking about how I can help other leaders in these incredibly tumultuous times. Since I was 17 years old, this is all I have ever done. In July 2019, we turned a new chapter in our story, and we became a part of the chapter with our new private equity partners. These days have been incredibly trying for all of us as we try to lead, navigate, consume knowledge, apply knowledge, report, digest, etc., etc., etc. I am positive that each one of us has spent exceedingly long days trying to find our path forward. For this reason, I wanted to put an email in your InBox that had no action item, nothing to follow up on, and that is a minor distraction from the rest of what is coming at you. It's about Perspective.

For Davisware, yesterday was named "Black Tuesday." For the first time in Davisware history, we had organizational level furloughs and RIFs. It was a day that our leadership team was required to figure out how to balance the organizational needs and come to tough decisions. On the same day, our first employee was diagnosed with COVID-19. God sure does have a way of upping the ante on the test of fortitude. This is a business that I spent the first (and only) 31 years of my professional life building alongside my husband. We have weathered many storms in those years, given birth to seven children, adopted three others. We've bought, and sold dozens of properties, stared bankruptcy in the face, buried our dads and his mom, and watched our fortunes ebb and flow. We failed at hiring and firing. We failed at outsourcing and selling. We failed at product deployment and customer partnerships. We have failed a lot. Those failures led us to success, sometimes via a very long and winding road. We created a team of employees who would stop traffic for us as we would for them because, at the end of the day, it was more important to have passion for what we did. It was that passion that translated into tangible results because passion always wins. Those results allowed us to be the "head-scratcher" 31-year start-up founded by teenagers. That passion, our failures, and our success are what have allowed Dan and I to live the textbook American dream.

I tell you all of this because I have learned that the world is driven by those with the right ***perspective****. Games are won, and teams are built by those who have the right* ***perspective****. There are far more talented companies with better products and services, but without proper* ***perspective****, none of that matters. As leaders, our* ***perspective*** *is the only thing we really can control. My* ***perspective*** *is that nothing worth having is easy. This chapter is unnamed in our book, but it is one we will look back on with a memory that we worked our asses off, made our best decisions (and hopefully the right ones), and we allowed these businesses to turn the page to the next chapter. My* ***perspective*** *is that these bad days are ones that many people in the world would kill for and trade for their best days. My* ***perspective*** *is that as a farm girl from Potosi, Wisconsin, from a high school graduating class of 48, I have done, seen, and achieved more than* *probably my entire class collectively, so I need to shut up and be grateful. My* ***perspective*** *is that if the worst thing we have to do is to sit in our perfectly conditioned and safe homes and ride out this storm, it is better than 99.99% of every storm every person in history has lived through. My* ***perspective*** *is that as the 6th of 9 kids, I was numerically irrelevant from the day I arrived, and that gave me the fortitude to build whatever I needed myself. My* ***perspective*** *is that we will all thrive out of this pandemic, not because it was easy, but because it was not. We will all be better at using technology to connect effectively and will find new ways of doing things with new people in new places that would have never happened if we had not been forced to. My* ***perspective*** *is that for the first time in my adult life, I have no calendar to tell me where I physically need to be, bookended by endless commitments that take me on the rat race of life every night. My* ***perspective*** *is that these family moments and stolen quiet moments are priceless gifts. My* ***perspective*** *is that we focus on the tragedy out of this pandemic, while there are so many gifts. Our world is forever changed. The new normal is yet to be defined. We can take our* ***perspective*** *and make it a reality. After all, this is what we've trained for. How many business leaders get to do that? Let's all go do that.*

#BExponential #Perspective #TeamDavisware #AllRockstars #NoBenchwarmers #StartRowing

Jennifer Davis

Co-Founder & CEO- Davisware

Portfolio CEO Freshman Class 2019

Finding the courage to send this letter was a defining moment in my career. Sadly, the world had always trusted Jennifer Davis far more than Jennifer Davis had trusted Jennifer Davis. My leadership throughout the global pandemic helped me learn what others saw inside of me. I was *Leveling Up* too.

It was on this same day; I committed to authoring this book. Everything I had was what the business needed. But, on top of that, it required a bit more.

The responses from this email were overwhelming. They were some of the most touching and meaningful feedback I had ever gotten. The gratitude was overwhelming. The sense of relief that they were not alone was profound. The strength I shared allowed others to find their strength and vice versa. I learned that the astute investors who had invested in our business also learned something from the freshman class of 2019. I found value in my perspective simply by sharing it. As a result, the tone of the communications changed between us.

The collaborative forums that were created gave everyone a forum to be vulnerable and safe. We could ask tactical questions about employee expenses, technology, and WFH transition plans (as well as WTF, if we are honest). We could ask anything we were struggling with operationally. We could ask strategic questions about borrowing money and safely brainstorm through scary "what if" scenarios. It was a place to find answers and sometimes to help you realize there were no answers to be found, and that's OK too.

This situation taught me the valuable lesson I had taught for many years but failed to learn myself. Leading Up is the most challenging form of leadership there is, but its value is priceless.

These CEOs became more *Exponential* because we learned so many of the fundamental principles of the *Exponential Mindset*. For example, we knew to Expect Conflict from the next wave of crisis the pandemic would bring us.

We learned to approach this new chapter in our stories with *Solution-Focused Flexibility*, understanding that just because our investors had helped us write a playbook, it didn't mean we had the luxury of following it.

We realized that although we felt we were at the top of our games, we had to Level Up, just as we asked our teams to do.

It meant that no matter how stormy the waters were, we had to be *Process-Driven* in creating and implementing our survival methods.

We had to accept the realization that where we were was absolutely at *The Slingshot Effect*. Our calculated pullbacks meant that our opportunity for forward success was great if we remained focused on our mission.

Most importantly, we were reminded that we are CEOs. We had to continue to *Triumph and Expect the Probability of our Defined Success*.

The decisions we made as a group made our companies stronger and our group more effective and resilient.

While I have always known that I wanted to write a book, I can confidently say that this wasn't the platform or the topic I would have chosen. Instead, I accepted the leadership challenge in front of me, and I used it to Level Up and *#BExponential.*

Chapter Summary – Chapter 9: Communications Under Crisis

Lesson Learned

- Crisis adds considerable complexity to every level of business communication.
- Moving meetings and group communications online required us to develop new presentation skills and our technical capabilities.
- The transition to virtual events eliminated many social elements, so our online presence had to be on target.
- We had to learn to use all four communication languages remotely. Words, body language, emotions, and appearance are all critical to engagement
- Quick, decisive glances into the camera give a sense to the audience of high engagement in a personal conversation.
- Online meetings meant the potential for fluctuating audiences and unknown engagement.
- Color matters. Choose the colors you wear based upon the hat you are wearing. Where black to feel authoritative. Blue is a relatable color, while plaid or patterns create a more casual atmosphere.
- Color mirroring of your audience is useful if you are trying to demonstrate being united with the audience or in presenting partnerships.
- Laughter is one of the most powerful tools of communication, so it was important to find this online.

- There was no value in succeeding through the pandemic without becoming a better organization as the outcome. Therefore, our leadership team had to proliferate what we were learning throughout the organization.
- Education 101 says that for people to learn you need to tell them what you are going to tell them. Tell them what you want them to learn and then tell them what they learned. Finally, it needs to be followed up by homework (recommendations to take action).
- The gift of delegating the HOW in a crisis is that we didn't have time to micromanage the HOW we wanted to do. Allowing our teams to own the HOW enabled them also to own the overall vision.
- Leading up is the most challenging form of leadership there is, but its value is priceless.
- The water cooler allows your mission statement to proliferate your organization.
- Use technology to stay true to your mission and proliferate the information throughout your organization.
- In times of crisis, every communication needs to tie back to the company's mission statement.
- Leading Up is the most challenging form of leadership there is, but its value is priceless.

Unveiled Discoveries

- Leading through a crisis is a gift to leaders. What did you learn in these times and how has it made you a better leader?

Statistics to Ponder

- Negative emotions are three to nine times more common in our brains than positive ones, so crisis leaders need to call them out to prevent our teams from creating their own reality, which is generally more negative than actual reality.

- Dr. Albert Mehrabian's 7-38-55 Rule of Communication teaches us that the words that we use only account for about 7% of the received message.
- 55% of all communication happens via body language, making the transition to on-line meetings more challenging than ever.
- According to the Institute of Color Research, people subconsciously judge a person, environment, or product within 90 seconds of initial viewing. Between 62% and 90% of that assessment is based on color alone—source: CCICOLOR - Institute for Color Research.
- The average power user of a cell phone uses about 8% of the embedded technology. Imagine what you could do if you expanded your use of that technology?

Action Plan

- How can you leverage the lessons learned you experienced during the pandemic to make you and your organization more effective?
- How can you improve the quality and effectiveness of feedback in your organization?
- How are you building laughter into your communications?
- Where can you get the feedback, you need to become a better leader?
- What are the most significant opportunities for you to manage up? How can you limit or eliminate the obstacles?
- Create owners of each technology tool in your business and help coach them on how to expand the use of the tool in your business.
- How are you empowering your teams to Lead Up?

Good Quotables

- *Tell a story to create a moment. It's the only thing your audience will remember.*
- *People and businesses get hurt when they play scared.*
- *Look where you want to go, not where you don't.*
- *Our success needed to be loud. The best way to silence critics is to outperform and outlast them. That is what we precisely what we did.*
- *God sure does have a way of upping the ante on the test of fortitude*
- *We have failed a lot. Those failures led us to success, sometimes via a very long and winding road.*
- *Our* ***perspective*** *is the only thing we really can control.*
- *I have learned that the world is driven by those with the right* ***perspective****.*
- *Our bad days are ones that most people in the world would kill for and trade for their best days.*
- *We will all thrive out of this pandemic, not because it was easy, but because it was not.*
- *Fear is the thief of joy. (Unknown)*
- *Do not allow compliments in my head or criticism in my heart. (Unknown).*
- *You have brains in your head. You have feet in your shoes. You can steer yourself in any direction you choose. You're on your own. And you know what you know. And YOU are the guy who'll decide where to go. — Dr. Suess*

Supplementary Learning Recommendations (Read/Listen/Watch)

- *Oh, the Places You'll Go* – Dr. Suess
- *Will Smith Skydiving* – YouTube
- *Never split the difference* – Chris Voss
- *Hello, Fears: Crush Your Comfort Zone and Become Who You're Meant to Be*—Michelle Poler

CHAPTER 10

Getting Started

If you are like me, you've read dozens of books that offer new strategies for the day-to-day challenges you face in business and life. If you're also like me, you've taken some nuggets from those books and have made positive changes in your life. But I'm sure that among all that you have learned, there are dozens of lessons that you took away with the best of intentions and are still filed away. The real test for any transformative strategy is not in the knowing but the doing. Knowing everything about *Living Exponentially* won't make your life better or your business more successful. But applying what you know so that you are living your life *Exponentially* will. I wrote this book in the hopes that you will do that. ***My success comes from yours.***

It's also worth mentioning that much of the context of this book assumes that you are a business leader or entrepreneur. While every chapter that I wrote about business has specific content they can directly apply to your organizations, you can use these concepts in your little league, your church, or often in your home. (Yes, I am often accused at home of operating it as a business. Not my proudest parenting moments, but yes, much of this content is relevant at home). The other reader that I wrote this for is the spouses of those who are leading companies. *Living Exponentially* is a journey for your life and whoever is in it.

Developing an *Exponential Mindset* and *Living Exponentially* are similar to starting a new weight loss or fitness program. Most people start and fail (usually in a matter of weeks) because they try to do everything at once! We are *all* guilty of this. When we fail, we punish ourselves by quitting, pressing the EASY button, and returning to what we did before. My goal is to prevent this from happening by giving you livable, life-size nuggets that you can execute, gain early wins, and keep the motivation to continue becoming *Exponential*.

Recently, a friend of mine started the 90-Day Challenge at my gym. He was very excited to find success. Having lived that journey, I was excited for him. After a decade-long battle with weight, I lost (and kept it off) over 90lbs throughout the course of a year. When you go through something that transformative, you are the best support network for those following you on their journey. He joined my gym, bought new running shoes and an entirely new fitness wardrobe. When I ran into him a month later and asked how his program was going, he shrugged his shoulders and said, "I've lost 30 days." No matter how much I wanted it for him, it's a journey only he controlled.

I have been contemplating this book for twenty years. I have been writing it in my head for the last five years. I have been writing this book actively for over a year.

My challenge was never the content, other than it was too much. My challenge was that I want you to be more successful than with every other self-improvement book you have read. My early readers have shared that this book is different because I framed it in the perspective of your whole life, not just your work and not just your personal life. It is not designed for a single person but for every person on the journey or supporting someone on it. I want you, your family, organization, work family, and anyone you touch to find more success and joy because of what you learned in this book.

I've given you many checklists of things to do (my nephew Brett reminded me that our family all thinks in checklists, so I apologize if there have been too many!). I AM GIVING YOU NOW THE MOST IMPORTANT CHECKLIST IN THE BOOK. This checklist will take these words and help them turn into life-changing methods for your life. To realize all the benefits *Living Exponentially* can deliver to your life and organization, you can start your journey with early wins and create the opportunity for success in *Living Exponentially*.

Become Aware

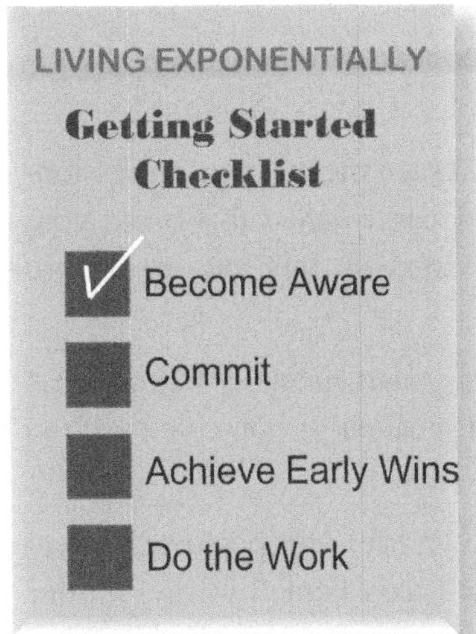

The biggest challenge in converting this book from a curious pursuit of how I accomplished what I did, was an awareness of what I did. The biggest challenge to developing an *Exponential Mindset* is the awareness of its need and where the opportunities are to execute. The number one inhibitor for most people is awareness. People don't realize how often they do the same repetitive tasks.

They don't realize how they could improve processes, and they don't see which things in their lives could be delegated or eliminated by using an *Exponential Mindset.*

Finding awareness is similar to the weight-loss journey- it is unique for each person pursuing it. By sharing my tricks, maybe you can apply some of them. Committing to anything new can be intimidating and overwhelming.

Every one of my failed attempts at weight loss happened because I committed without first becoming aware.

I needed to become aware of my body. The following questions helped me gain that awareness:

- What did I look like before?
- What did I want to look like afterward?
- What was the delta between the two? (This was a painful awareness).
- What did I use to do that I stopped doing that got me here?
- What did I start doing that got me here from where I was?
- What do people who live the healthy lifestyle I wanted do that I don't?

I've mentioned before that comparison is the thief of joy, so this is not an exercise in comparison. Instead, this is an exercise in self-awareness.

This step in the process toward *Exponentiality* you have already started- you picked up this book.

Whether you know me personally, have seen me on stage professionally, or are a random reader who somehow came across this book, your curiosity about *Exponentiality* is the first step on this journey toward awareness.

Without committing to change anything, start mentally noting areas in your life (personally, professionally, and spiritually) where you want to gain more joy and get more out of it.

Work to become an observer in your own life. This perspective may come by journaling at the end of the day. It may come by way of your calendar. Or you may find it in the silence of your head as you fold laundry, work on spreadsheets late at the office, or on your morning commute. Your goal is to discover where repetitive tasks are robbing you of time?

It could be minutes or hours; it doesn't matter. Adding just ten minutes per day of *Exponentiality* to your day will give you back nearly 2000 hours of your life back! Incremental changes make *Exponential* improvements in your life.

My journey in *Exponentiality* started naturally at home with a houseful of kids, wanting to be an active parent, having an unquenchable desire for adventure. I loved doing everything in my personal life and needed to keep the joy with the juggling act. In parallel, at work, I was juggling many hats, business travel, and leadership. So *Exponentiality* at home came naturally. At the office, it took much longer. Out of pure desperation, my assistant, and I decided to start tracking our time. We were both working far too many hours in a week, and our To-Do lists never got any shorter.

We went back to old-fashioned timesheets. This decision was one of the most profound moments in my 25-year career. Throughout the next few months, I came to realize what we actually did at work. For me, I was spending far too much time on H.R. (by the way, before this exercise, if you would have asked me how much time I spent on H.R., I would have said maybe an hour a week, not the nearly ten hours I was allocating). For her, it was scheduling. The majority of her time was planning, organizing, and scheduling meetings. In both cases, our awareness gave us solutions. Without awareness, we couldn't fix the problem. You can't fix what you don't know is broken. Our timesheets provided us the awareness of how to execute *Exponentiality.*

Allow yourself to become actively aware of the potential that is available for you to make *Exponential* changes. There is no wrong way to do this. Become a spectator in your day to see all of the things you actually do. Just like us, you may be surprised to find out how much time you spend doing things that don't get you closer to your goals and don't bring you joy.

Commit

Once you get to the awareness, the next step is Commitment. Unfortunately, most people and organizations, on any transformation journey, make the mistake of committing before they have perspective on what they are trying to solve.

They try to put the puzzle together without ever seeing the picture on the box. Failure in transformation usually happens, as it did for my friend at the gym, because we dive into a commitment before having a clear path to what we are solving. He wasn't solving only his exercise routine. He needed to solve his availability, his financial arrangement to join the gym, his eating habits, and his lifestyle in addition to the exercise.

He went hard at the exercise and just lost 30 days, not the 30lbs he hoped for. So please, *don't stage yourself for failure in this way!*

My definition of Commitment is, "Following through on a decision, long after the excitement of making it has left you." We all get so excited to get to the results; we commit without an awareness of what we committed to. You must commit yourself to the fact that *Living Exponentially* doesn't happen by itself. It doesn't happen overnight. You are never done, and you have to put focused work into getting something out of it.

Start your Commitment once you have a good awareness of

your opportunities. This part of the journey is the only part that I recommend you don't put a timebox around. You may feel like you want a complete inventory before you start. You may get overwhelmed when you think about a hundred places to create *Exponentiality*. When you have a comfort level with your awareness, commit. And don't wait. Commit.

Achieve early wins

Early wins are essential no matter what you do. Most self-improvement books have some reflection on finding wins. For example, Dave Ramsey, a seven-time #1 bestselling author on the topic of personal finance expertise, shares with 16 million listeners each week tips to take control of their money.

These early wins are essential. After becoming aware of the big picture around debts in Ramsey's coaching, he shares advice to pay off some low balances to "clean up" some debt and get an early win or two.[55]

Paying off that first card gives you an early win. Your start line in *Exponentiality* should be the areas of your life that your "whys" most strongly support. If you don't have enough "whys" for the area you are considering, wait. Don't invest the time. Instead, find areas of your life that align with your whys AND are an early win. Even if they are small, they will give you a sense of accomplishment and provide you with confidence in your journey to *Exponentiality* and maybe some joy along the way.

If you are trying to figure out where this is, look where you are struggling the most. You can likely answer this question in a single second and with conviction if you are like me. But, before blazing fearlessly down that trail, make sure that the area you are struggling with is the *actual* problem, not the byproduct of something else.

One area, for example, could be your kids calling you 30 times a day at work. Is this the problem, or is the problem that you are unreliably home at 6 pm and therefore they will bother you until you get aggravated and go home? If this is your story, as it has been mine, the problem I focused on was setting the expectation of when I would leave and then the discipline actually to do it.

Your concern could be first-time fix rates, technician recruiting, organizational issues, or even your healthcare. If you followed this Getting Started process, your awareness phase should have provided you an awareness of a dozen (or more) areas in which to focus. Put these to paper. I like to think of them in the following grid.

	High Impact	Low Impact
Quick Wins		
Big Rocks		

Sort them from quick wins to big rocks and then slide to low and high impact across the paper. I like this exercise because it allows you to see your list relationally. If you have a whiteboard, this is a great whiteboard exercise. If you are fortunate enough to have quick wins with high impact, you may want to start there. There is no best place to start; it's just important that you do.

I thought it might be helpful to give an example from my early *Exponentiality* journey. When our kids were little, I used to work from home multiple days each week regularly. My days were longer because of the interruptions, and my stress level was high. As much as I loved seeing their little faces, it made it challenging to stay focused, and what it ultimately did was robbed me of some of the joy I got to spend with them outside of work.

I started the solution with a glass office door. That way, they could visually see, not interrupt a call with a knock at the door.

Secondly, I had a little stoplight system that I used. If it was a green light, my kids could just come in, no need to knock. If it was yellow, they needed to wait for a physical thumbs up from me to enter. If it was a red light, there better be a broken bone or a robbery in progress. This simple system limited the unnecessary interruptions and ensured that it was for a good reason when I interrupted work. I found joy by working at home, saving a commute on the days I didn't need to go into the office. I got more accomplished while working and enjoyed my time being a mother. The kids knew what to expect, and everyone was significantly happier. This solution was a small rock with a huge impact.

Do the work

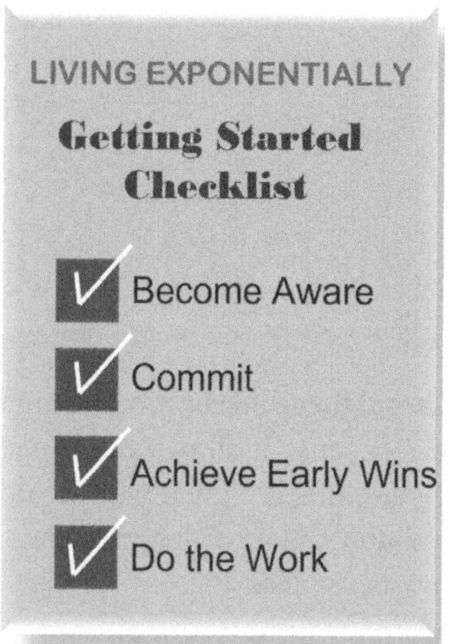

Jean, a long-time Davisware client, once told me, *"Nothing happens until somebody sells something."* In the same way, nothing happens until you do something.

The steps preceding this step are mental preparation, setting the stage, and gathering the ingredients.

They are in preparation for your *Exponentiality* journey. This journey will use the Step-by-Step to an *Exponential Mindset* process outlined earlier that includes:

- Assess your "whys" to determine the motivation for achieving the goal. If you don't have enough "whys," don't invest the time.
- Define success with a S.M.A.R.T. Goal (Specific, Measurable, Achievable, Relevant, and Time-Bound).
- Inventory your resources by listing/cataloging all the tasks required and timeboxing them to know what's available to you to achieve the goal.

- Analyze every task and step. Determine if it drives you toward your goal, impedes it, or distracts you from your destination. Assess whether these steps can be eliminated, delegated, combined, replaced, changed, or systematized.
- Develop a process tethered to the S.M.A.R.T. Goal, which includes a feedback loop- aka a check and balance so that if one element goes array, you know it as soon as possible and have an adaptation plan.
- Catalog the potential conflicts that may arise and what solutions may exist.
- Document & Implement the process/plan.
- Commit to ongoing improvement from the feedback loop.
- As a Leader

I've mentioned multiple times in writing this book that my goal in writing this book is the hope that others learn from what I have done and their *Exponentiality* journey happens better, faster, and with more joy than mine. Whether you are a leader in a business, an organization, or exclusively in your home, your job is to start. Getting started in your business, organization, or home needs to start with you.

Your personal Commitment will mirror your organizational Commitment.

Your personal success will do the same.

JP Morgan famously said, "The first step towards getting somewhere is to decide you're not going to stay where you are."[56] Your leadership is what those you lead are counting on, and your leadership is required to begin.

"The beginning is the most important part of the work."
- Plato.

For sustainable change to occur like *Exponentiality*, your example matters first. It also matters the most. First, *you have to develop an* Exponential Mindset. Once you do this, sharing that mindset will happen and grow in your execution plan to become *Exponential*. As you start to do things *Exponentially*, others will follow. The people in your house will follow. The people in your organization will follow and begin to develop. Lead by example.

Whether you know me personally or not, my biography and the pages of this book should give you a glimpse into the *Exponential Life* I lead. I lead it out of necessity and by design. I lead this life because I want to experience everything, do everything, learn everything, see everything and love everyone. I want to use my time and talent to the best of my ability and always focus on what I can do to make our organization, home, and the world a better place. My journey to *Exponentiality* has helped me make that happen. *Living Exponentially* has delivered rewards for me in giving me the gift of time and the power to use that time to create joy. Regardless of if your goals in life are to be an adventurer like me or your aspirations are less complicated than mine, an *Exponential Mindset* will bring more joy. You can set your sights on becoming a $100 million business or a one-person band. It doesn't matter. In all cases, in all walks of life, in all roles, in all places, *Exponentiality* can help get you there.

Your most precious commodity in life is time. You spend it and can never get it back. You can't expand it. You can't change it. You can't borrow it. Treat it like it's the most precious gift you have because it is.
– Jennifer Davis

Go #BExponential.

CHAPTER 11

What People are saying about Jennifer Davis and *Living Exponentially*

Josh Zolin

My name is Josh Zolin. In order of personal priority, I am a proud father & husband, CEO of Windy City Equipment Service, author of the best-selling book "Blue is the New White: The Best Path to Success That No One Told You About – Until Now" and host of the Blue is the New White Podcast. I have had the privilege of knowing Jennifer for a short time and am completely astounded by her knowledge of the industry, passion for the people in it, and unbelievable outlook on life. She is someone who truly understands the power of the present moment and how to unlock the potential in people. It didn't take but a few conversations for me to understand, not only how she became successful, but how she defines success. And both are equally important when striving to live a fulfilling life. There is absolutely no doubt in my mind that this book is written by the right person, for the right people. The knowledge, experience, and wisdom therein are so important to those who want to discover the power within themselves to achieve their goals, live their dreams, and understand the four most dangerous words in the world... *" I'll be happy when... "*

Thank you, Jennifer, for your incredible contribution to humanity. The world is ready for this.

Josh Zolin
Father, Husband, CEO, Author

WCE

BLUE IS THE NEW WHITE

JOSH ZOLIN

Adam Smith

Have you ever heard the phrase, if you want something done, ask a busy person? For those who know Jenn Davis, this phrase rings so true. Over the years I have known her, she has shown her ability to accomplish so much not just with her career, but also with her very large family and her community. What is even more impressive than how much she is able to accomplish is that she is able to do with a work life balance or integration that so many people aspire to achieve. Living Exponentially is so many great leadership books combined into one. As leaders of companies, families, and communities, we have seen the rate of change increase dramatically. Jenn's story will help you find ways to thrive on these changes while enjoying the journey of Living Exponentially!

Adam Smith

Vice President, HB McClure.com

Melissa Ross

As Jennifer's much younger sister, my beautiful, smart, and confident sister has molded me into the person I am today. I have admired Jenn in so many ways- many she probably doesn't even know. Growing up Jenn always took the initiative to be involved in my life without care for the effort it took. I fondly remember the days where Jenn would take my other sister Molly and I to her college dorm for extended visits. It was quite impressive how she managed her two younger sisters and college at the same time! Her Possibility Mindset found childcare, bent rules to have us in class and created memories for all involved, I am sure! After college, I had the opportunity to briefly work at Davisware, directly for Jenn. In those years, I learned so many skills not only in business but in life as well. I got to see firsthand how a real Exponential life works! She gave me the ability to shadow her and evolve my life, molding future opportunities and adventures for me! Now, as a business owner and entrepreneur, I can reflect on my success and where I am today, knowing how I was influenced by Jenn. I was her first student of the Exponentiality Movement! My current successes happened by following the guidebook that Jenn laid out for me.

This book really embodies the life skills that you need to Live Exponentially! All of the things that Jenn has taught me in my life has made me into a better business owner, wife, sister mother and friend.

Melissa Ross

Sister, Wife, Mom

President, Fitchburg UPS Store

The UPS Store

Heather Price

Jennifer is an inspiring trailblazer and a truly refreshing role model for women. She has inspired so many people in our industry and beyond. Enjoy your journey to Living Exponentially!

Heather Price - Executive Director, Commercial Food Equipment Service Association

Dr. Mitchell

I have known Jennifer for the past 10+ years and the most appropriate description that comes to mind is "Superwoman"! I have worked with her in both a professional and personal capacity and she never ceases to amaze me with the ease at which she transitions between the two. As I read this book, it put better clarity around my relationship with Jennifer. She is one of the most genuine human beings that you will ever meet, and this book exemplifies that trait. This is not a how to book on how to organize your life, but a blueprint of who to be in life. I am truly honored to know Jennifer. She has been and is my true measuring stick for my own personal and professional relationships, my expectation is that after reading her book, you will know exactly why!

Thomas M. Mitchell DC, CCSP
Founder and Clinic Director
Chicago Institute for Health & Wellness

Rich Malachy

The food equipment service industry is a challenge every single day. Our company, Malachy Parts & Service, based out of Bayonne, NJ provides services not just on equipment but to people. The core of our business is people. It was important for me to start with that because I've known Jennifer for over a decade now and since day one, she has been such a supportive, positive role model in my life, for my business and in our industry. Technology is at the forefront of what we're doing here and without S2K and now S2KVision, we would not be able to support our customers in the fast-paced world we all live in. The software she created with her husband Dan has been Exponential for Team Malachy. (Pun intended!)

Jennifer has been involved in the food equipment industry for several decades and she knows the challenges we all face. She has been engaged in conferences and meetings during that time as a partner of our industry, get to know her customers and get to know what's important to them. I've also had the pleasure of seeing her speak passionately about "Being Exponential". She commands the room. You are immediately focused on her message that has become her mission- To Live Exponentially. This book is a testament to her commitment to her family, her employees and her customers across multiple industries and will give tremendous insight into her leadership. She has left a lasting impact on me, and I'll be forever grateful for her wisdom, support, and friendship. Our industry is better because of the Exponentiality movement.

Rich Malachy
CEO Malachy Parts & Service

Lalita Janke

As a mother and wife, and as a part of my 45 year professional career in the field of medicine, the book Living Exponentially would have paid dividends in every area of of my life. This book has the tools, skills, systems and knowledge I needed to make the highest and best use of my time. As the past president of the United Nations Women USA, I was thrilled for Jennifer to join our board of directors, where she can be a striking example for women and girls (as well as men and the men who support them) to fierlessly combine kindness, bravery, success, empathy, patience, creativity, strategic thinking and power- she is the archetype of the new woman.

What makes this book valuable is the transparency in which Jennifer has shared her journey. By seeing her failures, alongside of her successes, we can all gain confidence in our own journeys. This confidence is gained by learning the methods of Living Exponentiality. The unique time management lesson in this book is to see all of our time, not segregated time personally and professionally. Had I read this book 50 years earlier, I would have found myself sooner and realized quicker that it was okay to fail at many things, let go of others things and fiercly hold on to the right things.

The timing and release of this book aligns itself with Jennifer's broader mission. 2020 was a time of global unrest, physcological and physical fears, shifting priorities, emotional pandemonium, and unpredictable changes. Many people withdrew , revealed their dark sides, floundered and suffered through emotional and spiritual paralysis. Jennifer is amoung those who decided to do something different. She used the global pandemic to grow and prosper.

Adventurous and brave of heart, Jennifer took this challenge to inspire others as a forward thinking corporate leader. The crisis wasn't a time to retreat. It was a time to a elevate. Living Exponentially is the sharing her life experiences and teaching people how to lead their best lives.

Soon to be best-selling author, Jennifer's story is more than a story. It's a lifestyle that I have personally witnessed, through engagement with her family, friends and even employees. This book exemplifies why I behold her as the queen lioness; the force that holds the pride together. Her pride includes her family, clients, employees and friends. Like a lioness, she is;

mother, leader, keeper of the pride, provider, protector, creator of new paths. She instills cooperation, is courageous, is always true to herself, has excellent instincts, is patient, daring, loyal to her tribe, understands social order, and is responsible to the death. She knows how to conserve energy to achieve her goals. She is deliberate methodical and uses her strengths in everything she focuses on. Her Exponential Mindset keeps her committed to her duty and does not require that she seek approval of others. She is an influencer in her field. As a lioness, she is not intimiated by challenges and knows it is her duty to use her strength, bravery, creativity, passion and beauty to change the world around her. She will conservatively sacrafice of herself, to teach, mentor and coach, knowing the results in other is the true measure of success.

In a quick read what does not jump out of her book is her foundation, her core belief; devotion to God. Service to Him is her Northstar. This is a must read anyone who wishes to create a life that influences and uplifts others. This book provides validation for any women that possible is not impossible and serves as a roadmap for men who are championing women on their missions.

Through Living Exponenailly, Jennifer Davis is exponentially changing the lives of women and children locally and globally. Get started. The world can't wait to see how Exponential looks on you.

Lalita Janke, *Past President*, UN Women USA

Jodie Charlop

As a leadership coach for 20 years and nearly as many years prior as an executive, I have experienced and worked with many emerging and executive leaders on their leadership journeys – all unique, talented, and growing. Yet from the moment you meet Jennifer Davis, there's something very special about the experience. Yes, she has a keen business mind. She is, obviously, a capable business leader and successful entrepreneur. Yet - the moment you meet – you feel that she's so, so, so much more. She's full-hearted mom, friend, and world servant to helping others be better versions of themselves. Jennifer invests in people - she dives head on into knowing you, and when you meet, you are enveloped in connection, warmth, compassion, and authenticity. She inspires you to be the best version of you, even for me as an executive coach. Jennifer faces the world with courage, possibility, and amazing humanity. This book is a treat to read and inspirational reminder that we all only have 24 hours in a day – that failure is not fatal but fuel for learning – and that all things are possible with an Exponential mindset. If you take away only one thing from this book, you will bounce out of bed tomorrow inspired to do more joyfully – be more joyfully. You will believe you can get the most out of life and business without sacrificing love, joy, and harmony. Jenn is a role model for living and leading with possibility. Enjoy the read. Savor the inspiration!

Jodie Charlop, NCC, CMC
Executive Coach & Managing Partner

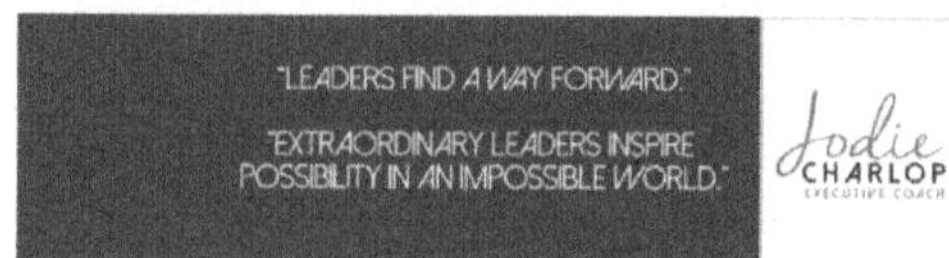

Sue Vrzak

Thundering through every storm, seeing challenges as opportunities, and valuing each differing perspective as an opportunity to embrace informed and compassionate positions on today's issues is what we all ideally wish for our organizations and society. Putting this in to practice in everything we say and do is a challenge that is Exponentially more challenging than individual thought and action. It's something that we all hope our children embrace. A true leader makes these concepts synchronistic with their lives. Jenn Davis is an inspiration as to how authentic leadership does not end when she exits the boardroom. She lives every aspect of her life Exponentially.

Sue Vrzak
Lieutenant Col, United States Army (Retired)
Director, Supply Chain Program Management
Northrop Grumman Corporation

Jean Choquette

My name is Jean Choquette, and I am a principal and Chairman of the Board of Transport Lyon Incorporated, located in Montreal, Canada. I am a 2-time Davisware customer, having used their products to grow my business, Key Food Equipment Services, LTD., located in Western Canada. I acquired that business in 1997 and grew it tenfold under my leadership, and through the use of the technology tools Davisware provided.

In 2002 while attending the Commercial Food Equipment Service Association (CFEA) conference in Chicago, I was first introduced to Jennifer Davis, during her presentation to our association. Her thought leadership in the industry was evident, and the commitment that she and her husband Dan had to their customers was exactly what we were looking for in a technology partner. After reviewing multiple products, we, became a Davisware customer, during which time, the improvements we partnered on became indispensable in our business and to others in the industry. Their solutions were so impactful that upon the sale of Key Food, I purchased the software again to grow my next venture.

Jennifer helped make the adaptations and features happen because she understood the industry and how to impact a business on a bigger scale. She was teaching us about “Exponentiality” before we knew it was her mission. She has been a pioneer in the industry in helping people realize the real potential of their business.

Over the years, we became friends, and occasionally stayed with the Davis’. One day, I wandered around the kitchen, and I saw a series of calendars on the wall. I quickly realized that all ten kids, their parents. and whoever was in the house to help on a weekly basis was basically on that calendar. It was a printed copy of ever every hour of where everyone was supposed to be, including all coaching, meetings, and the kids’ after-school activities. If Dan or Jenn were coaching, it was on there too. It was then that I realized that Jennifer used the same organizational skills to run the family she did to manage the business. She had truly found the way to balance life with a career and #BeExponential.

This book shares her passions for work, family, and the balance of the two. This book shares what I have witnessed the Davis’ do in their lives to influence others to get the most out of their business and their lives. Enjoy the book.

Jean Choquette, P. Eng.
Président du conseil d'administration, Montréal-Est, Québec, Canada
2-Time Davisware Customer

Madhuri

My journey with Jenn began in 2005, as one of the founding engineers of the Davis Software Solutions, Pvt. India organization. From our first meeting, she has led by an example on how to be exponential, never forgetting to have empathy and kindness to people around her. She has taught me personally how to be better organized and always leaves me surprised as to how she balances work, kids, customer relations and leads organizational culture. My mom gave me my talent and the push to use all of it comes in no small part from Jenn as successful leader, loving wife and mother, and proactive leader in the business and in the world. I am so proud to have her next to me and thankful to God for making her part of our life. This book is a mirror that will be inspiration to many, especially women on how to become successful leader with balanced life and really have it all. Good luck on your journey. You will be inspired.

Madhuri Bhogadi
Director of Product Engineering, Davisware

Janet Friederick

I have known Jenn for 32 years since I dated and married her favorite brother. She has been a mentor for me with survival pregnancy, breast feeding and parenting advice for the last 19 years. Jenn has a lot of positive energy and is always on the go. She is definitely Go Big or Go Home! You could catch her doing a handstand anywhere in the world! She has given both of our children the gift of adventure and opening their eyes to *wonder.* Just like her Dad, Don Friederick, Jenn is willing to help anyone who needs in her spirit of philanthropy with her time, talent, financial support or being a part of her home. She welcomes anyone who needs a place, regardless of what it is, making sure they feel welcome and loved. The Exponentiality movement is sharing how it is possible to be everywhere, do everything and still find joy to share with others. I hope you enjoy the book as much as I have enjoyed witnessing it in real life.

Janet Friederick
Sister-in-Law
School Nurse, Dubuque Public Schools, Dubuque, IA

Unpaid CFO, Friederick Excavating LLC, Potosi, WI

Bryan Dodge

Jennifer is a living example that time is more valuable than money. You can acquire more money, but you can't acquire more time. Her new book, *Living Exponentially - Unlocking the Power of Every Moment in your Business and Life,* is a book that reflects not only what she knows, but also how she lives her life each and every day! Her success as a Business Owner, Leader, Mother, and Wife is proof of that and who she is as a person. Success is not to be pursued—it's to be attracted by the person you become. This is a must read for all those that are looking to get the most out of themselves and truly want to maximize their hidden potential in all phases of life."

Bryan Dodge
President/Owner/Author
Dodge Development Inc.

Rick Schulte

My name is Richard Schulte, I am a founding partner of Wright & Schulte LLC, a national civil litigation firm prosecuting some of the most important cases in the United States. My professional life has blessed me with the opportunity to meet, work with and understand some of our country's best leaders, including Jennifer Davis.

I received the gift of Jenn as my first cousin, close friend, and in my inner circle of people I rely upon for advice and friendship. For more than 30 years I have watched, studied, and observed as she has grown professionally and personally. Jennifer has many of the skills you expect to see in great leader. She has vision, motivation, confidence, adaptability, intensity, focus, and trustworthiness. She is a quick decision maker, hard worker, and most important of all, is not scared of failing. But there is something she has that most leaders do not have or diminishes once they ascended to the top of their professional. She has a high level of emotional intelligence, and it permeates all that she does. Her ability to quickly perceive, understand, and empathize, with the emotions and thoughts of all those she encounters is unmatched. It is as if she reads minds, knows what one is going to say, knows what one thinks and always know what to say. I have watched her deploy this skill on repeated occasions over the years and become better at it over time. Strategic thinking is easy for her, as she is always two and three steps ahead of everyone else.

When I learned that she was writing her first book about how to live "Exponentially", I could not wait to read it. Jenn is in her prime, and there is no better time for her to share her insights. To learn from someone who has built a significant company from the ground up while gracefully meeting every obligation of motherhood and relationships is something that can benefit us all. It is in that vein that I encourage all to carefully consider her roadmap to living "Exponentially".

Richard Schulte
Founding Partner

Connie Cetrusi

My name is Connie Certusi, and I am the CEO/President of an Atlanta based SaaS technology company, FieldEdge, that provides Field Service Management software to contractors throughout North America. Our paths crossed several years back, and I got to know her as we were acquiring one of Jennifer's business lines. In the world's view, we are competitors. In our mutual eyes, we are comrades in making the industry a great one to be a part of. Before, during and after that transaction, she always worked to be the best partner possible to her customers, her employees, and our mutual brands. It was obvious throughout that process, that the foundation of her success has always been and will continue to be her commitment to the teams that got her to success on so many levels.

Since then, our relationship grown to a friendship, both personally and professionally, spending time discussing deep topics such as faith and worldviews… to business strategies… to lighter more humorous family stories that are inevitable in Jennifer's world of raising ten children.

Jennifer's journey has been an amazing one to witness firsthand. She has had the rare tenacity to stay true to herself and her priorities, while finding business and leadership success in so many venues. She has never lost sight of what matters - keeping her priorities in check while balancing the often-competing priorities of being a mom, wife, friend, coach, community servant, and business leader. Her authenticity is an inspiration to everyone she meets. Her ability to juggle the pressures of life by continuing to live in the moment while simultaneously and strategically calming the future seas and putting others first. It is mind boggling. In fact, I'll apologize in advance if this sounds corny, but the words "Super Woman" comes to mind whenever I think of Jennifer which is why I am so excited about the launch of this book.

I'm convinced that the "secret sauce" Jennifer shares within will help us all live life exponentially!

Connie Certusi
CEO/President
Field Services Xplor Technologies, Atlanta GA

JD

If you believe time is money – this book is for you! What Jennifer so eloquently does in these pages is saves us from ourselves. Exponentiality is the disciplined practice of establishing the guard rails around your precious time to get the most out of every moment in life and business.

What gives Jennifer's take on Exponentiality so much meaning is the way I've seen it play out in my lifetime of friendship with her. From weekends with her and her family in her hometown of Potosi, WI to basketball games, car rides and hunting trips — if you didn't know Jennifer was the CEO of a multi-million-dollar, international software company, you would think she was a stay-at-home mom. Jennifer's obsession with her family driving everything she does. This love for her family (all 10 of her children, 20 siblings and all ~113 of her nieces and nephews) overflows into a love of her staff (manifesting in the moments she pushes them to be their best or offers a helping hand in their darkest moments) and is paramount in every relationship she has with her customers (loving on their kids, their customers, and their families).

Not often do you get the opportunity to learn from a woman who's collaboratively built a company from the ground up, while keeping her family and marriage intact. Not often do you hear about the ways to optimize what you're already doing every day. Small changes and a slightly different approach create more joy in every moment. Not often do you learn all of the tips and tricks about becoming more Exponential as a person and leader... until now.

You'll love what you learn, because you're not just getting better – you're able to be more joyful and do more, better. So, what are you waiting for? You're holding in your hands the Guru's guide to Exponentiality. Time is money, so get reading!

JD (Jonathan Davis)
Founder / Executive Creative Director, Unknown Certainty
Former Head of Production, Uber Freight

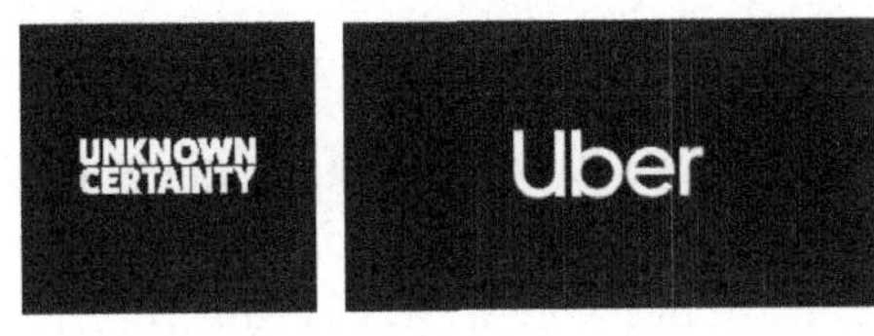

Christina McAdams

In my role as an Air Traffic Control Supervisor for both Chicagoland Airports, my teams and I have proudly navigated Jennifer's safety to and from her many adventures. With unconventional wisdom, she is the only passenger that I've ever met who took the time to send a quick text of gratitude, thanking us for making sure she arrived and departed safely.

My connection to Jennifer extends far beyond O'Hare to our small hometown of Potosi, Wisconsin. When we met in 6th grade, I knew that this beautiful, fun, intelligent, caring, fearless, real, positive, humble, Twizzler-loving, goofy person I know as Jenny, would change the world. Words cannot capture how proud I am of her and her accomplishments. The adventures she seeks in life and her uber empathy for others I was a part of from the beginning. Whether we have spoken yesterday or not for a year, the conversation doesn't change, and we will be belly-laughing in the first minutes. We played chess, suffered through first boyfriend and mosquito bites together, all of the time knowing she had my back in an unparalleled way. Through lots of terrible childhood ideas including candy/cookie making episodes, grape juice spills, and sledding down the Kamikaze Hill, (that I found out years later she actually hurt herself on), together we found a special adventure that, in my adulthood, I learned was a mindset that decided to have joy in all we did. She always found joy for herself and for everyone around her.

Nothing Jenny does surprises me because I have witnessed her strength and courage since we were 11. In awe of? Yes. Surprised? No.

Too busy isn't in her vocabulary if it comes to making the world a better place. In a recent conversation where she was leading a company through a global pandemic, authoring her first book, and managing a plethora of complexity with her tribe of kids, she mentioned that she was working with her brother Jason on putting together a scholarship program for kids in our hometown who will not attend college. Her bewildering selflessness and desire to better others is an inspiration to me. Surprised? No. During world chaos seems like a perfect time to take on something else. Simply said, Jenny is an inspiration to me.

Gaining an early access to this book, I have taken Small Changes Big Impact to heart. For 31 years starting as an Air Traffic Controller in the military, then advancing my career to become a supervisor for the

Chicagoland area, I have succeeded working a rigorous schedule in a demanding career while raising three boys. After the world's reaction to the global pandemic shut the nation down and air traffic dwindled to record lows, we switched to a more normal schedule. For the first time in my adult life, I had a moment to just breathe. In the book she said it perfectly, "Our lives are now blank slates. We can write our own scripts". These words gave me a new perspective and gave me the courage to change my career path to join a wonderful new team, training others from my years of air traffic control work, become Exponential myself. I am giving back to the career that gave me so much, and at the same time gaining back my life and joy.

Her book is engaging and very on topic for what the nation needs to read **right now**. I will always cherish memories with Jenny and grateful for every new memory we make. My new journey to an Exponential Life will give me the time to do just that. Jennifer Davis is a force to be reckoned with. I hope your journey to Exponentiality is as rewarding as mine has been so far. EnJOY the journey.

Christina Brown McAdams
Air Traffic Control Supervisor
Chicago Terminal Radar Approach Control Facilities (TRACON), Elgin, Illinois
Air Traffic Control for O'Hare & Midway Airports

Curt Cain

Over the summer of 2019 I first met Jennifer Davis, and she immediately impressed me with her unique approach to life. Over the next several months, we worked side by side each day as I was serving as a consultant and Interim Chief Financial Officer for Davisware during a key period of transition within the business. During our long hours, I had the special privilege of seeing her up close both professionally and personally, including being invited into her home for dinner with her family (who are also amazing). I saw her live out this concept of Exponentiality in her work, family, and community. Clearly, she has the proven and unique credibility to write this book.

We all have the same 24 hours every day. Jenn has somehow figured out how to get more out of it than any other human being that I know. And this concept is not just about productivity at work - that concept has been overplayed and overshared in so many other books. Jenn is sharing her concepts about overall life. She is an amazing individual. I'm looking forward to exploring her insights further in this book and figuring out how to apply them to my own life.

Enjoy her book and the journey of living life Exponentially.

Curtis Cain
Partner, TechCXO

Hugo J. Martinez

What you are about to read in the pages of this book, I have witnessed firsthand by interacting with Jennifer. Growing a friendship and receiving mentoring from her has been one of the most unexpected blessings to my life in the last five years.

Jennifer's principled approach to work, family, and life, in general, has caused me to pause and re-think several crucial decisions I had made for myself. What I learned from her put me on an unexpected and much better track to fulfill my goals. After a few course-altering conversations with Jennifer, I decided to take a closer look and spend more time learning from her. These "sessions" have created an impact in my life that have accelerated my overall maturity and business growth in orders of magnitude I was not expecting.

The most significant benefit that I have gotten from my time with Jennifer has been receiving some pointed inspiration and advice to accomplish one of my most important goals. I want to develop a successful business career that does not require sacrificing my family in the process.

Getting to know Jennifer provided me with a clear example that it is indeed possible to create a business venture that allows for more opportunities to invest in my family and also provides me with resources to do something about the problems I have noticed in the world. She showed me that it is as I suspected: I can create a business that empowers and serves my life instead of one that enslaves my life. We all need to work and have a balanced life. Many of us want to win at home and in our careers, but not all of us have the wisdom needed to accomplish both successfully. Jennifer's approach has impacted me, and I hope you have the same results by reading this book.

Hugo J. Martinez
Managing Partner, Elevation Consulting, Santiago, Dominican Republic

Terry Moore

As a business advisor and in my board role at the Global Leadership Network, I am consistently surrounded by successful leaders and entrepreneurs. Over the last 5 years, I have been engaged with Davisware, as they evolved to be a private equity backed organization. It was immediately clear to me I was engaging with an exuberantly empathetic, talented, driven, high-capacity individual. My perspective is not just on what she has accomplished, but how she has succeeded through the team they have built. Ultimately, value creation comes from investing in people for sustainability and growth. Jennifer has succeeded where many never arrive. She has built a solid, market-leading organization with a broad customer base. What has always amazed me is she seems to have a personal relationship with each and every one of her hundreds of customers. I have witnessed firsthand the authenticity of these personal bonds time and again. Beyond self-interest, she invests her precious personal time to gain a knowledge of what is going on in their lives and has a genuine interest in their well-being that far transcends the niceties of usual business relationships. Why does this matter? It's simple. People care about you when you demonstrate you care about them and ultimately people build their professional networks around people they know and trust. She is a trusted business partner and friend to many.

Her personal commitments withstand the test of priority, despite her workload. She keeps a pace that humbles my very brisk pace with the only objective being to live life to the fullest, by making the most of the time God has given her, leaving every situation better than she found it, and creating a positive difference in the people's lives she touched. She coaches sports, is an avid spectator of her children's endeavors and travels the country to be with her many children wherever they are. She embodies servantry in her family and community with her time, talents, and treasures.

Her plate is full with these commitments. So how is it she is doing all of this while leading her senior management team and running an international organization? How does one become so effective in so many varying circumstances? Again, it comes back to investing in people in all facets of your life. If you show you care and that you will be there when you say you will, others will respond in kind. The community with you is far more effective than anything you can accomplish on your own.

One could say with all that she has accomplished, is there anything else needed for her to be better as a role model? To feed Jennifer's growth-oriented mindset, I introduced her to the Global Leadership Summit several years ago, inviting her to attend the annual two-day event of international leaders, sharing their experiences and insights. Her quest to always be the best she can be, to be humble and quiet in spirit, to listen and learn from others in all walks of life, has been fun to watch. She does this personally and applies it exponentially, by turning the GLS into a companywide event, helping others become better leaders.

When she told me she was writing a book (in the midst of a pandemic), it didn't surprise me that this would be the next hill for her to climb. The message she has to share has much to offer to so many. I am sure this book is just the start. Whether you are young or not so young, new, or seasoned in your leadership, the insights she shares in this book will be thought-provoking and lessons for all of us to consider. The gift of Living Exponentially is one that she is giving to each of us through this book.

Terry Moore
Consultant, Best Way Advisors
Board Member, Global Leadership Network
Chairperson, Finance Committee

Dr. Mark Turner

As the co-founder of The Turner Method, my wife Colleen and I work to identify injury risk and mitigate through corrective exercise, nutrition, medicine and mental health protocols. It was through these services, I was first introduced to Jennifer as a result of a serious trauma to her lower leg in a bike accident. After complicated surgical intervention, our team set out to regain her pre-injury, highly active status, which was deemed unlikely. Through her positive mental attitude during the months of painful treatment and therapeutic exercise, she defied all expert opinions by completing a marathon run just months after her surgery.

During this interaction she learned of our technology needs to create Exponential impact on athletes. After two failed attempts, our organization was trepedious about finding a solution. In spite of having no experience, she and her husband Dan volunteered their organization to collaborate with us on the project. The fearless engagement in this endeavor parallels the 7 Fundamentals of an Exponential Mindset in so many ways. Together we created a first in class software that systemitized our business. Their efforts impacted our business as well as every athlete who evaluation was succesffuly executed.

During this time, I thought that our experience was unique. However, in getting to know her better, I have learned that this is a way of life, not a unique experience. In everything Jennifer touches, she is looking to create Exponentiality, regardless of the effort or personal reward. Our goal at The Turner Method is to help each person who walks through the door an Exponentially better life through empowerment. We empower our clients in the same way this book can empower you. Congratulations on "Living Exponentially". This is work well-done.

Dr. Mark Turner
Founder
The Turner Method
www.theturnermethod.com
We Empower You!

From the Perspective of Exponential Kids (Big and Little)

Mary Therese

From the moment I was chosen to be a part of our family, it was always demonstrated to me how to make moments count and to know everything is possible. In third grade, we drove to Florida in a Ford Fiesta with no air conditioning, no radio, and no money. The ride was almost as fun as the amusement parks we visited because you encouraged us to enjoy the ride. You encouraged us to sit upside down and put our feet out the window, because it was more important to have joy than it was to follow the rules precisely. Having no money to take us on a vacation didn't deter your generosity or willingness to make sure it was the trip of a lifetime.

I learned from the example of responsibility and hard work. My children have the same standards to get their driver's license that I was given. They can check their oil, change a tire, and drive a manual shift car. The standards expected of us never strayed from what you expected of yourself. You expected us to be exceptional.

We were taught to address the world head on and to be bold. We learned to be fearless when we could, and admit when we couldn't and the confidence to know you'd never let us fall harder than we needed to. We were taught that the best start to a day is a made bed and that every mistake is an opportunity for a lesson learned. You expected us to be so much more than ordinary. The valuable lessons of our childhood are contained in the pages of this book. I am so proud of your new title. I love you so much!

Mary Therese Lempke
Kid #1 (No matter how you count 😊)
Proud wife of Troy and mom to Madison, Troy, Aiden, and Jake

Hannah "Pearl"

My mother is dope. She is a perfectionist who is always pushing me to be the best version of myself. She gives me great advice and is definitely my go to person for how to Live Exponentially. Read on if you are ready to learn for yourself.

Hannah Pearl
Kid #4 (#2 or #3, depending upon your math)
Social Media Influencer
Dog mom to Ellie

justpearlythings

Gabrielle Davis

One of the biggest flexes in my life is something I was born into, or shall I say out of. It's having Jennifer Davis as my mother. She is someone I brag about constantly and consistently, and have no shame in the matter. This is for one simple reason. She decided how she wanted to run her life. He life didn't happen to her. She decided what it was going to be. She decided she wanted to Live Exponentially. She didn't measure this by anyone's standards but her own. She decidedly choose extraordinary over ordinary. My mother has ten kids and is a force to be reckoned with in all she does. Together with my Dad, she started and ran a successful technology company. She has been a coach on dozens of athletic teams and all the while pushing everyone else around her to do better, to be better, to work hard, and to be the truest versions of themselves. I never had to be like my siblings. I had to be the best version of myself. Living Exponentially means just that. For me it was my mother who pushed me to have that drive. At 19 years old, I am starting to see the value of what was just our normal life (trust me, I didn't always see it this way).

For you, reading some of her words will help you to see a new perspective and to understand the world a little more Exponentially. It isn't easy but it's worth the work. Get going. What are you waiting for?

Gabrielle Ann Davis
Kid #: Not even sure. I'm in the middle of the middle.
Collegiate Volleyball Player
Proud sister, neat freak and speed racer (I learned this from my mom)

Living Exponentially Glossary

7 Fundamental Elements of an Exponential Mindset

Includes the following:

#1 - Expect the possibility/probability of Defined Success.

#2 - Leveling Up. Expect others to meet you at your level.

#3 - Goal-Driven Focus.

#4 - Jenga. Solution-Focused Flexibility

#5 - Expect Conflict. Confront Conflict. Get Comfortable in Chaos. Expect Solutions.

#6 - Slingshot Effect.

#7 - Process-Driven. Always Drive Toward Process.

Administrative Timeboxing Negotiation Exercise

The process of segregating administrative activities from other activities and then identifying ways to reduce the time or level of effort to do them through systems, procedures, or delegation.

Basket Syndrome

Lighting candles and putting baskets over them, rendering the value of the candle useless. Translated to Davisware, we loved to create new and profound technology and not share the news with anyone outside our organization.

Closed-Loop Communications

A technique used to avoid misunderstandings. It focuses on people/teams in organizations exchanging clear and concise information, acknowledging receipt of that information, confirming its correctness, following up when promised, and repeating until the issue is closed.

Communications in Crisis (7 Biggest Entrepreneurial Challenges #6)

Changing communication styles and strategies to reflect the demands created by a crisis. In an emergency, all affected people take in information differently, process information differently, and act on information differently. As a leader, you need to know that the way you usually communicate with your community may not be effective during and after it suffers a crisis.

Conscious awareness

The individual and subjective awareness of your unique thoughts, memories, feelings, sensations, and environments. Your understanding of yourself and the world around you.

Core beliefs

Fundamental beliefs about ourselves, other people, and the world in which we live. They are things we hold to be absolute truths deep down, underneath all our "surface" thoughts. Essentially, Core Beliefs determine how you perceive and interpret the world.

C.P.I. (Continuous Process Improvement)

Ongoing efforts to make incremental or breakthrough improvements of products, services, or processes.

Culture on Purpose

Deliberately creating a culture that communicates who you are, what you do, why you do it, and how you do it. Designing every aspect of the culture to embrace the organization's vision, values, mission, strategies, and goals.

Defined Success

Having a clear and specific definition of what success looks like when achieved.

ERP Software (Enterprise Resource Planning software)

A type of software used by organizations to manage their day-to-day operations. It is designed around a single defined data base to ensure information used across the organization is normalized and based on common definitions and user experience.

Evolutionary Mindset

Allowing the mind to adapt to new and different perspectives of the world. Many people are in a "fixed model" of self. Since the mind accepts whatever reality you give it, it will continue to process the events of your life according to that framework. An evolutionary mindset opens the mind to new possibilities and opportunities.

Ex·po·nen·tiality /ˌek-spohˈnen shuh-a-letee noun

Using skills, tools, and technology to make the highest and best use of an individual's time and talent. *Exponential Mindset* means making a conscious effort to get the most out of every moment, every minute, and every interaction. In business, it is creating replicable processes with skills, tools, and technology. *Living Exponentially* is living life to the fullest.

Exponential Life Balance by Design (7 Biggest Entrepreneurial Challenges #1)

Consciously creating a lifestyle that allows you personally and professionally to make the highest and best use of your time and talent. Rather than reacting to circumstances, you can live your life based on conscious choices.

Exponential Mindset

Using skills, tools, and technology to make the highest and best use of an individual's time and talent. It is creating replicable processes with skills, tools, and technology. An *Exponential Mindset* means making a conscious effort to get the most out of every moment, every minute, and every interaction.

Exponentially

Growing or expanding at a steady and rapid rate.

Four Communication Languages

Words, body language, emotions, and appearance.

F.U.D. Factor (Fear, Uncertainty, Doubt)

A condition that shakes accepted paradigms that provide boundaries or rules for success leading to hesitancy and indecisiveness.

Goal-Driven Focus (7 Fundamental Elements of an Exponential Mindset #3)

Staying focused on the original goal or objective. Not getting distracted by obstacles or redefine what success is.

Go-Lives

Making operational or becoming available for use. An example of Go-Live is allowing employees to use a new software program once it is installed.

Highest and best use of time

Participating in activities and tasks that best utilize your talent and are consistent with your most important values and priorities.

Holistic *Exponential Mindset*

Applying an *Exponential Mindset* to every aspect of your life.

Hyper-focused over multi-tasking

Concentrating on doing a singular task very well rather than spreading your attention over several.

In-Person Timeboxing Negotiation Exercise

A process for determining the best way to optimize in-person requirements for a project, task, or job. It requires that you identify all in-person demands and deciding which are negotiable and non-negotiable. Then, manage the non-negotiable commitments through scheduling, logistic, or concessions.

Inventory of Resource

A physical listing of all the resources available for a given project, task, or job.

Jenga. Solution-Focused Flexibility (7 Fundamental Elements of an Exponential Mindset #4)

Looking at a problem as though there *are* solutions and how those solutions have flexibility. Taking this approach helps avoid making a faulty assumption that limits the solutions considered and how you can apply them to the current circumstances.

Jenga

Jenga is a game that requires physical and mental skill built into the simple premise of stacking interwoven wooden blocks. The object of the game is to extrude wooden blocks without causing the tower to collapse. These towers remind me of *Solution-Focused Flexibility*. If we looked at the blocks like they would come tumbling down in our *Jenga* game, we would never pull the bottom piece out, when really, that was the only one where there was no pressure. In *Solution-Focused Flexibility*, we must look at the situation as though we can move every block, and then one by one, we stress-test them, poke at them if you will, to see if we can make them move to get the result for which we are looking.

Joy Triangle

A pyramid-type graphic that demonstrates the relative importance of every step of an Exponential journey. The highest valued and most important step is placed at the top. Because each step is foundational to the next and builds upon the previous successes, the other steps are set below based on their relative and foundational place in the journey.

Knowledge Ubiquity

Having knowledge available to everyone, everywhere, simultaneously creates a single source of truth in an organization. A single source of truth provides employees, employers, and stakeholders with the most precise picture of their decision-making information.

Leading with your Hair on Fire (7 Biggest Entrepreneurial Challenges #3)

Treating all decisions and actions with a sense of hair-raising urgency. By focusing on putting out fires, leaders have no time to find ways to prevent them.

Level Up or *Leveling Up*. Expect others to meet you at your level (Fundamental Elements of an *Exponential Mindset* #2)

Requiring others to meet a higher standard or set of expectations, asking people to perform at your level or standard rather than lowering your expectations to theirs.

Living Exponentially

Living a life built on core beliefs and a decision to execute an Exponential Mindset in all areas of your life.

Modus Vivendi

Modus vivendi is a Latin phrase that means "mode of living" or "way of life." It often is used to mean an arrangement or agreement that allows conflicting parties to co-exist in peace. Modus means "mode", "way", "method", or "manner". Vivendi means "of living." The phrase is often used to describe informal and temporary arrangements in political affairs. For example, suppose two sides reach a modus vivendi regarding disputed territories, despite political, historical, or cultural incompatibilities. In that case, the accommodation of their differences is established for the sake of contingency.

Non-Negotiables

The areas of your life that are most valued and important and are not open to discussion or modification. They are areas of your life that you would drop everything else to attend to.

Process-Driven. Always Drive Toward Process (7 Fundamental Elements of an Exponential Mindset #7)

Continuously identifying ways to increase performance or value by implementing or improving procedures, systems, or processes.

Protagonist Power. Expect Conflict. Confront Conflict. Get Comfortable in Conflict Chaos. Expect Solutions to Conflict (7 Fundamental Elements of an Exponential Mindset #5)

Great protagonists of the world like James Bond, Bugs Bunny, Darth Vader, Rocky Balboa, Marty McFly, Scooby-Doo, and even Shrek are characters that expect conflict and find ways to make solutions happen. *Protagonist Power* means expecting conflict and challenges on the road to success and welcoming the chaos that comes with them. These go hand-in-hand both in your business and personal life. Once you have set the expectation that these can and will happen, the most crucial element is being willing to confront them.

Resource Inventory - Inventory of resources

A physical list of all the resources available for a project, task, or job.

R.O.I. (Return on Investment)

A ratio between net income and investment. A performance measure used to evaluate the efficiency of an investment or to compare the efficiencies of several investments.

S.M.A.R.T. Goals (Strategic-Measurable-Attainable-Realistic-Timely)

An acronym to ensure that goals are specific achievable.

S.O.R.

System of Record – A powerful source of data that businesses value as the *single source of truth* because this is the origin of all the company's data.

S.W.O.T. (Strengths, Weaknesses, Opportunities, Threats)

An analysis of internal strengths and weaknesses and external threats and opportunities to help organizations make operational plans and strategic initiatives.

The Slingshot Effect (7 Fundamental Elements of an Exponential Mindset #6)

Using a setback as a tactic for achieving a different and possibly more significant goal or objective. In business, there will always be times to step back, pause, or make sacrifices. Using these setbacks strategically can provide new opportunities and options. Setbacks in business are like the pullback when using a slingshot. When using a slingshot, the farther you pull it back, the farther forward the object goes.

Source transactional data

Ensuring that you create all data as close to the original source as possible.

Sway

The rhythmic movement used to maintain balance while keeping a line of gravity. When pushed in one direction, we must move in the opposite direction to regain our center of gravity (or risk falling). These oscillating movements allow us to accommodate the pushes and pull we encounter in life.

Symbiotic

A mutually beneficial relationship between different people, organizations, or groups who work or live together.

Tactical Empathy

Deliberately influencing a negotiating counterpart's emotions to build trust-based influence to win the negotiation.

TExponential (7 Biggest Leadership Challenges #2)

Using technology and an ***Exponential Mindset*** to create a more efficient and effective business and personal life. The integration of technology into your business and personal life creates time. How you spend that time determines how *Exponential* you are.

The Great Re-Define

Provides a new perspective on the traditional take of work-life balance. Instead of two separate lives competing for equality, The Great Re-Define delivers a picture of *one life* balancing the changing demands of work and family.

Timeboxing

Allocating time to activities in advance and then completing them in the allotted time.

Tribal Knowledge

Any unwritten information not commonly known by others within an organization. This term is used most when referencing information that may need to be known by others to produce quality products or services. The information may be crucial to quality performance, but it may also be totally wrong.

Triumph. Expect the possibility/probability of Defined Success (7 Fundamental Elements of an Exponential Mindset #1)

A mindset that a goal or end result can and will be achieved, no matter what.

Unsolvable Problem (7 Biggest Leadership Challenges #7)

A problem that can't be solved using past strategies or resources as they were used in the past. Confronting the Unsolvable Problem needs to be done through a different perspective, seen through a different lens and often with other tools and maybe even different people.

W.I.I.F.M. (What's In It For Me)

An acronym used to remind salespeople, leaders, and speakers that the unspoken question people have when listening to a presentation is, "How can this benefit me?"

References

[1] Donna J. Kelley, C.G.B., Andrew C. Corbett, Mahdi Majbouri, *GLOBAL ENTREPRENEURSHIP MONITOR*. 2020.

[2] Council, S. *Facts & Data on Small Business and Entrepreneurship*. 2018 August 20, 2021]; Available from: https://sbecouncil.org/about-us/facts-and-data/.

[3] Betterrelationships. *CORE BELIEFS AND SELF ACCEPTANCE*. 2021 August 20, 2021]; Available from: CORE BELIEFS AND SELF ACCEPTANCE.

[4] Ford, H. *Henry Ford*. 2021 August,20/2021]; Available from: https://www.thehenryford.org/collections-and-research/digital-resources/popular-topics/henry-ford-quotes/.

[5] CBINSIGHT. *The Top 12 Reasons Startups Fail*. 2021 August 26, 2021]; Available from: https://www.cbinsights.com/research/startup-failure-reasons-top/.

[6] POZIN, I. *10 Best Reasons to Be an Entrepreneur*. 2021 August 26, 2021]; Available from: https://www.inc.com/ilya-pozin/10-best-reasons-to-be-entrepreneur.html.

[7] vivendi, M. *Modus vivendi*. 2021 August 20, 2021]; Available from: https://en.wikipedia.org/wiki/Modus_vivendi.

[8] Wikipedia. *Balance*. 2021 August 26, 2021]; Available from: https://en.wikipedia.org/wiki/Balance_(ability).

[9] Reid, L. *I alone cannot change the world..." - Mother Teresa*. 2019 August 20, 2021]; Available from: https://www.theskippingstone.com/blogs/news/i-alone-cannot-change-the-world-mother-teresa.

[10] Collinsdictionary. *Ubiquitous*. 2021; Available from: https://www.collinsdictionary.com/us/dictionary/english/ubiquitous.

[11] IBM. *Cognitive University for Watson Systems SmartSeller*. n.b. August 20, 2021]; Available from: https://www.ibm.com/support/pages/cognitive-university-watson-systems-smartseller.

[12] DocuWare. *How to go paperless: The practical guide to a paperless office*. 2021; Available from: https://start.docuware.com/guide-to-a-paperless-office.

[13] CheckIssuing. *What are the Different Types of Bank Checks?* 2021; Available from: https://www.checkissuing.com/the-cost-of-issuing-checks/.

[14] dloo. *Federated Search: The Importance of Being Able to Find Information.* 2013 August 26, 2021]; Available from: https://armedia.com/blog/federated-search-the-importance-of-being-able-to-find-information/.

[15] USA.VISA. *Digital Transformation for SMBs*. 2021 August 20, 2021]; Available from: https://usa.visa.com/run-your-business/small-business-tools/small-business-digital-transformation.html.

[16] Med, M.J. *https://www.ncbi.nlm.nih.gov/pmc/articles/PMC3438148/*. 2004 August 20, 2021]; Available from: https://www.ncbi.nlm.nih.gov/pmc/articles/PMC3438148/.

[17] Thorne, B. *How Distractions At Work Take Up More Time Than You Think.* 2020 August 20, 2021]; Available from: http://blog.idonethis.com/distractions-at-work/.

[18] PLUMMER, M. *You Probably Check Your Email More Often Than You Should. Here's How to Stop*. 2021 August 26, 2021]; Available from: https://www.inc.com/matt-plummer/you-probably-check-your-email-more-often-than-you-should-heres-how-to-stop.html.

[19] Whitney, L. *How to use the Search tool in Windows 10 File Explorer*. 2019 August 20, 2021]; Available from: https://www.techrepublic.com/article/how-to-use-the-search-tool-in-windows-10-file-explorer/.

[20] Shan, W. *How Not Using Keyboard Shortcuts Makes You Lose 64 Hours Every Year*. 2021 August 26, 2021]; Available from: https://www.lifehack.org/561663/wen-shan-how-not-using-keyboard-shortcut-make-you-lose-64-hours-every-year.

[21] King, R. *More than 110,000 eating and drinking establishments closed in 2020*. 2021 August 26, 2021]; Available from: https://fortune.com/2021/01/26/restaurants-bars-closed-2020-jobs-lost-how-many-have-closed-us-covid-pandemic-stimulus-unemployment/.

[22] Reynolds, M. *The Tyranny of the Urgent*. 2021 August 20, 2021]; Available from: https://barbell-logic.com/the-tyranny-of-the-urgent-2/.

[23] Covey, S.R., *The 7 habits of highly effective people: Powerful lessons in personal change*. 2004: Simon and Schuster.

[24] News, C. *Borders books to close, along with 10,700 jobs*. 2021 August 26, 2021]; Available from: https://www.cbsnews.com/news/borders-books-to-close-along-with-10700-jobs/.

[25] Appolonia, A. *How BlackBerry went from controlling the smartphone market to a phone of the past*. 2019 [cited August 20, 2021; Available from: https://www.businessinsider.com/blackberry-smartphone-rise-fall-mobile-failure-innovate-2019-11.

[26] Tan, M. *The Downfall of Blockbuster*. 2021 August 26, 2021]; Available from: https://medium.com/an-idea/the-downfall-of-blockbuster-da69f6c8a536.

[27] Oomen, M. *Netflix: How a DVD rental company changed the way we spend our free time*. 2021 August 26. 2021]; Available from: https://www.businessmodelsinc.com/exponential-business-model/netflix/.

[28] Producthabits. *How Netflix Became a $100 Billion Company in 20 Years*. 2021; Available from: https://producthabits.com/how-netflix-became-a-100-billion-company-in-20-years/.

[29] Cohan, P. *How Netflix Reinvented Itself*. 2013 August 20, 2021]; Available from: https://www.forbes.com/sites/petercohan/2013/04/23/how-netflix-reinvented-itself/?sh=474b48862886.

[30] Davis, J. *Knowledge Loss: Turnover Means Losing More Than Employees*. 2018 August 26, 2021]; Available from: https://hrdailyadvisor.blr.com/2018/07/18/knowledge-loss-turnover-means-losing-employees/.

[31] Hyderabad. *Hyderabad: Tourist Attractions in Hyderabad: HITEC City Hyderabad*. 2021; Available from: https://www.hyderabad.org.uk/tourist-attractions/hitec-city.html

[32] Center, R. *Pew Research Center*. 2009; Available from: https://www.pewresearch.org/hispanic/2009/05/12/ii-introduction/.

[33] Archie. *The History of Archie*. n.d. August 20, 2021]; Available from: https://history-computer.com/software/the-history-of-archie/.

[34] CLIFTON, J. *Are You Sure You Have a Great Workplace Culture?* 2017 August 26, 2021]; Available from: https://www.gallup.com/workplace/236285/sure-great-workplace-culture.aspx.

[35] Hsieh, T., *Delivering happiness: A path to profits, passion, and purpose*. 2010: Hachette UK.

[36] Goldsmith, M., *What got you here won't get you there: How successful people become even more successful*. 2010: Profile books.

[37] Church, O.L. *5 Days of Leadership with Pastor Craig | Day 1: Value-Driven Culture*. 2021 August 26,2021]; Available from: https://open.life.church/training/337-5-days-of-leadership-with-pastor-craig-day-1-value-driven-culture.

[38] Heard, E., *Walking the talk of customer value.* National Productivity Review, 1993. **13**(1): p. 21-27.

[39] Franz, A. *7 Pillars of a Strong Culture*. 2017 August 26, 2021]; Available from: https://www.business2community.com/human-resources/7-pillars-strong-culture-01947495.

[40] Max, R. *A rising tide lifts all boats meaning*. 2020 August 26, 2021]; Available from: http://readymax.com/kkfbb/a-rising-tide-lifts-all-boats-meaning.

[41] https://www.coachinggreatness.com/. *Coachinggreatness*. 2021; Available from: https://www.coachinggreatness.com/.

[42] Buffett, W. *AZ Quotes*. 2021 August 26, 2021]; Available from: https://www.azquotes.com/quote/40692.

[43] HARTER, J. *Employees Want a Lot More From Their Managers*. 2021 August 26, 2021]; Available from: https://www.gallup.com/workplace/236570/employees-lot-managers.aspx.

[44] Philosiblog. *The single biggest problem in communication is the illusion that it has taken place*. 2012 August 26, 2021]; Available from: https://philosiblog.com/2012/01/06/the-single-biggest-problem-in-communication-is-the-illusion-that-it-has-taken-place/.

[45] Meetings, T.S.S.B.S.R. *Steven G. Rogelberg*. 2020 August 26, 2021]; Available from: https://sloanreview.mit.edu/article/the-surprising-science-behind-successful-remote-meetings/

[46] penguinrandomhouse. *Thanks for the Feedback*. 2021; Available from: https://www.penguinrandomhouse.com/books/313485/thanks-for-the-feedback-by-douglas-stone-and-sheila-heen/.

[47] Stanley, A. *Quote*. 2017; Available from: https://globalleadership.org/quote/leading-others/qi201710676/

[48] Smith, W. *What Skydiving Taught Me About Fear*. 2018 August 26, 2021]; Available from: https://www.youtube.com/watch?v=bFIB05LGtMs.

[49] Voss, C. *Tactical Empathy*. 2021 August 26, 2021]; Available from: https://www.masterclass.com/classes/chris-voss-teaches-the-art-of-negotiation/chapters/tactical-empathy.

[50] PSYCHOLOGY, F.H. *80 % of Thoughts Are Negative…95 % are repetitive*. 2012 August 26, 2021]; Available from: https://faithhopeandpsychology.wordpress.com/2012/03/02/80-of-thoughts-are-negative-95-are-repetitive/.

[51] Belludi, N., *Albert Mehrabian's 7-38-55 Rule of Personal Communication*. 2008.

[52] Belludi, N. *Albert Mehrabian's 7-38-55 Rule of Personal Communication*. 2008; Available from: https://www.rightattitudes.com/2008/10/04/7-38-55-rule-personal-communication/.

[53] Sung, Y. and S. Kim, *The Effects of Colors on Brand Personality in Advertising*. The Journal Of Advertising And Marketing Research, Prieiga per internetą: http://www. japr. or. kr/index. php, 2013.

[54] Snyder, C. and K.M. Pulvers, *Dr. Seuss, the coping machine, and "Oh, the Places You'll Go."*. Coping with stress: Effective people and processes, 2001: p. 3-29.

[55] Ramsey. *Your Top Debt Snowball Questions Answered.* 2021; Available from: https://www.ramseysolutions.com/debt/top-5-debt-snowball-questions-answered.

[56] Morgan, J.P. *J.P. Morgan Quotes*. 2021 August 26, 2021]; Available from: https://www.goodreads.com/quotes/223825-the-first-step-towards-getting-somewhere-is-to-decide-that.

About the Author

Since the age of 17, Co-Founder and former CEO of Davisware, Jennifer Davis, has been at the epicenter of business technology transformations in thousands of field services businesses throughout her more than thirty years in the technology business. Davisware, co-founded by Jennifer and her husband Dan, has partnered with its customers since 1988. They strategically focused on operational efficiency and analytics solutions supporting their clients' field services businesses' growth and success while providing best practices to help scale these companies. Since inception, thousands of contractors manage, organize, and grow their businesses through Davisware technology and are supported by their global team of nearly 200 empathetic and creative problem-solvers.

Through the humble beginnings of a family HVAC business, Dan used his first-hand industry knowledge to create scalable, industry-leading technology innovation for field services businesses from startup to enterprise level. Their mutual passion for the trades motivated them to develop solutions that exponentially impacted the growth of these very non-technical businesses.

Their 31 years of passionate pursuit of business excellence created the three professional assets that were the formula for their success - their teams, customers, and culture. These assets allowed us to produce great technology solutions and create the opportunity for private equity investment in 2019. Jennifer recently stepped down as CEO, maintaining an active role in the business with her passion for the industry and customers in the position of President.

Business success is a page of Jennifer's story. She grew up professionally and personally during her career, adding ten kids residing in 8 states to her vast professional responsibilities. Outside of demanding work and home schedules, Jennifer and Dan have been passionate coaches and community servants, having coached nearly 100 youth sports teams and thousands of athletes.

The key to her success is also the title of this book, *Living Exponentially*. It reveals how entrepreneurs and business leaders can leverage their time, energies, and talent to enjoy building the successful business of their dreams and create joy in their lives.

Made in the USA
Columbia, SC
07 November 2021